SHEER MISERY

SHEER MISERY

Soldiers in Battle in WWII

MARY LOUISE ROBERTS

THE UNIVERSITY OF CHICAGO PRESS

CHICAGO AND LONDON

The University of Chicago Press, Chicago 60637
The University of Chicago Press, Ltd., London
© 2021 Mary Louise Roberts

Published 2021
Printed in the United States of America

30 29 28 27 26 25 24 23 22 21   1 2 3 4 5

ISBN-13: 978-0-226-75314-0 (cloth)
ISBN-13: 978-0-226-75328-7 (e-book)
DOI: https://doi.org/10.7208/chicago/9780226753287.001.0001

Library of Congress Cataloging-in-Publication Data

Names: Roberts, Mary Louise, author.
Title: Sheer misery : soldiers in battle in WWII / Mary Louise Roberts.
Description: Chicago : The University of Chicago Press, 2021. |
Includes index.
Identifiers: LCCN 2020039055 | ISBN 9780226753140 (cloth) |
ISBN 9780226753287 (ebook)
Subjects: LCSH: United States. Army—Infantry—Health and
hygiene. | Great Britain. Army—Infantry—Health and hygiene. |
World War, 1939–1945—Health aspects—Europe, Western. | Soldiers—
Health and hygiene—United States. | Soldiers—Health and hygiene—
Great Britain. | World War, 1939–1945—Campaigns—Italy. |
World War, 1939–1945—Campaigns—Belgium.
Classification: LCC D810.H4 R63 2021 | DDC 940.54/7520973—dc23
LC record available at https://lccn.loc.gov/2020039055

♾ This paper meets the requirements of ANSI/NISO Z39.48-1992
(Permanence of Paper).

For Elizabeth

In a dark time, the eye begins to see.

THEODORE ROETHKE

CONTENTS

Axis country
Axis-occupied

DENMARK
SWEDEN

North Sea

NORTH

IRELAND

NETHERLANDS

MAP 4

UNITED
KINGDOM

GREATER
GERMAN REICH

London ●

Berlin ●

BELGIUM

English Channel

● Prague

Luxembourg ●

SLOVAKIA

● Paris

Vienna ●

SWITZ.

HUNGARY

FRANCE

Bay of Biscay

YUGOSLAVIA

ITALY

MAP 3

● Rome

SPAIN

200 MILES

200 KILOMETERS

Mediterranean Sea

PORTUGAL

TUNISIA

MAP 2

MOROCCO

ALGERIA

BLACKMER MAPS

INTRODUCTION

Marching victoriously across France with his infantry regiment in 1944, GI Leroy Stewart had neither death nor glory on his mind. Instead he was worried about his underwear. "I ran into a new problem when we walked . . . the shorts and I didn't get along. They would crawl up on me all the time."[1] Complaints like Stewart's pervade infantry memory of the European theater of operations during World War II, whether the soldier was British, American, German, or French. Wet, freezing misery with no end in sight—this was life for millions of infantrymen in Europe. Creeping underwear may have been a small price to pay for the liberation of millions of people. And yet, in the wretchedness of the moment, soldiers like Stewart lost sight of that end.

Like death, misery exercised perfect equality, taking no side. Officers planned the battles; foot soldiers suffered them. As a result, officers and infantrymen had different views of the soldier's body. "Snow, ice and cold were more brutal enemies than the Germans," noted Major General Ernest Harmon of the cold in the Ardennes. "By the end of the battle Jack Frost had put more than twice as many of my soldiers in the hospital as German guns." Harmon sees the cold in strategic terms: as an enemy taking men off the line. By contrast, British tank driver Bill Bellamy described the same weather this way: "It was too cold to see without goggles and yet impossible to wear them as they froze on to your nose. If you took them off in order to have a clear view, your eyes filled with tears, which either froze to your face or failing that, your eyelids froze shut."[2] Bellamy knew his body as a source of sensation. His eyes were tearing; his eyelids were freezing; his vision was impaired. The major general, on the other hand, knew Bellamy's body as an abstract unit of violent force. If a body suffered too much cold, it could be rendered nonviolent.[3]

The difference was by no means clear-cut. Officers at lower levels of command—platoon leaders, sergeants—not only witnessed infantry suffering but experienced it themselves. As the war progressed, these officers gained commissions, rising through the ranks. Even when they had more authority, they could not forget what they had seen and felt on the front lines. In taking on intermediary command positions, they were forced to balance competing objectives: to keep everyone alive at the platoon level while completing missions at the division level and above. All commanders wanted their men to be warm, rested, and well-fed, for these factors favored victory. Visiting wounded soldiers in a Sicilian hospital, General George Patton told his diary that he had "emoted" out of admiration for their nobility of sacrifice. But in speaking of one badly wounded soldier, he warned himself: "He was a horrid bloody mess and not good to look at, or I might develop personal feelings about sending men into battle. That would be fatal for a general."[4] Patton claimed that leadership *required* abstraction of men's bodies. But that did not mean he didn't recognize or care for them as human beings.

Still many infantrymen complained that high command didn't give a damn about their misery. Infantry soldiers resented the disparity between their dirty foxholes and the tidy beds of their superiors. GI George Neill remembered sitting with his buddy at Bastogne in December 1944. The cold went through their bodies as they each lay in a fetal position and shivered. While "turning, trying to find relief from the overwhelming discomfort," Neill promised his friend he would write "a detailed account of this suffering after the war. The public and the rest of the army should know what this is really like."[5]

What *was* it really like? Answering that question is in one sense impossible. We can never really know how the war sounded or smelled, what misery felt like. War memoirs are notoriously subjective and often inaccurate, particularly those written several years after the war.[6] And yet "what is remembered in the body is well-remembered," as one critic has claimed.[7] In the 1990s, Robert Conroy gathered testimonies of his company's engagement in the Battle of the Ardennes. He noticed that while memory of the *facts* of various battles had dimmed, "the details with respect to record-breaking cold weather, inadequate clothing and equipment, body-weakening dysentery, frozen feet, horrific sounds of incoming shells and bullets snapping through nearby trees, hunger, bone-weary fatigue" were still sharp. It was "just as if it all happened yesterday," wrote Conroy. "I consider these images seared on the brain." While personal testimony is often unreliable, sense memories are indelibly vivid.[8]

What we can recover are shared meanings about the sounds and smells of the battlefield; the taste of rations; the dirt, cold, and wet of the front; war injuries and wounds; the sight of a corpse. How, for example, did soldiers use their senses to *make sense* of new forms of artillery? What did dirt signify in basic training, and how did that change in the wet and cold of the Italian mountains? Why did some soldiers consider it unmanly to be treated for an injury? How did cold injuries such as trench foot come to symbolize both endurance and betrayal? What kinds of wounds did men consider the best and worst to get and why? Soldiers created a language of sense meaning in order to make comprehensible—and hence to negotiate—the alien world into which they had been thrown. As one historian has put it, "Meaning comes to a great extent through the senses."[9] How frontline soldiers understood their bodies—as well as the dirty, dead, and wounded bodies around them—shaped their experience of the war. Despite stark differences of ideology, language, and culture, such meanings showed remarkable consistency among soldiers of different armies. If misery transcended national barriers, so did the meanings made of misery.

What follows is a loosely structured set of essays that aim to recover these shared meanings. Together they compose a field of historical knowledge: a somatic history of war. The enormity of the conflict demands a limited focus; thus, this book attends to Europe during the last two years of battle during World War II. In that place and time, three campaigns left high-water marks for infantry misery: the 1943–44 winter campaign in the Italian mountains, the summer 1944 battles in Normandy, and the 1944–45 winter battles in northwest Europe.[10]

In the winter of 1943, unceasing rain and a stubborn German war machine battered Allied soldiers in the Italian Apennines. After success in North Africa and Sicily, the Allied army's goal was to move up the Italian mainland, capture Rome, and arrive in the heart of Hitler's Third Reich. It proved easier said than done. The campaign started in September 1943 and dragged on until the very end of the war, with an estimated 300,000 casualties. Among the many challenges facing the Allies was the Italian geography, a torturous mix of mountains and rivers. Soldiers on both sides fought high up in the mountains, where there were no foxholes to dig and only rocks for shelter. Mules climbed up the mountain with supplies, then clambered down the mountain with corpses.

The following year was just as wretched. During the summer of 1944, the Allied army encountered tough German resistance in Normandy on the Cotentin Peninsula and in the city of Caen. The wounds suffered by British soldiers in this campaign form the basis of chapter 4. After the Allies trapped their enemies in the Falaise area, they moved briskly across northwestern Europe. Everyone began to hope the war would be over by Christmas. Again they were disappointed. In border French cities such as Colmar and Metz, as well as in Holland, Belgium, and the Rhineland, Allied soldiers met a diminished but still determined German army. Christmas week offered no celebration. The US Army staggered to respond to a surprise offensive in the Belgian Ardennes Forest. The battle took place in some of the worst weather Europe had ever seen, including subzero temperatures and abundant snowfall. When storms blocked supply lines, foot soldiers fought on empty stomachs with blue fingers and black feet.

Europe during these years was only one hell among many other hells. The Second World War was a global conflict that brought physical misery to soldiers and civilians all over. Suffering varied enormously depending on weather, terrain, climate, as well as type and stakes of battle. The discomfort endured by soldiers in Italy, for example, was unique to its mountainous terrain, wide rivers, and rainy cold climate. In the hot, humid jungles of Guadalcanal and Burma, Allied soldiers endured an altogether different hell.

All foot soldiers, however, had one thing in common. As they were all too aware, they were inducted, trained, and sent into combat primarily as bodies. New recruits had to pass an exam evaluating their bodies' aptitude for war-making. The US Army induction exams assessed every organ, muscle, and bone in a man's body. At the beginning of the war, soldiers were required to have young bodies—aged between eighteen and thirty-eight. Size counted: bodies had to be a minimum of 105 pounds and five feet in height; the chest had to measure at least 28.25 inches.[11] To be classified as "1-A," a body needed to meet certain requirements. The upper extremity bones, muscles, and joints had to be capable of "hand-to-hand fighting." The lower extremity bones, muscles, and joints had to be able to march and stand for long periods of time. There were standards defining strength, stamina, agility, and range of motion as well as specifications for the eyes, ears, mouth, nose, trachea, esophagus and larynx, skin, spine, scapulae and sacroiliac joints, heart, blood vessels, and abdominal organs.[12]

British soldiers were assessed much the same way. As war broke out in 1939, again it was young bodies—aged twenty or twenty-one—that were wanted. As the war went on, that range expanded from eighteen to fifty-one.[13] At induction centers, recruits stripped off their clothing and moved in a long queue from one medical doctor to the next. "There were a number of doctors in the hall and we were told to strip off and proceed along the 'conveyor belt' after prime documentation," recalled E. J. Rooke-Matthews. "One doctor examined head and ears, another chest and back, another (using a ruler) inspected the private parts and checked our cough, another knees and feet, and so forth."[14] A recruit's body was then assigned one of four grades, A–D. By the end of the war, there were roughly ninety-two subcategories and four grades.[15] The goal was to assign the right soldier to the right job, using their bodies in the most efficient way possible. As Colonel S. Lyle Cummins of the Medical Corps explained in 1943, in wartime "it becomes essential to utilize to the full all available material."[16]

What began at recruitment intensified in training. In boot camp, a recruit was more or less reduced to his body. David Holbook described military training: "None of them felt he was himself any longer. Personality was subdued to the driven life of the body and even the body could barely keep up—all else that was human in them was relinquished."[17] The recruit was taught to abstract his own body from himself. He learned to endure physical agony without stopping, to ignore his body's distress signals. When he was sent into combat, he became Major General Harmon's unit of violence.

But there was a problem. The foot soldier was foremost a sentient being vulnerable to illness, injury, and death. Try as it might, military command could not transform a human body into a blind, mechanical unit of force. The winter campaigns of 1943–44 in Italy and 1944–45 in Belgium revealed the futility of this attempt. In the terrible conditions of the front, soldiers' bodies began to break down, stubbornly declaring their need for warmth, rest, and good nutrition. Feet became swollen, frozen, and black. Walking became difficult, sometimes impossible. Diarrhea stained underwear and pants. Stomachs and abdomens cramped. Fingers became too frozen to pull triggers. In sum, the soldier's body began refusing the demands placed upon it. Some soldiers endured it "like a man." Others made good use of the power of their bodies. They deliberately contracted trench foot or frostbite to get off the front line. They irritated or reopened wounds to lengthen a hospital stay. In other words, they exploited their *ungovernable* bodies as a means to resist command.

Misery loved company. Bonds of solidarity were forged around sense perceptions and bodily events. Men on the line shared expertise about artillery noises, bitched about the bad food, and smelled death on their uniforms. They shared tips on keeping their feet dry, their stomachs full, and their bodies warm. Cartoonist Bill Mauldin's famous infantrymen Willie and Joe depended only on each other to relieve their distress. Rear officers they discounted as hopelessly out of touch. In this way, misery helped forge a brotherhood among men.

War is "the most radically embodying event in which human beings ever collectively participate," one critic has claimed, because injuring and being injured constitute its essence.[18] Why then do we know so little about how it felt to be a body in combat? Perhaps we were meant to know little. Photographs of dead GIs were censored except when necessary to boost war bond sales.[19] To maintain morale, the British Army transported wounded soldiers in the dead of night. Military command presented casualties in list form. The wounded were known only by their name and service number. And yet the sounds of a man in pain, the sight of an opened body, the smell of pus, the taste of blood—these sensations were known to every infantryman. Dead bodies were also erased from view as armies made aggressive efforts to "sweep" the battlefield. Nevertheless, infantrymen were constant witnesses to death. For them, the corpse was a complex symbol of the war. Upon the dead body was written a multitude of signs—about what the war meant, why it was being fought, and what its consequences were.

Studying sensations and bodily events can tell us much about how frontline soldiers saw their world and communicated with one another. Eating, sleeping, hearing, smelling, and other bodily functions were human givens. Yet in this place and time, they took on unique meanings. Consider the example of defecation and urination. Due to the unsanitary conditions of the front line, dysentery was a fact of life.[20] The smell of human shit pervaded the battlefield. Men on the line preferred the word "dysentery" to "diarrhea," according to GI William Condon, because the word "dysentery" had "more class than diarrhea."[21]

As infantry officer Paul Fussell was parading his platoon one evening, "terrible cramps forced out a cascade of liquid shit before I could scuttle to the side of the road and drop my trousers." After fifteen minutes trying to clean himself up with pages from his official Field Message Book, Fussell ran to catch up to his men, one of whom immediately commented, "Lieutenant, you stink!" Fussell remembered, "I have not often been so miserable, so humiliated, so profoundly unable to put on an impressive front."[22] Fussell's shame came not only from his body's failure but also from his inability to overcome that failure.[23] To shit in your pants meant you could not discipline your body to behave in a civilized manner. In a very real way, it made you feel like a child again, unable to control your bowels. The stench carried an even worse stigma if it resulted from diarrhea produced in fear. To soil yourself in an artillery assault or in battle was to signal weakness. The GIs called cowards "pants-shitters." For this reason, men rarely confessed to losing control of their bowels.[24]

Urination was another matter. In March 1945 when the Allied troops had finally penetrated Germany, Winston Churchill insisted on being taken to the Siegfried Line, the so-called impenetrable line of fortifications also called the West Wall. Once there, Churchill ceremoniously exited the car and, followed by his staff, headed toward the wall. Fumbling with his fly, cigar in his mouth, a huge smile on his face, he proceeded to urinate on the fortification. "Gentlemen," he beckoned, "I'd like to ask you to join me. Let us urinate on the great West Wall of Germany." Three weeks later, General Patton echoed Churchill's gesture by pissing into the Rhine River. While Churchill had refused to be photographed (arguing that "this is one of those operations connected with this great war which must not be reproduced graphically"), Patton allowed photos (fig. 1).[25] Soon every GI in the Third Army wanted to urinate in the Rhine. As Walter Brown put it, "anointing" the Rhine was "a top priority project." "It didn't make the river rise any, but we had the satisfaction of doing what we had all been bragging we'd do for a long time."[26] Urination became a favored way to celebrate Allied conquests. While the ritual had deep roots in Western culture, it took on unique meanings in this time and place.

For soldiers who fought, the war was above all about their bodies. It was as bodies that they had been recruited, trained, and deployed. Their job was to injure and kill bodies but also to be injured and killed. "I am now what my civilization has been striving to create for so long," claimed British lieutenant Neil McCallum, "a technically valuable, humanly worthless piece of flesh and blood, animate,

FIGURE 1. George Patton urinating in the Rhine.

responsive, and supposedly faithful until death."[27] McCallum's body became what the war made it—technical, submissive, faithful. But the anger he expressed tells another story: how men on the front line used their bodies to challenge military discipline as well as to insist on their humanity.

1

THE SENSES

The Second World War battlefield, with its massive firepower coming from all directions, did violence to the human senses.[1] The war exposed human eyes to unknown horrors, ears to strange noises, and noses to unfamiliar odors. To British soldier G. W. Target, the mountain battles in Italy were first and foremost a crushing cacophony of sound: "The prolonged grating screamings of metal on metal or on stone, explosions, shatterings, shoutings, cryings, mechanical roarings and thunderings, convulsions, shudderings of earth or of flesh in agony, splinterings of wood or of bone, near or distant shellings, sudden crackings, gunnings, bombings, days, nights, nightmares." Conceived by commanders as pins on a map, these battles materialized for Target as howling maelstroms of fire and death. Donald Burgett of the Eighty-Second Airborne endured the same sort of hell in the Ardennes. "All you can do is lie there and listen to the shrieking, screaming shells coming in and the loud explosions they make when they hit. Your throat dries up and your lungs burn as you breathe in the burnt powder, dust and acrid smoke caused by the blasts."[2]

Target and Burgett were not atypical. Infantry memoirs convey men incomparably alert to the sense-scape of the battlefield. The sound of an incoming shell, the smell of cordite and burnt powder, the sight of decaying bodies, the taste of blood—these sense memories overwhelm all others.[3] Why do sense memories dominate infantry testimonies? Scientists believe that the human brain links perceptual and memory systems so that each triggers the other.[4] And the high flow of adrenaline common to men in combat intensifies their sense memories. In British A. G. Herbert's first artillery barrage, he recounted how he "leapt a foot into the air, and my heart pounded in fright, my nerves were taut because all the sounds were new at that stage."[5] During combat, infantrymen lived in an intensely focused present. As British Peter White put it, "Our life was occupied with the passing minute." Brian Harpur noted, "One was conscious only of what life held for the next ten minutes or for the hour."[6]

Orders came down from army commanders to corps, from corps to division, from division to brigade, from brigade to battalion, from battalion to company, and from company to platoon. In this downstream current, the infantryman was, as Harpur described him, "a lonely island of uncomprehending isolation."[7] "Infantry," British Rex Wingfield explained, "originally of necessity and finally from sheer habit, had the ability to look forward only to the next meal, or, at the most, to the next day." "What was happening in the 'bigger picture,'" observed White, "we could only usually sift from rumours." "I don't believe that there was any unit in the army that was more sheltered from the big picture as to what was happening in the war as was the Infantry platoon," American GI Arnold Whittaker agreed; "most of the time we existed in our own little world of preservation." GI Frank Denison admitted, "We often had no idea where we were, or what any 'big' plans were or why we were there."[8] According to one officer, French foot soldiers were doubly handicapped in knowing the operation. Not only did they see just a fraction of the front from their foxholes, but they were too tired and afraid to remember anything accurately.[9] An infantryman's understanding of the war extended no further than his field of vision.[10] "You have no sense of the grander scale," wrote Patrick Morrisey, "a soldier is only aware of what is happening in his little area. . . . He focused on the demands each day brought."[11] For infantrymen, the war was a series of short-term commands that more or less exhausted your body.[12]

If sense impressions predominate in infantry memory, what can they tell us about foot soldiers and their lives on the front lines? To hear an incoming shell, to smell a buddy's blood, or to eat frozen food for weeks at a time—these miseries have been seen as a "given" of war with no history of their own. Yet sensory meaning does have a history inasmuch as it emerges from a particular context recoverable through first-person accounts. How you heard an artillery sound, for example, depended on where you were, which way the wind was blowing, the kind of bomb coming at you, how well you had been trained, and how much time you'd spent on the line.

A soldier's senses were one of the few things he could call his own. Military life challenged a man's personhood. Absolute obedience was the rule. A soldier had little power over his movements. Both the clothes he wore and the food he ate were issued, not chosen. Most importantly, he knew his body to be "war's most necessary and most necessarily expendable raw material."[13] In all these ways, a soldier's superiors owned him and could expose him to danger and death. His senses, however, were his alone.[14] By making meaning of what he heard, smelled, saw, and tasted, he kept a fragile hold on his sense of self.

1

When it came to surviving the front line, hearing was the most important sense.[15] On a battlefield where artillery was largely out of sight, and where *to see* the enemy was also *to be seen by* the enemy, visual self-orientation could prove deadly.[16] Instead the soldier listened to the sounds of battle to map his position relative to that of his enemy. Being able to isolate and interpret noises made by guns helped him locate himself in a field of danger. Listening became a matter of survival, with battle noises actually helping a soldier save his own life.[17]

Men on their way to the front measured its distance by sound. "The noise came first," recalled British infantryman Tom Perry. "I was sure that a thousand gates on rusty hinges were being opened, the sound amplified a million times." In a letter to his mother in early 1945, one German soldier explained how he was measuring his proximity to the front by artillery noise.[18] At night, the sounds of exploding mortars reminded you that, even behind the lines, you were vulnerable.[19] Noise demarcated the space of the battlefield, reinforcing the boundaries between front and rear, danger and safety.

On the battlefield itself, noise came from all directions. Sometimes the racket emanated from above, as it did during Mack Bloom's first night at Anzio. "Suddenly a howling came from the sky above us and the noise grew louder and more terrifying as a plane that was hit came rocketing toward the ground. With a terrible crash, it landed so close, everything in our hole bounced up and down. My ears seemed to spring a leak." Sometimes the noise swept in from a distance. Fighting in Italy, Major H. W. Freeman-Attwood described a noise coming "like an express train, the din becoming louder and louder until I thought my head would burst." "Suddenly death comes screaming," wrote German infantryman Hans Stock from Monte Cassino to his family.[20] Also in Italy, a French artilleryman recorded in his diary how the guns were always "barking and groaning."[21]

The noise could be overwhelming. On July 9, fighting in Normandy, Brit Eric Codling wrote in his diary that "after a while the battering on our eardrums caused us to reel about like drunks such was the deafening noise." "We were both shaking and shivering and crying and praying all at the same time. It was our first barrage," remembered one infantryman in the US Ninth Division. "I shall never forget the brain-splitting shock wave as mortar bombs detonated," recounted Brit Sidney Jary. "I felt as if each whistle was seeking me out personally, and the bombardment of explosions was like the blows of a sledge-hammer against the imperfect resolution of my will," recalled British doctor Stuart Mawson. GI Raymond Gantter's internal organs began to "quiver and dance" during one night barrage: "It's as though heart and lungs, stomach and liver were suspended in Jell-O, and the bowl being shaken violently."[22] Many soldiers could not "take it" and had to be removed from the line altogether.[23] "One poor fellow who had lost his nerve lay shaking and weeping on the ground," observed a British stretcher bearer. According to another soldier, "Even battalion commanders would crack up, begin to cry and refuse to fight."[24]

Artillery fire assaulted both body and soul. In the war, it inflicted roughly half the battle casualties.[25]

Allied soldiers disliked the German 88 mm gun in particular. "It had a screaming sound," explained US Sergeant Ed Steward. "At first it's absolutely frightening, it's a nightmare."[26] Robert Kotlowitz said he often got an erection when the 88 exploded; "a panicked rush of blood was released in my groin that was almost Pavlovian in its reliability."[27] One French soldier had such a phobia about the 88 that he carried around a large sailor's bag in which to bury himself during barrages.[28] One reason soldiers hated the German 88 was because it presented no "calling card to tell you to duck." It was so fast, observed a French infantryman, that "no sooner did you hear the departure thump than 'S-H-H-H-H-I-V' it has arrived."[29] Because the gun had a flat trajectory, the noise came only when it was upon you.[30] The American cartoonist Bill Mauldin wrote that the GIs hated "those that come straight at him more than those that drop, because the high ones give him more warning." "It's the one you don't hear that gets you," agreed Leroy Coley.[31]

But the 88 was merciful, in fact, *because* of its speed. For many soldiers, the worst moments were the seconds before the shell hit. "One could hear the shells approaching for a few seconds which seemed of interminable length," recounted British Geoffrey Picot. "The swisssh grew louder and more violent. One's heart panicked and one's knees shook." GI Lester Atwell's memory focused on the same moment: "There'd be that long wild shrieking, growing louder and louder—it seemed to be seeking you out, knowing exactly where you were lying. . . . With the whole world filled with that sound, there'd be a split second of intolerable wait and then would come the enormous deafening smash of the explosion."[32]

When barrages occurred at night, it was impossible to sleep. "No sooner had one dropped into oblivion," remembered Brian Harpur, than "something always happened to shock one back into the most miserable consciousness. It could be the ear-shattering explosion of a mine, shell or mortar bomb nearby."[33] Worse still, darkness made artillery sounds seem closer.[34] Sleep behind the lines came poorly to D. G. Aitkin, for example, because "every sound is rather of a terror."[35] After a while one grew accustomed to the sounds of war. A night barrage deemed intolerable to a newcomer might not affect the sleep of a veteran soldier.[36] British medical officer P. J. Cremin wrote his wife on June 14, 1944, that "there is plenty of noise going on most of the time. But we are now quite used to it."[37] In this way, one's ability to tolerate noise took the measure of time spent on the line.

The barrage was intentionally relentless. One artillery strategy was to fire as many as two hundred guns simultaneously at a relatively small target.[38] A "concert of death" was how Maurice Piboule described a night barrage in Italy in May 1944. At Colmar, French tanker Jean Navard estimated that twenty guns went off per second: "The woods are hammered at an infernal pace." A diary found on a German paratrooper fighting at Cassino contained this entry: "What we are enduring here is indescribable. I never experienced anything so bad on the Russian Front. Not a second's peace, only the constant thunder of guns, mortars as well as planes overhead."[39]

The idea was to terrorize the enemy by creating a small, contained hell with no hope of escape. "One felt literally hemmed in by the prospect of death or serious wounding and quite unable to end the onslaught."[40] British soldier Rex Wingfield summed it up this way: "The barrage swelled and slammed its doors behind us." The noise and force of exploding shells made GI Richard Byers feel as if he were trapped inside an enormous bell "while giants pounded it with sledgehammers."[41] An artillery assault was an extreme version of the war itself: one was trapped with no recourse but to confront death.

Noise exhausted the soldier because he was constantly using it to locate himself on the battlefield. As Mauldin put it, "The doggie becomes a specialist on shells after he has been in the line awhile."[42] Short-range field guns such as mortars and howitzers were backed by long-range, major-caliber artillery. Because artillery targets were communicated by phone or radio, barrages were aimed at unseen targets from locations several miles behind the front. Learning how to distinguish one noise from another as well as hear trajectories of sound became vital skills. One had to listen intently to isolate and identify sounds on the battlefield, then determine their direction. "One could keep track of each sound and visualise the moves made by the enemy mortar crews in the process," noted Brit Peter White. In this way, one's ears became one's eyes. "Thinking became difficult," recalled British Trevor Greenwood, "every single fibre and nerve being too occupied in trying to see from where the shots were fired." Another trick was to learn to distinguish, as did French soldier Louis-Christian Michelet, between the smoke coming from artillery, mortars, and tanks.[43]

These methods were hardly foolproof. At times, confessed White, "so many guns were firing that the individual noise of each shot and explosion on arrival, combined with the incessant shriek of passing shells like droves of giant wildfowl in flight, made it impossible to identify any individual sound except short shells or enemy shells landing nearby." For the most part, however, frontline men determined their position based on sound. In the end, of course, knowing whether or not you were going to be hit did not do you much good. The "most terrifying part of an artillery attack," claimed GI Roscoe Blunt, was "knowing that the next shell will land on top of you." Fighting in the French First Army, writer André Malraux was more philosophical: "In war, if it was necessary to worry about every noise you heard, you would not survive."[44]

Nevertheless, locating yourself on the map of fire gave you the illusion of control. The origin and target destination of artillery fire was one line of expertise. While Steward was initially terrified of the 88s' screaming sound, he eventually became oriented enough to make sense of it. "The sound itself is replaced by the need to make a judgment about it. . . . So then you become preoccupied with that. You almost begin to like the sound because this gives you some information."[45] Behind the lines, men walked around with one ear cocked to the sky.[46] When you heard the 88 shell overhead, you knew it was *not* aimed at you. As Mauldin wrote, "If the flat one misses him it keeps on traveling, while the dropped one can kill him even if it misses him by dozens of yards."[47] To hear the German "buzz bomb" or V-1 missile overhead was also good news. Because its rear diesel flame made an audible vibrating sound that "cut off" a few miles from the target, noise meant danger was not headed your way.[48]

Even if you were as good as dead, calculating sound made a barrage less terrifying. For one thing, it gave you something to do besides just waiting to get killed. "All the time you're *listening*," explained GI Mel Lowry, "because you know the difference, the different sound, between a shell going out and a shell coming in. Also a shell that's going to go over, a shell that's going to go to the side, and a shell that's going to come close to you! They all make different sounds, and you very soon learn these." Writing about the Battle of the Bulge, Burgett recounted "that it takes long-range artillery a good bit of time to reach the target. Sometimes you can hear the booming of the guns before you hear the sound of the incoming shells. Other times you don't hear anything until you pick up the sounds of shells rotating and screaming just about at the top of their arc from cannon to target. If you live long enough, you can learn to almost pinpoint the spot of impact where high-trajectory shells will hit, just by the sounds they make." If you then heard a swish, warned Brit Arthur Reddish, the shell was dangerously close. The formula was simple for GI Jesse Caldwell: If you hear a crack and then a whiz, the shell was outgoing. But if you hear a whiz and then a crack, you should hit the ground.[49]

Infantrymen also became expert in mortar sounds. They began as a "click, click, click," according to GI Mac McMurdie. You then had about ten seconds "to do whatever you wish."[50] "The higher the pitch at the beginning, and the longer the scream continues, the closer the shell is coming," observed another GI.[51] The best possible outcome was to hear the "Brrr . . . ing" of steel passing over your back.[52] Mortar sounds changed depending on the terrain so that sounds had to be interpreted differently depending on location. "Crump, crumpcrum', crumpcrumcrump, crump" was the sound H. W. Freeman-Attwood used to describe mortars hitting Italian rock. In the Hürtgen Forest, they exploded in the trees, creating a "fire burst" with a splitting, cracking sound, "like a crashing explosion in a huge barrel that just won't quit," remembered GI Francis Ware. For the rest of his life, British Lieutenant E. A. Brown felt a chill up his spine every time he straightened a pack of cards on edge; the sound reminded him of the "report" of a mortar.[53]

The most hated German mortars were the Nebelwerfers, nicknamed "Screaming Meemies" or "Sobbing Sisters" for their sound. The French called them "lions" because they roared.[54] The Nebelwerfers demonstrated how a sound could itself become a weapon of war. The "diabolical weapon" fired six rockets at one-second intervals.[55] While in the air, the shells were rotated in such a way that they made an ever-louder eerie, "ungodly sound."[56] "If you have never heard the screamin meeny [sic] . . . you don't know what being scared is," claimed GI James Hagan.[57] "What made the weapon so terrifying is that each shell *sounded* like it was going to hit you even if it didn't."[58] "As they flew in on us," declared GI John Khoury, "they sounded like an express train chugging in the sky, and then they made high-pitched screaming sounds before they landed."[59] "While sobbing they bring death" was how French journalist Fernand Pistor put it. British soldier Chester Wilmot tried to look on the bright side: "At least they do announce their coming unmistakenly."[60]

The screaming meemie made your blood go cold and your body hair stand at attention. Harpur described it as the "most unnerving noise I personally have ever heard. . . . At night when one was already sick with anxiety and up-tight with just plain terror, the addition of this awful sound and the menace behind it was paralysing." GI Ross Carter observed how his friend Willie's Adam's apple "pistoned his dry throat" every time he heard a meemie. "They made a horrible noise when fired and while streaking through the air," noted Ralph Schaps. "They had a high explosive charge and really didn't do that much damage but the eerie screaming noise scared hell out of us." The Nebelwerfer had a bark worse than its bite, as Schaps recalled, but it was not all talk: John Clayton dubbed it "a six barreled organ playing purple heart blues." Cartoonist Mauldin swore he "never drew pictures about 'screaming meemies' because they just [weren't] funny."[61]

Front soldiers could also interpret the sounds of small gunfire. According to Jary, there were the "monotonous, repetitive bursts of the Bren, the hysterical shriek of the MG42's furious rate of fire and the lethal chatter of the Stens and Schmeissers." Tracer bullets, he continued, "approached almost lazily until suddenly, like a swarm of fiery demons, they accelerated directly past one's head with earsplitting cracks."[62] If you heard the report of a rifle, the danger had passed because a bullet travels faster than sound. A bullet whizzing past you gives out a "vicious hiss" or a "dreaded thwack ... when it hits a human being."[63] The German rifle made a distinct noise, "like a snap of the fingers when passing directly over you."[64]

In the Hürtgen Forest, GI Leroy Stewart had second thoughts about firing at a soldier behind a tree when his gun "didn't sound right."[65] The soldier turned out to be an American rather than a German.[66] The Allies named the German machine gun after its sound: it was a "Burp" gun because it shot bullets so fast it went "brrrrrb."[67] To John Davis, it sounded "like canvas ripping." Davis also remembered hearing "a clank and then a hissing in the snow" as the Germans replaced the barrel. Davis took advantage of the break, which would last about ten seconds, to change his position without fear of fire.[68]

Unlike music, the noise of a shell coming at you was not open to creative interpretation. Each shell had a precise sound that could be taught and learned with time *if*, as Burgett emphasized, you lived long enough. Making meaning out of sound was one of the first lessons that veteran soldiers taught replacements. Infantrymen could expertly mimic the sounds of a mortar or a buzz bomb.[69] The appearance of a wide-eyed, clean-shaven replacement on the line created a turbulent mix of feelings among "old-timers," among them grief for dead buddies and anger about the risks posed to the entire company by such green soldiers. To pass on the meanings of sound bridged the gap between "old" and "new" men. Sharing expertise also shed a flattering light on your own qualities as a soldier. In all these ways, sense meaning created camaraderie.

While weaponry dominated the battle soundscape, there were other terrible noises. As the battle progressed, you could hear the sounds of human distress. You knew how the fighting was going, noted British Peter Ryder, by gauging the number of cries around you. "Groans all around indicated that the guns had done their work."[70]

"Screams of pain . . . gave us the grim tally of the casualties as we pushed on toward the road," explained GI Milo Green.[71] "Suddenly it was all over [and] an unearthly quiet reigned, broken only by the moans of the wounded," recalled British L. C. Pinner. Worse than the sound of the wounded was the silence of the dead. "C'est le silence, un silence inimaginable," observed French writer André Chamson.[72]

Then came the cries for help from the wounded. After a bombardment in Italy, GI Carter lay trembling on the ground and heard "the nerve-tightening scream of 'medic, medic, for God's sake send a medic, three men hit!'"[73] Freeman-Attwood referred to the "dreaded call of 'stretcher bearer.'" "Around me men were being wounded or killed and the cry of 'stretcher-bearer' could be heard on all sides," remembered British David Evans. According to GI Peter Bepulsi, "Those left wounded on the field would cry for help and scream to each other in pain, sometimes for hours after a battle was over."[74] The wounded soldier begging for something "à boire [to drink]!" haunted a French doctor's memory.[75] There were prayers, Hail Marys, and Our Fathers recited "loud and clear," as well as cries for "mama," "mutter" and "mum."[76] Navard recalled both French and German soldiers "calling out for their mother, screaming with pain."[77]

Such sounds signaled the terrible toll of war, its horror and suffering, its arbitrary imposition of death. A German soldier admitted in his diary one night that he got drunk just so he didn't have to hear "loud screaming anymore."[78] At the same time, cries were not considered sounds of cowardice, as they might be in times of peace. Instead they were welcomed as sounds of life.

2

Unlike sound, the smell of battle had little strategic value. Rather than attend to smells carefully, as they did with sounds, soldiers tried to ignore them. This was because frontline odors evoked the traces of battle. If sound meant something was coming, smell meant something had come and gone. The meaning of smell was the war's power to wreak havoc with human life. GI Nat Frankel remembered the "crackle and stink" of human flesh, the malodor of sweat and decomposition. The "stink of a suffering humanity" was how a frontline French doctor described it.[79]

Like sound, smell demarcated the battlefield. As GI Robert Gravlin moved toward the Ardennes front, "the distinct smell of death" warned him that he was getting closer to the line. When Donald Burgett returned to the front at Bastogne after several days' leave, he dreaded the stench of the front line: "We needed time away from killing and the smells of the battlefield: the smells of gunpowder, of the freshly killed, of raw iron in fresh blood, and of burnt human flesh." Because the stink of death was everywhere, recalled a British infantryman, you "got used to that smell." But then if you went off the line for a few days, forgetting it, "it would hit you again" when you returned. "Terrible."[80]

The stench of war transcribed its chaos. Frontline odor combined smells from divergent sources: chemical weaponry, burnt wood, wounded bodies, and decaying corpses.[81] "The smell of war is the smell of cordite, a scorched smell," declared GI Bill Scully. It was all over the Italian mountains after a mortar barrage, recollected Freeman-Attwood.[82] A combination of cordite and pus, gunpowder and fresh blood, flaming metal and the stink of human flesh, war's stench mixed the source of destruction (firepower) with its effects (wounding and death).

Soldiers remembered the battlefield precisely as this odd mix of cause and effect. British Bert Isherwood described the Reichswald Forest, "The smell of cordite still lingered, mixed with the stench of the putrefying flesh of men." "My memory is well stocked with smells," observed Sidney Jary, "the metallic stench of dead cattle in Normandy, the pungent odour of German prisoners and the vile, penetrating chemical smell from a newly ploughed shell crater." "Smells are usually held to be one's most evocative memory," noted another infantryman, "and I can still smell today that mixture of wet earth, burnt cordite, brick and plaster dust, and pus that permeated those days."[83]

When US Sergeant Robert Conroy's buddy died in his arms, he suffered "the fetid, obnoxious stomach-wrenching odor produced when blazing hot metal, residual gunpowder and human flesh come together." "The hilltop smelled of cordite," Dale Lundhigh recounted, and also of "powder-seared flesh in the crisp, damp, frosted air." "I learned that the smell of rotting flesh, dust, burned powder, smoke and gasoline was the smell of combat," explained German soldier Siegfried Knappe.[84]

Because battle sounds were about strategy and function, danger and death, they remained neutral in terms of moral value. Battle odors, by contrast, assigned social place and moral worth. To smell was to be lowly and wretched, particularly in the case of dysentery. The faint stench of diarrhea pervaded the line at almost any time. Although every effort was made to keep food and latrine areas as sterile as possible, living and eating in the open air exposed soldiers to airborne or insect-transmitted illnesses.[85] This is likely the moment when "the GIs" as a phrase for diarrhea took root.[86] Aid stations passed out paregoric "by the quart," according to Richard Stannard, but its effect was only temporary. While dysentery was not frequent in the Italian or Normandy campaigns, an epidemic broke out in December 1944 during the fighting in Germany and Belgium.[87] In the combat chaos of the Hürtgen and Ardennes Forests, inadequate sanitary facilities, poor food, stress, and extreme cold all made diarrhea common.[88] "You could easily follow our company," recollected Harry Jubelirer, "by tracking the brown spots in the snow." "From the amount of action on the road, dozens of us had intestinal diseases," recalled William Condon, "what a trail we made!" The Germans were no different. As they began to retreat in the Ardennes, the GIs traced them by the trails of bloodstained feces.[89]

The reek of diarrhea was humiliating. Soiling your pants was not uncommon.[90] "The back of my pants are warm now," confessed an infantryman, "but as they get warm, I begin to stink."[91] The stench meant that you had lost control over your body, a terrifying realization in an already precarious situation. At nighttime soldiers would repeatedly leave their foxhole or tent, risking their lives in the wind and snow to avoid the incriminating odor.[92] When Mother Nature sent Arnold Whittaker, prostrate in the snow, "a telegram that the

K-Rations you recently deposited in your stomach must leave immediately," he asked himself: "Did I want to take the chance of dying with my pants down?" Lundhigh avoided the foul smell by using his trench knife to cut away the pant seat of his long underwear when he had an accident. He was often wearing several pairs of such underwear only from the knee down. Paul Cunningham's Ardennes buddies also used their knives for the same purpose, although it often meant they froze because they were down to just their outer pants.[93]

The stigma attached to malodors became a way to denigrate the enemy. "They didn't smell—they stank," declared Conroy about the Germans. "Never, never, did I smell anybody as foul as those machine gunners. . . . Words cannot describe how repulsive their body odor was. I was afraid I would throw up." Soldiers like Conroy made much of an "all-pervading peculiar German stench" in the air and along the line.[94] Wehrmacht prisoners were particularly bewailed for their smell.

At the same time, no one could deny that the Allied soldiers also stank. "The enemy could have smelled us if he himself hadn't stunk just as bad," claimed Leroy Coley. As trash, mud, excrement, and stained underwear accumulated and mixed with sweaty bodies, foxholes became stink holes.[95] George Biddle remembered them reeking of sweat and vomit. "God we're a mixture of smells, mostly bad," admitted the narrator in William Wharton's novel about the Ardennes. When Conroy tried to save a friend's life, he "learned a new fact of battlefield life—wounded men smell! Stink horribly! AND so do their clothes." Lack of fresh water "meant a good deal of body odor," noted Ronald Lewin. GI Michael Bilder almost threw up when he entered an Allied fort in the Ardennes: "There was no running water so there were no working toilets or showers, and the smell from human waste and body odor, combined with gunpowder, trench foot, and infected wounds, was enough to make the devil himself retch." Summertime was the season of foul smells. "We found that the stench in the tank was almost unbearable at times during the hot summer days," observed British tank driver Stephen Dyson.[96]

Like sound, stench bound infantrymen together. "We all knew what each of us smelled like," recalled British tank driver Arthur

Reddish. Luckily, he added, everyone joked about it.[97] The sharpness of a soldier's smell, like the sharpness of his ears, took the measure of his time on the line. Tolerance prevailed, as did resignation. Everyone was in the same boat; no one could really help it; and perhaps most importantly, smell became another badge of an experienced soldier. "You were afraid to take your boots off next to anybody, the smell would knock the bugger out," joked a British soldier. "But you didn't care if others smelled because you knew that you smelled."[98] To put up with your buddy's stink meant that you, too, would be forgiven for your bad odor. British David Evans called to mind a soldier named Frank who had soiled himself as a result of fear from a sudden mortar attack. His comrades lay him on the ground and pulled off his trousers. "God, what a mess! His underpants were flung away as being past redemption, some of the lads began to clean his trousers as well as they could, using grass, while others attended to his legs and body. The stench was awful." Although this soldier came under ribbing on other occasions, no one ever mentioned this incident again.[99] Humiliation over not being able to control their bodies united these men, even if they rarely spoke of it.

The most pervasive smell of the battlefield came from the dead. No amount of training prepared soldiers for the "ghastly stench of death," according to British Captain Henry Pearce.[100] A corpse could not move or talk, but it could emit a smell—an eerie final act. The odor of the dead, like that of the living, erased enemy lines. German, American, and British corpses all smelled the same. "There's only one stink and that's it," observed a Graves Registration official. Graves Registration people were experts on the smell of bodies. As one put it, "The ones who stink the worst are the guys who got internal wounds and are dead about three weeks with the blood staying inside and rotting."[101]

The reek of a corpse was invasive. "You never get used to it and after a while the stink gets into your clothes and you can taste it in your mouth."[102] "The odor of the tomb invaded my nostrils and made me nauseous," declared Fernand Pistor. "An unbearable stink" was how Louis-Christian Michelet described a pile of decomposing bodies.

"The smell of rotting flesh has a way of lingering on in the clothing," agreed British A. G. Herbert. "The stench of death clung to our nostrils for days," recollected British Raymond Walker.[103] When US officer Charles MacDonald ordered some of his men to bury corpses, they returned with "the scent of death" on their own bodies. It "quickly filled the room and was nauseating." At the Falaise pocket in Normandy, where thousands of German infantrymen died, soldiers had to deal with the "Falaise smell," which reached even Spitfire cockpits fifteen hundred feet above. "It was during our stay at Coffin Corner," recalled Walker, "that our senses of sight, sound and smell became acute."[104] In its reminder of death, the corpse rallied the senses to life.

3

The intoxicating smell of onions cooking on the stove, the reassuring warmth of a pot roast with family, special cakes made lovingly by mothers—these types of food attachments followed men to the lines. Army rations broke them.[105] With little to offer but a hole for a bed, the front line was no luxury hotel. What had been linked with comfort came to represent its absence on the line. If food had stood for pleasure back home, it now stood for misery at the front. The monotony and blandness of military food came to represent an infantryman's boredom and anonymity on the line. Scanty or poor-quality food assaulted the soldier's sense of self-worth.

In a world where bathing, touching, and sexual stimulation were either forbidden or absent, food remained a singular source of physical gratification. Perhaps this is why, as Paul Fussell has pointed out, food is a primary preoccupation of all soldiers everywhere.[106] A common joke in the Thirty-Fourth Infantry Division played on the similarity in sound between "chow" and the Italian greeting "ciao." "There's nothing like saving time," went the joke, "to say hello and ask for food with the same word."[107] Even a brief glance at unit newspapers such as the *Red Bulletin* or the *45th Division News* reveals an infantry fixated on food. Fresh white bread with C rations, delicious lamb chops left behind due to sudden troop movement, a KP cook who burned a stew while fighting a battle—this was the stuff of front-page news in unit papers.[108] "We talk nonstop about food," noted French Jean Navard in his diary, "as if we had nothing else to do."[109]

Letters home, journals, and diaries evoke food as an object of intense interest. Thousands of soldiers wrote their families about what they had been eating, particularly on holidays. On Christmas a French soldier boasted in his diary that he had eaten lamb and milk-fed pork with a good bottle of wine. J. A. Garrett reported his Christmas bonus: "a rum issue, 5 bottles beer, 50 Player's cigs, an apple, pear, orange and bag of sweets which we give to the local kindergarten."[110]

British Colonel W. S. Brownlie was not so lucky. In a letter to his family dated December 25, 1944, he complained that the cook had come up with supper in containers "stone cold." GI Lester Atwell knew by heart everything he had eaten when food ran short near Metz: "a tiny dab of stew or very limp corned-beef hash, two narrow ration crackers, a cup of coffee and, with luck, a single spoon of canned fruit salad." Wounded British soldier L. F. Roker recorded every bite he took while convalescing in the hospital. On December 13, 1944, for example, he had tea, porridge, one sausage and potatoes, and two slices of bread with margarine for breakfast. Dinner was potatoes, meat and peas, and sponge cake. Tea brought two more slices of bread and margarine, a slice of toast, and some pease pudding. The day ended with a supper of soup, two slices of bread, and margarine and cheese. This fixation on food evinced boredom but, more importantly, a profound need to be nurtured. Good food meant comfort. After a particularly tough night of combat, with his company all but wiped out, GI James Graff recollected how the kitchen jeep appeared with breakfast. "I remember we had pancakes."[111]

Certain foods symbolized home and normality.[112] If the GIs obsessed about tender juicy steaks an inch thick, it wasn't just about being hungry. J. R. McIlroy longed for a "good old American hamburger or my mother's home cooking." Cartoonist Bill Mauldin observed, "In the misery of the battlefield, men tended to cling to anything—any little nicety—that could take them back to civilian life, even for a moment." GI Oakley Honey looked over at a soldier in the next foxhole who had laid out a breakfast setting with a white cloth, utensils, a plate, and a coffee cup. "You would think he was at the Waldorf Astoria Hotel," commented Honey. When the soldier's foxhole suffered a direct hit, his life was saved by the fact that he had ducked into the hole for some salt and pepper.[113]

Food was also the subject of dreams and fantasy. While GI Leroy Stewart was fighting his way into Germany, he started having a recurrent dream. Wounded by artillery, he would gain consciousness in a hospital eating a big hot dish of mashed potatoes with gravy. While holding out on one can of beans per day in the Ardennes, John Davis woke up in his foxhole and "saw a giant platter of steaming turkey floating through the air." On a long march, "while trotting through the mud with clanging mess gear, en route to what was sure to be another unsavory arrangement of spam and green beans," Raymond Gantter distracted himself by thinking of his favorite meals back home.[114]

The problem with rations was quality not quantity. For foot soldiers who had grown up in the Depression years (particularly in Germany and the United States), food scarcity had been a fact of life. Luckily, except for rare occasions when supply lines were cut off, the Americans and the British were amply fed. By contrast, German soldiers faced the last battles of the war on empty stomachs. One of their chief incentives in 1944 was to make the Allies retreat hastily, so they could eat any rations left behind.[115] Hubert Gees knew to look in the inner edge of the camouflaged covering of foxholes to ferret out C and K rations. Erich Nies remembered having "agonizing pangs of hunger" on Christmas Eve 1944.[116]

Even if army rations were almost always available, Allied soldiers loathed them. "Wherever they served, regardless of background or upbringing," claimed historian Sean Longden of the British Army, "most soldiers agreed on one thing—they hated army food."[117] The Royal Army Service Corps (RASC) provided British soldiers with their food. Off the line, the men ate field kitchen "dixies," named after the large pots used for cooking meals.[118] Otherwise they lived on compo rations, including tea and biscuits, vitamin-enriched chocolate, pudding, and tinned meat and cheese.[119] The reviews were not all bad. Fred Glasspool recalled the compo packs as having "a superb variety of tinned foods." Some of the puddings also received high praise. Harpur described "an absolutely delicious creamed rice and creamy sultana roll for which I used to trade my bully beef, or even my precious cigarettes."[120]

In general, however, British soldiers deemed the food awful, particularly the porridge served without milk or sugar and the hardtack biscuits, commonly called "dog biscuits." These the soldiers used to line the floor of their slit trench in order to keep it dry.[121] "How do they expect anyone to live on this bloody stuff?" asked an infantryman nicknamed Popeye. "My pigs get better grub than this." "The fighting man's breakfast," sneered one officer.[122] Only hunger, soldiers claimed, forced them to eat. The compo meat and vegetable soup was "too fatty." The salmon was "grade 3 and of poor quality." The oxtail stew was "too foul to be true," riddled with bones, and "very greasy." In general, the meat was "tasteless, insipid and nauseating." Finally, the marmalade pudding was "soggy and indigestible."[123] The first time Arthur Jarvis entered the mess hall, he caught the smell of the food and walked out. When he complained, a corporal told him to wait a week. He would be hungry enough to eat anything. "And I was," confessed Jarvis. In their lighter moments, soldiers joked about their rations. Bill Scully used to roll the cheese down a hill for a joke. "It were [sic] solid," he jested. When Peter Ryder saw that his dinner had arrived on the Arnhem line, he asked in mock seriousness, "What happened to the buttered crumpets?"[124]

The American C ration was also widely reviled. US Army rations were developed by the Quartermaster Corps of the Army Technical Services. "The rations were garbage especially the C rations," according to Bill Buemi. "I ate C rations Morn. Noon. Nite. I got to a point of where I would open up a can of C rations—'get the smell' and throw up, then eat the scrap. I can understand in combat you are not going to get steak."[125] The C ration was particularly bad when eaten cold because the grease congealed on the top and had to be scraped off.[126] It had three canned "meat units" representing three daily meals.

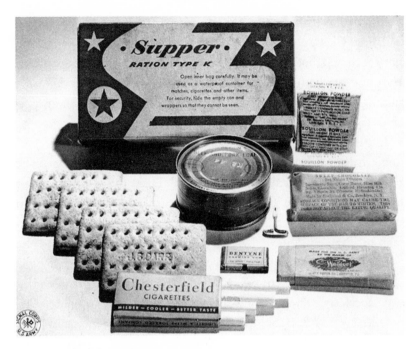

FIGURE 2. The daily K ration.

They were meat and beans, meat and vegetable stew, meat and vegetable hash.[127] All three menus received negative reviews. Stuart Kline
thought they "looked and smelled like dog food." "The odor was so
repulsive" that David Reagler could not eat them. As for the meat and
vegetable stew, Larry Collins could "eat a bit of it if I just have to—a
little of it."[128] Lester Atwell also passed on the stew despite his terrible
hunger. It was the meat and vegetable hash in particular that, according to the Quartermaster Corps, "was not well received." That was
putting it mildly if we consider Collins's letter home from Italy: "The
third type is meat and vegetable hash, and only those on the verge of
starvation or those with perverted appetites and tastes can eat it."[129]

Neither did the K ration get any love (fig. 2). A GI instructed to
give K ration crackers to a German POW joked, "I thought there was
an article of war forbidding torturing of prisoners."[130] The K ration
was also distributed to the French army, where it garnered decidedly
mixed reviews.[131] Although K rations were designed to be eaten in the

field for two to three days, infantrymen were often forced to down them for weeks at a time.[132] After a stretch of eating the "Ks," you would get diarrhea from "real food."[133] Packaged to fit inside a uniform jacket and resembling a Cracker Jack box, the K contained biscuits and crackers, powdered eggs, tinned meat or cheese, chocolate, a lemon drink, one stick of gum, and four cigarettes. Industrially produced, the K lacked any fresh ingredients to give it flavor. According to Atwell, the hardtack biscuits "tasted as if they had been dipped in preservative, or a weak dilution of rat poison." "Terrible" and "horrible" was how Julian Jacobs described the powdered eggs.[134]

The complaints were unending. "We are eating so many of those 'delicious' C-rations," Mack Bloom observed, "that when we look at them we get the GIs—in the Army that is the back-door [censored]." "There is nothing quite so tasteless as cold C rations (I could only get two meals down today)," Robert Snyder wrote in his diary in Italy. Peter Bepulsi called them "the cold, canned C, 'ugh' rations."[135] "Why was it called 'C'?" asked Morris Courington. "Because it was c—p." According to Mauldin, German prisoners screamed when given C rations because they were supposed to get the same food as their captors, and they refused to believe that the GIs ate such food.[136]

It is fair to ask: Why did the food taste so bad? We often assume that army rations, like hospital food, will just be generically horrible. But, in fact, army food was terrible for good reasons. A great deal of sincere effort went into making decent food for Allied soldiers, but there were insuperable obstacles to producing tasty meals. American rations were a case in point. First, they were designed for function rather than flavor. In the British and American cases, the goal was to provide enough energy to keep the infantryman fighting. As the US *Soldier's Handbook* put it, the rations were "especially selected to build up your body and give you the energy and endurance which will carry you to success on the battlefield."[137]

Taste was sacrificed in pursuit of this higher goal. For example, early in the war, the Quartermaster Corps contracted with the Hershey Company to make chocolate bars for the K ration. It specified that the chocolate itself must taste "just a little bit better than a boiled potato." If the chocolate tasted too good, the Corps reasoned, the soldier would "eat it like candy rather than retaining it for energy use."[138] The reviews were predictable. "If you had a good stomach," noted Gerald Creehan, "maybe you could eat it." You had to eat it "like a rat chewing and gnawing its way through a ridge plank," recalled Cliff McDaniel. British chocolate was also designed for energy rather than taste. Thick, black, and bitter—it was forbidding in flavor. "I never saw anyone eat a whole bar of this stuff in one go," swore B. A. Jones.[139]

The Corps was determined not to cater to "sectional appetites," another problem.[140] Deemed unacceptable was any food considered "ethnic"—for example, Mexican cuisine. In 1941 the Subsistence Research Lab (SRL), acting under the aegis of the Corps, refused a company making tamales without even so much as testing a bite. Instead the SRL developed menus according to a vague concept of "American food." This bland meat and vegetable diet stripped food of all traditional or regional meanings. Although it was called "American," it had no real place in American food habits.[141]

Furthermore, both armies operated under the limits of portability and sustainability. Their task was global in scope: to deliver rations to soldiers fighting in climates all over the world. To do that required canning, dehydrating, and packaging food—all of which destroyed its flavor. To dehydrate food was to deprive it of water, the very symbol of life. *Yank* joked about how eating dehydrated foods could actually "shrink" soldiers (fig. 3). All Allied soldiers were desperate for fresh foods and went to great lengths to get them. Even on D-Day, it was rumored, British soldiers scooped up fish killed by explosions and stored them in their helmets to eat later.[142]

The cold weather made infantrymen crave hot food. Fires were forbidden because their smoke revealed a unit's position. "One of the best inventions of the Second World War" was how a British soldier described the beloved self-heating soup distributed to their lines.[143] Lit by a cigarette, a heating agent in the center of a can warmed the soup in four minutes. When US mess sergeants brought food up to the line, they wrapped it in straw and blankets. But when kitchen crews

FIGURE 3. *Yank: The Army Weekly*, February 25, 1945.

were delayed or considered the front too dangerous to approach, cold food became a dreary fact of life. "Gravy turned to grease in mess tins, potatoes were like iced balls, and pudding congealed," complained Peter Ryder. In the Ardennes, American foot soldiers sometimes ate frozen C rations for weeks at a time.[144] "We would take our bayonet and break off some frozen rations and put it in our mouth to melt so it could be eaten," recollected Leroy Stewart. "I remember the frozen canteens, frozen C Rations, especially the solidified grease in the stew or hash," wrote Ray Rulis. Byron Reburn hated the ice crystals "woven into the lard and meat; it was like eating greased ice."[145]

GI Leroy Coley was ecstatic when his platoon reached the assembly place and "a *hot meal* was awaiting our Platoon, and the rest of E Company. Yes, a hot meal! We had hot C-rations. . . . This was the same food we had been eating since Christmas day, except the food was hot. Everyone appreciated the warmth."[146] J. J. Kuhn recalled the night in France that "they sent up mashed potatoes and ground beef. A good, solid meal! From K rations to a good, hot meal! That night I guessed that maybe I wouldn't have to live on cheese forever and that maybe my GIs would go away with something solid in my system."[147]

Rations offered little choice. British compo boxes had repeating menus—namely, tins of stewed lamb, oxtail and green beans, beef and kidneys, steak and veggies, or salmon.[148] Similarly, the C ration had three canned "meat units." Soldiers ate these same menus over and over again. British tanker Stephen Dyson referred to the "hated selection of 'same again' tinned food and hard biscuits in the composite ration box." "The main trouble with K and C rations was their monotony," remarked Mauldin.[149] GI Ross Carter described the average Joe eating in Italy:

> The joker gets hungrier. He is always hungry. He drags a supper ration [from] the shelf of his dugout. Although he knows the lettering on the box by heart, he reads it again to pass the time. He even counts the words that begin with M and then those that begin with N. He pries the end off the box with his bayonet, tears the waxed paper off the crackers, surveys the corn pork loaf with hatred, and puts the stick of stale gum and small chocolate bar in his jacket pocket to chew on outpost that night. . . . He munches the crackers slowly in his saliva-less mouth and stares straight ahead with the vacant expression of a cow.[150]

If food had been about pleasure before the war, rations stood for its utter absence on the line. They sucked all the color and joy out of eating—just as the war sucked all the color and joy out of life. They also evoked the tedium of the front line—the endless hours waiting to move out or watching for the enemy.[151] There was nothing distinctive about these foods. Rations reminded you of your anonymity in the army.

Most importantly perhaps, rations affronted your dignity. Holidays were painful. Because a special meal was expected, the decidedly non-special meal would provoke anger. GI Bepulsi wrote with bitterness about a Thanksgiving in Belgium. The turkey presented to him was so awful, he threw it on the ground in anger. "All the guys of my section looked down at it and we all felt like kicking it around like a football from being so damn disgusted with not only having to fight the damn war but being given a half frozen turkey."[152]

The infantryman's frontline position, his barking sergeant, and his hideous living quarters—all reminded him every day, day after day, of his lowly status. US infantrymen often considered themselves the "sludge" of the military forces.[153] "As I think back on it," wrote GI Bernard Friedenberg, "I believe we envied everyone who was not in the infantry because we in the infantry were at the bottom of the ladder." "It was a shock to be sent to the infantry," recalled Ray Millek. "Nobody wants to be in the infantry." GI Grady Arrington expressed his indignation: "Why should we stand facing the enemy while the sailor glides lazily about on the cool, clean ocean, and the air corps speeds overhead, high above the din of battle, returning to comfortable quarters miles away from the messy mud and slime of the front?"[154] As for the British version, it was called the PBI, or "poor bloody infantry." "Nobody wanted to have anything to do with the old-fashioned foot slogger," admitted Gerald Kersh.[155]

The infantryman preserved his pride by scorning everything. Food was no exception. Gantter complained about food in this way:

Here's a sample of our breakfast menu while we lay in the woods near Bastogne: one-half ladle of hot cereal, one-third canteen cup of coffee, one small teaspoon of sugar (you could choose: either in your coffee or on your cereal), one tablespoon of milk (same choice), four dog biscuits (hardtack about the size of graham crackers) and one slice of bacon. I admit that this menu represents one of the bad days and often we ate better. But sometimes we ate worse, and there were many days when even the daintiest eaters wholeheartedly agreed with the wit who said "In this goddamn army you don't get enough to eat in a week to have one good bowel movement!"[156]

Gantter was writing from Bastogne during the Battle of the Bulge. For several days, snowy weather had prevented supply planes from dropping food and ammunition for the First Infantry Division.[157] Yet Gantter took the food situation personally. Expected to triumph over the German war machine while sheltering in the freezing cold and eating "dog biscuits," he saw his choices reduced to a teaspoon of sugar and a tablespoon of milk. Gantter demanded the right to be treated decently even if he was in the infantry. "Living like animals in holes in the ground, eating C and K rations for long periods of time and being treated not much better than galley slaves," recalled Robert Bowen, "turned most of us off the infantry life all together."[158] To bitch about food was to insist on the humanity and dignity of the foot soldier.

4

The infantry relied on yet another sense—the instinctual sixth sense. In Mignano, Italy, a sleeping William Kunz was jolted awake at one in the morning by his buddy digging a new trench some feet away. "I got a little annoyed because we had to move the field phones and some radio gear," remembered Kunz. "He said he had dreamed his mother had told him to move! I said he'd been in the line too long." Two hours later, an artillery attack destroyed the vacated foxhole.[159] The sixth sense—a feeling that "something was not right"—protected soldiers on the front line. Soldiers who followed their instincts often saved their own lives.

The sixth sense also forecast death. Although paratrooper Donald Burgett claimed not to be superstitious, he saw the sixth sense work repeatedly at Bastogne: "A soldier's premonition of death in battle is usually pretty accurate." "I couldn't shake the feeling that something was going to happen to me before the next day was over," noted rifle-man Stanley Smith. "Call it a preminition [*sic*] or something else." In fact, he was wounded that very day, barely surviving. British infan-tryman John Thorpe wrote in his diary on October 15, 1944: "This day is different, I feel this is my last day." And it was; he left the front with serious wounds, never to return again. "Next week, a few hun-dred miles north of here, there's something waiting for me with my name on it. . . . I feel it . . . ." sensed J. H. Burns's fictional GI about the Italian front.[160] John T. Jones likewise "felt a premonition that some-thing bad was going to happen" on March 30, 1945, the day he was wounded by shrapnel. The night before Ed Wadd was killed, Ralph Schaps found him crying in his foxhole. Schaps was surprised given that Ed was a "happy-go-lucky type of guy." Ed explained that "he had a premonition that his number was coming up the next day." And it did. Jack Reeder's buddy Joe Bonnaci turned to him one day and said, "Reeder[,] this is our day. This is it." Over and over he said it. He died five minutes later. When British glider pilot Bovey Tracey told his buddy Sid Carpenter, "I wish I could see my wife and baby daugh-ter once more," Carpenter reassured him they would survive and go home soon. Not only was Tracey not consoled, but he was killed soon after.[161]

Even when presentiments did not mean death, they deeply spooked soldiers on the line. When Rex Wingfield attacked a German-held house in Belgium, it brought back a dream he had had in Ypres, in which he was shot seven times in the throat. Terrified, he concluded the same thing was now happening in real life: "I was going to die and I couldn't do a thing about it." In fact, it was the soldier behind Wingfield who was shot in the throat—seven times.[162]

Like the other senses, the sixth one helped make meaning of the front line. Profoundly vulnerable, infantrymen went to great lengths to stop the gnawing of fear. To tie your death to a particular date transformed an endless succession of days into a narrative with a beginning and an end. "Under combat conditions, every day, week or month becomes the same," noted GI Roscoe Blunt. "Why bother keeping track of the date?"[163] Predicting your death resolved the story of your role in the war, giving it shape and meaning. More importantly, knowing your day had come gave you at least the illusion of control. If the front line was a lottery, it helped to pick your number.

5

Then there was the suspension of senses altogether. As Nat Frankel put it, "There's a condition common to all wars, which in World War II we called the two-thousand-year stare. This was the anesthetized look, the wide, hollow eyes of a man who no longer cares."[164] So overwhelming was the sense-scape of the battle that sometimes the foot soldier simply checked out. One American infantryman recollected a barrage in which he started shaking and crying, then banged his head against a tree: "I lost my senses. I couldn't hear anything. I don't remember exactly what happened, but I was walking down the road and I remember seeing this soldier crawling out of a tank with both arms shot off. I remember helping him, and then I don't remember anymore. I guess I must have gone off my nut."[165]

For this soldier, losing his hearing and losing his mind were pretty much one and the same thing. He shows us just how decisive the senses were to war-making. "Battle exhaustion" or "guardsman's hysteria," as the British called it, resulted from the extreme overstimulation of the senses. Doctors recognized it as the "shell shock" of the First World War. British psychiatrist H. A. Pamer explained a soldier's condition: "His central nervous system lets him down at this stage, and he may develop a condition of vague dissociation."[166] GIs referred to the stupor as being "bomb happy"—what Peter Ryder described as "not knowing or caring, and oblivious to danger."[167]

The telltale sign was the blank stare. In Normandy, sapper Ned Petty came across a group of eighty-five soldiers who had been in combat for three weeks. They had originally numbered six hundred. "When they got up, I thought there was something wrong with them. They just stood still, staring. They were all very dirty and stood as though they were still asleep." After a long stretch of combat in Italy,

Morris Courington looked into his mirror to shave and was startled by what he saw. "I expected to see the dirt and long beard, but my eyes showed an older guy who had a very strong, dull, empty stare. I looked at others and found the same thing." "Look at an infantryman's eyes and you can tell how much war he has seen," wrote Bill Mauldin. Edward Arn saw an old buddy from his boot camp days during the Battle of the Bulge: "He was filthy and his eyes were glazed. Beck was in a complete state of shock." "Coming off the line after weeks of tension, lack of sleep and exposure to death," recalled Ralph Schaps, "we often had the staring look of Zombies—a numbness and indifference to anything."[168]

The pervasiveness of battle fatigue reminds us that the human senses suffered extreme violence on the front line. The noises, smells, and sights of the battlefield sometimes (or eventually) defied meaning. Once the senses gave out, the soldier became extremely vulnerable. No longer able to orient himself in space, he had to be removed from the battlefield. Away from the noise and the stench and the killing, soldiers usually recovered. Sometimes they didn't. But before being overcome, the senses counted among their best friends. The accurate interpretation of artillery noise allowed a soldier to distinguish between friend and foe, place himself on the field, and duck for cover. The sounds of suffering told him how the battle was going. Instinct, "the sixth sense," proved to be a trusty guide. Sense-making also created camaraderie. As infantrymen shared their sense impressions and gave them collective meaning, they developed a culture separate from that of their superiors. Complaining about food became a declaration of communal pride. Stinking, starving misery not only loved company; it created it.

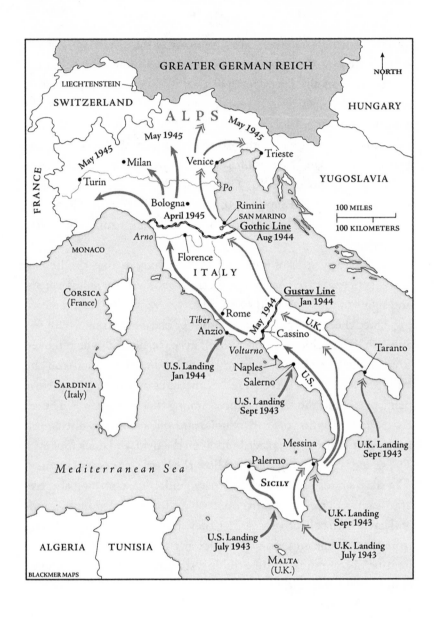

GREATER GERMAN REICH

NORTH

LIECHTENSTEIN

SWITZERLAND

A L P S

May 1945

May 1945

HUNGARY

May 1945

•Milan

Venice•

•Trieste

FRANCE

•Turin

Po

YUGOSLAVIA

Bologna•
April 1945

Rimini
SAN MARINO
Gothic Line
Aug 1944

100 MILES

100 KILOMETERS

MONACO

Arno

I T A L Y

Florence

Gustav Line
Jan 1944

CORSICA
(France)

Tiber

•Rome

U.K.

Anzio•

May 1944

Cassino

Taranto

U.S. Landing
Jan 1944

Volturno

Naples•

U.S.

SARDINIA
(Italy)

Salerno•

U.S. Landing
Sept 1943

Messina

U.K. Landing
Sept 1943

Mediterranean Sea

Palermo•

SICILY

U.K. Landing
Sept 1943

ALGERIA

TUNISIA

U.S. Landing
July 1943

MALTA
(U.K.)

U.K. Landing
July 1943

BLACKMER MAPS

2

THE DIRTY BODY

On February 27, 1945, the cartoonist Bill Mauldin found himself standing at attention on the carpet in front of General George S. Patton. Sergeant Mauldin drew a comic strip called *Up Front* featuring two dirty, unshaven GIs named Willie and Joe, for *Stars and Stripes*. The cartoon duo had so offended Patton that he threatened to ban the US Army newspaper *Stars and Stripes* from the Third Army area if Mauldin wasn't fired, a warning not welcomed by Eisenhower, who believed in the value of an independent GI newspaper.[1] Headquarters sent General Oscar Solbert to talk to Mauldin. Solbert confessed to the cartoonist that Patton had "got a fixation about this thing." As *Time* magazine put it, Patton would not be satisfied until the comic's "well-plugged uglies tidied themselves up."[2] Was it possible, Solbert asked Mauldin, "to clean up those characters of yours a little. . . . Some of these kids fresh from the States as infantry replacements think they've got to roll in a muddy ditch and grow whiskers before they're socially acceptable." To further quell tensions, Eisenhower aide Captain Harry Butcher called Patton to see if he would meet with Mauldin in person. "If that little son of a bitch sets foot in Third Army I'll throw his ass in jail" was Patton's reply.[3] Finally, however, the general did agree to a meeting with Mauldin. For his part, Butcher was hopeful "there could be a meeting of their minds leading to delousing of the characters."[4]

Mauldin shaved and cleaned himself to a polish, and was then transported by jeep to Patton's quarters in Luxembourg. He later described the trip as a "suicide mission." The "four meanest eyes I'd ever seen" was how he remembered the general and his bulldog Willie as he entered the office. Patton lost no time screaming at Mauldin about "those god-awful things you call soldiers." Waving a clip of the cartoon, he loudly accused Mauldin of treason. "You make them look like goddamn bums," he shrieked, "what are you trying to do, incite a goddamn mutiny?" Without a tidy appearance, he continued, armies "couldn't fight their way out of a piss-soaked paper bag." Mauldin should get a medal from the Germans for helping them "mess up discipline for us." Patton urged the cartoonist to teach respect to soldiers instead of encouraging them "to run around with beards on their faces and holes in their elbows."[5]

A West Point graduate and a career army man, the general linked cleanliness with discipline, filth with depravity. A dirty soldier, in his opinion, was a mutinous degenerate. Much more than other generals, Patton was known for his insistence on tidiness. As infantryman Paul Fussell bitterly put it, many of Patton's soldiers died with their neckties tucked properly between the second and third button.[6] Despite the scolding, the general did not win what Butcher called the "battle of Mauldin." The meeting, Butcher told his diary, was "a case of 'no hits, no runs, one error.'" Shrugging off the bruising, Mauldin went back to Paris and continued to draw *Up Front* just the way he wanted. As he told *Time* magazine, "I came out with all my hide on." Willie and Joe, reported the weekly, "remained unwashed, unsquelched."[7]

How was David able to triumph over Goliath? The answer is simple. Three stripes beat three stars because *Up Front* was so popular among the GIs. As one journalist put it, Mauldin had become the "idol of combat men" up and down the lines in Italy and France.[8] It was *refusing* to print *Up Front* that would have caused a "goddamn mutiny" in the Third Army. A two-time Pulitzer Prize winner, Mauldin is widely considered to be the most important cartoonist of the war. Contemporaries considered him and Ernie Pyle to be the only journalists telling the truth about life for the average GI Joe.

Even today historians view *Up Front* as a window onto the front line. "This is the authentic voice of GI Joe," claimed Stephen Ambrose. "For anyone who wants to know what it was like to be an infantryman in World War II, this book is the place to start—and to finish."[9]

Willie and Joe were beloved for their muddy, disheveled appearance. In this sense, Mauldin did produce a mirror of infantry life. Front soldiers got dirty and stayed that way. At the same time, dirt acquired a new meaning in *Up Front*. General Solbert urged Mauldin "to clean up" Willie and Joe because "some of these kids fresh from the States as infantry replacements think they've got to roll in a muddy ditch and grow whiskers before they're socially acceptable." If infantry replacements were intentionally rolling in ditches, that was because Mauldin made the dirty body the thing to have.

In boot camp, soldiers were held to extremely high standards of cleanliness. A dirty body was considered a sign of moral depravity. In *Up Front*, however, filth served as a badge of the true warrior. Mauldin's pair of infantry soldiers had endured the fire and danger of battle; they had the mud to prove it. According to journalist Ernie Pyle, Willie and Joe represented the "tiny percentage of our vast army who are actually up there in that other world doing the dying."[10] They were, in other words, the real deal. Cleanliness, not dirt, carried the biggest stigma in *Up Front*. The sergeants and lieutenants appearing in the cartoon frames may have sported spotless uniforms, but their spiffiness was held against them. In Mauldin's world, a clean soldier was a man hiding in the rear and sparing himself the war's real dangers.

Mauldin's greatest achievement was to help GIs deal with the physical changes they experienced on the front line. There soldiers became unrecognizable to others, even to themselves. Take the case of Grady P. Arrington. In France, Arrington ran into a friend from back home:

> I shall never forget the appearance of one friend in particular, a boy whom I had known back at the University of Arkansas. He had always been well groomed, smooth shaven and had a word of wit for

everyone. Seeing him that day was a shock. His clothes were dirty, wet, and torn by the concertina wire that stretched all along the Siegfried Line. His hair was matted and hung long and shaggy; his beard seemed to pierce rather than grow out of his soot-covered face; his eyes were sunken and red-rimmed; his hands were grimy, cracked open and hardened from exposure and dirt during the time he had crawled like a reptile under enemy fire. . . . Evidently my own schoolboy complexion had undergone quite a change, for I had to tell my buddy who I was. An astonished expression crossed his face and I wondered how long such a life could be endured by men who had once considered themselves human beings. Would we ever regain our sense of decency?[11]

By making filth the mark of the true warrior, Mauldin gave Arrington another way to understand his sunken, shaggy look. A cake of mud not a bar of soap, the cartoonist suggested, was what made the best soldier. Except, of course, in Patton's Third Army.

1

The links between cleanliness and morality were forged in the early nineteenth century. At that time, there arose a new social intolerance of dirt and its smells. Municipal officials of cities began to clean away human filth. They installed sewers and indoor plumbing, created parks, and established institutions of public health.[12] Increasingly, hygiene was connected with good health and morals. As germ theory gained acceptance, so did the belief that dirty habits threatened not only your health but also that of others. Patton grew up in a world where foul odors had been stigmatized and removed, a practice sometimes called "deodorization."[13]

Military institutions were among the first to impose squeaky-clean standards of hygiene. By the 1940s, the military had made discipline both a precondition and a product of good hygiene practices.[14] "Battle physical training will be wasted if personal hygiene is not practised diligently," claimed a 1944 British Infantry training manual.

"Ignorance of, or slackness in hygienic rules," it continued, "will soon incapacitate not only individuals but armies." "Sanitation is an indispensable part of the training of every soldier, and sanitary discipline is most important," declared an American training manual. "Keep all parts of the body scrupulously clean. . . . Bathe frequently and don fresh clothing after every bath." Notions of filth and cleanliness fed each other in a spiraling obsession. Filth had to be stigmatized to justify an elaborate regime of cleaning; higher standards of hygiene, in turn, further vilified dirt.[15]

Obviously, the Allied army wanted to keep its soldiers healthy and strong. By the 1940s, the links between health and hygiene had become indisputable. Dysentery and trench foot were only two of the many diseases produced by unhygienic practices, and officers felt a moral responsibility to ensure the well-being of their men. The meticulous care of the body also instructed soldiers in attention to detail. That skill would be crucial for innumerable tasks once they were deployed.

At the same time, the insistence on cleanliness was a way to regulate a soldier's body even in its most intimate functions.[16] American instructional manuals meticulously listed the body parts to be washed: scalp, ears, eyelids, eyes, nose, armpits, hands, feet, crotch, rectum, and genitals, including under the foreskin. Teeth were to be brushed "on the inside and outside, away from the gums and towards the cutting surfaces of the teeth." Bowels were to be moved "regularly once each day at as nearly the same time as possible" to keep the digestive tract clear of toxins.[17]

Both British and American recruits were penalized if their uniforms were not immaculate, their beds not properly made, their boots not shined. Although British recruits were often trained in castles and barracks without running water, their uniforms had to be "spotless," their room "swept and polished and all the beds arranged as book."[18] "There was always emphasis on personal cleanliness. Whatever the pressures it was always a priority to have a shave and a wash first thing in the morning," remarked W. S. Brownlie.[19] Even men with no facial hair were required to shave daily.[20] David Holbrook remembered a fellow soldier put on "punishment parade" because the inspecting officer found a "dirty" spot of gun oil on his pocket flap. H. C. Abrams recalled "the ridiculous charade" of rolling his mattress to the head of the bed so that the NCO could see if his bed space was spotless. George Neill wrote his parents that as soon as they finished dinner, they had a "GI Party" at the barracks. "This consists of taking all the beds outside and scrubbing the floors, washing windows, etc."[21]

These practices became the butt of British humor. Promoted to lance corporal in training camp, Douglas Sutherland joked how he had "become acclimatized, and even happy, in my role as mentor to young militiamen on such weighty military matters as achieving the exact patina on the toe-cap of an ammunition boot or the correct use of the button-stick so that buttons could be brightly burnished without impregnating the serge jacket with Brasso." Anthony Cotterell recollected an "adjectivally fiery speech" from his sergeant major on "the disgraceful state of the area round our hut. There were matchsticks there and he had personally seen an empty cigarette carton. It seemed to have ruined the day for him." As for inspections, Cotterell declared: "I have never been looked at so much in my life." "I had scoured myself from head to foot, sharpened my trousers to a knife-edge, polished my boots and brasses, spring-cleaned my webbing, and shaved myself so conscientiously that I broke out in a rash," wrote Gerald Kersh.[22] (The cleverest soldiers "acquired" a second kit set for use only at inspections.[23]) When Kersh was asked to create a pamphlet on infantry training for the British War Office, he came up with the title *They Die with Their Boots Clean.* Unsurprisingly, it was deemed unfit "to bear the imprint of His Majesty's Stationery Office."[24]

Dirt was not only degrading—it was seditious. Patton scorned Mauldin's dirty infantrymen as "mess[ing] up discipline for us." Dirt meant that something—mud, dust, grease, food—was not where it was supposed to be. Conversely, cleanliness meant everything was in its proper place. It represented order and hierarchy, the bedrock principles of an army. An unclean army might turn into a mutinous one. "Cleanliness is considered to have great moral value. Slovenly persons lack self-respect," a British manual argued, "good health, good discipline, morale and self-respect cannot survive in the midst of filth. Unclean habits make you both objectionable and dangerous."[25] At stake was not only the health of recruits but also their moral well-being. To have a dirty body was a disgrace.

2

But there was a problem. To be successful on the battlefield, soldiers had to get dirty. "You don't fight a kraut by Marquis of Queensberry rules," as Mauldin put it.[26] High standards of cleanliness were feasible in training camps, less so in the field. The Italian campaign was a good example. In the late fall of 1943, as the Allied troops made their way slowly north to Rome, a continuous rain transformed combat into a deadly form of mud-slinging. GI Milo Green remembered the mud of the Volturno River as being "everywhere . . . you walked in it . . . ate in it . . . often slept in it."[27] According to French Georges Gaudy, commander of the Moroccan *tirailleurs*, the US Thirty-Fourth Infantry Division camp was "swimming in liquid terrain. . . . Sixty bulldozers would have been required to clean the surface and establish a sleeping place which would last." "The mud got thicker and deeper, until in parts it reached up to my thigh," wrote British soldier Brian Harpur. Scots soldier Walter Elliott recalled bailing out slit trenches all night so they could stay safely underground during daylight. But "the mud was so sodden" that the trenches filled up again, leaving him soaked to the skin. Journalist Fernand Pistor described French soldiers in Italy as "mud shaped in the form of men."[28]

Ironically, given the torrents of rain, there was also a water shortage. When infantry followed the Germans into the Italian mountains, water became a precious commodity. Every drop had to be hauled up to the troops, usually by mule. In such circumstances, personal hygiene became a luxury no one could afford. All water was used for drinking; the men stopped shaving and grew beards. Uniforms became caked with grease and dirt; faces were blackened by burnt gunpowder.[29] As GI Ralph Schaps recalled: "We lived for months like wild animals in a fierce world where the certainty of death was always present. We were filthy, unwashed, unshaved and slept on the ground without any blankets or covers."[30] "The worst part was the filth, the hunger, the cold, and the life of living like an animal," wrote GI David Reagler.[31] Nicknames for US infantrymen such as "dogface" or "doggie" branded them as animals.

Being smelly and dirty was no fun. No one wanted crusted shit in their underwear. "It is difficult to imagine a more miserable group of men than we were," wrote Ross Carter of his time in Italy. In seventeen days on the front, he remembered, "we had never washed our hands or shaved or taken off our boots more than three times." German infantryman Hans Stock complained to his family that for weeks his company had been "unwashed and neglected."[32] Showering became the purest of pleasures. When shower trucks got to the Italian front, GIs would wait in long lines to undress, shower for five minutes, dry off, and be issued new clothes. Carter and his buddy Sokal "emerged with shining faces." "Egad, Mac," said Sokal, "I feel like a sixteen-year-old after his first kiss."[33] In early 1945 Captain D. H. Deane took leave with the intention of going straight to Florence "for a bath, haircut and shampoo—eighth heaven bliss." "Hurrah, had a bath, the first warm shower since that one in Normandy," Briton John Thorpe recorded in his diary on October 1. "Showers over here are wonderful," declared Richard Sanner from Alsace. "Imagine if you can, men who haven't shaved, brushed their teeth or washed for a week. Get these same men together, give them a shower and a chance to shave and brush their teeth and the moral[e] is built up 100%."[34]

Besides the pleasure of getting clean, a shower and a shave put emotional distance between a soldier and the war. Shaving had a tonic effect on soldier morale because, in Sean Longden's words, "it was a joy for them to scrape away with razors—as if the stubble was a symbol of all the accumulated dirt and exhaustion. To have a clean face was one final link with civilisation, and to shave was a liberating experience, symbolically distancing them from the corruption of war—if only for a few minutes."[35] Brit Stuart Mawson also enjoyed "the feeling of civilized security" that shaving gave him.[36]

At the same time, there was something sinfully delicious about being dirty. For one thing, it meant you had dodged the holy commandment†of squeaky clean. "The only way to escape most of the chickenshit was to be in combat and so far forward as to be virtually unreachable and surely uninspectable," remembered Paul Fussell. Longden mused that the appearance of British foot soldiers in Normandy "would have had their drill sergeants in paroxysms of fury." But when officers saw no reason to let up on the rules, they looked more like petty autocrats than managers of health. French Pistor noted with satisfaction that men still managed to shave in the icy Italian mountains. B. A. Jones recalled a cold December morning in 1944 when two soldiers showed up on parade unshaven. They were taken to the decontamination unit, where they were placed in ice-cold water and scrubbed down with floor brushes. After being up all night on watch, Patrick Delaforce ran into his commander, Norman Young, who asked him if he had shaved. "Sod off, what the hell do you think we've been doing all night?" Delaforce wanted to say. Instead he managed: "Imminently, Norman. Imminently." "I supposed our appearance was about like that of a tramp or homeless person," GI Wayne Kirby said of the mountain fighting. "Anyway a message came down from above, ordering every man to be clean-shaven within a day. I remember how stupid we thought it was when we were getting about a quart of water per day."[37]

To soldiers in battle, hygiene rules looked more and more like control for control's sake. As such, they generated mutinous disapproval. British soldier Harpur portrayed a soldier's attempt to shave on the Italian mountain as masochistic: "He had taken off his boots and jacket so he was blue with cold. He had hung up his socks hopefully to dry which already bore the pearly stiffness of incipient icicles. He was jabbing a razor in frozen water and . . . trying to shave himself. The places where he had hacked through the stubble were marked with spots of congealed blood."[38] Soldiers upholding these standards became the butt of jokes. In December 1943, the *45th Infantry Division News* mocked a GI named Edward Smith for attempting to remain pristine even as he fought. "Sanitary," as the newspaper nicknamed Smith, was "much impressed by the lectures handed him during his first days in the army." He "somehow" kept his clothes pressed, and "not wanting to get his feet dirty by getting out of the tub," stayed in his bath during an artillery attack.[39] Here the word "sanitary" carried the connotation of being stupid and effeminate. A dirty soldier, by contrast, was one who faced the realities of the battlefield. By the end of 1943, the meanings of filth and cleanliness were beginning to change in Italy. It was Mauldin who would make this transformation decisive.

3

Advancing north in Italy with the Forty-Fifth Infantry Division, Bill Mauldin was dealing with his own fair share of mud. Born into a poor family in New Mexico, the future cartoonist was rarely without paper and pen. After only one year of art school, he tried to make ends meet designing menus and drawing illustrations for rodeos. Unable to survive, he joined the National Guard in 1940. Once the war started, he entered the infantry and kept his hand in drawing by submitting work to his unit newspaper.[40] His cartoons, appearing under the rubric "Star Spangled Banter," became so popular among the GIs that in February 1944 he was asked to join the staff of *Stars and Stripes*. Mauldin was given his own jeep and free rein to travel in Italy, where he followed the front lines northward to Rome.

Infantry filth inspired *Up Front*. Mauldin drew the cartoon to channel his anger about how infantrymen were treated when they returned from the front. In Naples, where Mauldin worked on the *45th Division News*, a soldier would come down from his mountain post to take leave. "His shoes were muddy, his clothes were filthy, torn and often bloody, he needed a shave and haircut, and you could smell him a block away," remembered Mauldin. Considering these soldiers noxious, the US commander of the city would put them in jail for "insubordination" as soon as they entered town. As the cartoonist put it in a speech after the war, the commander and his "over-zealous MPs arrested haggard infantrymen, back from the front for a rest, by the truckload, and threw them in jail for dirty uniforms before they even had time to change." After a four-day "leave" in jail, the soldiers were shaved, showered, and sent back to their foxholes.[41] At Anzio some months later, Mauldin again watched MPs picking up infantrymen at the dock for a five-day leave in prison.[42] As Mauldin pointed out:

> It was not enough, the doggies felt, to live in unspeakable misery and danger while these "gumshoe so-and-sos" worked in the comfort and safety of the city. Hell, no. When they came back to try to forget the war for a few days, these "rear echelon goldbrickers" had to pester them to death.[43]

Witnessing these incidents strengthened Mauldin's determination to "give voice to the lowly soldier" and bring some modicum of pleasure to the "shivering dogface."[44] The doggies repaid him with love.

If infantrymen were treated like dirt in Naples and Anzio, that was because dirt was the root of class stereotypes. Both the British and the American working classes were stigmatized by their personal "filth." In the 1930s, George Orwell argued that the "secret of class distinctions in the west" could be summarized in "four frightful words. . . . The lower classes smell."[45] Because a majority of infantrymen came from poor or poorly educated populations, many had already experienced the prejudice attached to their "filthy, torn and often bloody" clothing.[46] African Americans, Jews, and non-European peoples were all similarly branded. A common anti-Semitic slur was a "dirty Jew."[47] Once again, personal cleanliness defined the line between the civilized and the uncivilized. If you had dark skin, whether due to pigment or dirt, you were on the wrong side of that line. Infantrymen were considered criminals by virtue of their filth, which explains why their commanders felt they belonged in jail.

Maudlin's *Up Front* countered the stereotypes by proposing that "these strange, mud-caked creatures who fight the war" suffered self-consciousness about their appearance. They did not want to be dirty. Their mud was simply "a curse which seems to save itself for war." "They wish to hell the mud was dry," the cartoonist claimed, "and they wish to hell their coffee was hot."[48] In one frame, Willie's brush

"No thanks, Willie. I'll go look for some mud wot ain't been used."

FIGURE 4. *Stars and Stripes*, June 21, 1944. Copyright by Bill Mauldin (1944). Courtesy of Bill Mauldin Estate LLC.

and razor, apparently defeated by the task before them, stick out from his soaped-up beard. "By God, sir, I tried," he swears to an unseen officer. In another cartoon, three GIs are up to their ankles in mud as a bunch of airplanes fly overhead. "It aint th' glammer I'm jealous of," says one, "it's jest that they're within fifteen minutes of a bath!"[49] In another frame, Willie and Joe are on the line facing each other. Their coats are covered with mud, and their helmets are black tangles of stems and leaves. "I got a hangover. Does it show?" asks Willie. In a famous drawing, Willie bathes in a mudhole, which he offers to share with Joe. "No thanks, Willie," Joe replies. "I'll go look for some mud wot ain't been used."[50] The unlikely Hotel Taft towel slung over his arm and the bar of soap in his hand suggest the futility of high standards in the field (fig. 4).

Dirt could, in fact, be a friend. At Anzio in 1944, Mack Bloom remembered, "One would dig a deep place in the ground, put some tree branches and a shelter-half over it, pile the dirt back over it and Happy Days 'home.'" Still another *Up Front* frame shows Joe digging a foxhole in France while proclaiming, "Me future is settled, Willie. I'm gonna be a perfessor on types o'European soil." In fact, many Allied soldiers collected soil samples from places where they had fought—North Africa, Sicily, Italy, France. As Peter Schrijvers has remarked, "Foot soldiers always stayed close to the soil. They ran heads down, they stooped, they crouched."[51] During artillery attacks in particular, a dogface "hugged" the ground. "Hit the dirt!" became a survival call.[52] The phrase appeared in one of Mauldin's most well-known cartoons featuring a priest hastily finishing prayers as shells began to arrive: ".... forever, Amen. Hit the dirt." Infantrymen under fire learned to nestle into "Mother Earth" as snugly as they could. The mud sheltered them from death and danger as well as from rain and wind.

4

Mauldin assuaged dogface shame. At the same time, he acknowledged the mutinous quality of being dirty or, in Patton's words, its power "to mess up discipline." In one cartoon Willie passes a jug of water to his comrades on the Italian mountain front. "Drink it all boys," he says, "th' guys wot put out the order about shavin' ain't comin' up here to inspect us."[53] Not only are the officers out of touch, Mauldin implies, but they didn't care—or dare—to climb up to the front line. No reason to worry, then, about the rear echelon's "chickenshit" on the

STAR SPANGLED BANTER   By Bill Mauldin

"I need gravel haulers, wood choppers, ditch diggers, mud scrapers, and rock busters.
We wanna make this th' best lookin' rest area in th' regiment."

FIGURE 5. *45th Division News*, January 22, 1944. Copyright by Bill Mauldin (1944). Courtesy of Bill Mauldin Estate LLC.

mountain. Here Willie's refusal to shave comes from battle experience rather than slothful habit. His beard acts as a symbol of reasoned disobedience. What looks like resistance to command is based on a higher logic.

In a January 1944 cartoon, Mauldin drew an infantry company resting in a bombed area in Italy (fig. 5). The soldiers sit around unshaven and exhausted. When their sergeant (himself unshaven) orders them to clean up the camp ("I need gravel haulers, wood choppers, ditch diggers, mud scrapers, and rock busters. We wanna make this th'best lookin' rest area in th'regiment"), the men do their best to ignore him.[54] The joke is on the sergeant, whose efforts only reveal the limits of his authority.

That joke is perhaps what Patton found so threatening about *Up Front*. The general was smart enough to recognize in Mauldin's dirty bums the limitations of his own command. Not that Mauldin set out to directly challenge army standards. Although he did on occasion refer to his cartoons as "seditious" and "insubordinate," he mostly wanted to make people laugh.[55] He was foremost a strong believer that the foot soldier and his miseries should not go unnoticed.[56] "I'm convinced that the infantry is the group in the army which gives more and gets less than anybody else," he wrote in 1945. "I draw pictures for and about the dogfaces because I know what their life is like and I understand their gripes."[57]

Even after Mauldin joined the staff at *Stars and Stripes* in early 1944, he followed the infantry in his jeep, splitting his time between the front and the newspaper offices. When a *Stars and Stripes* reader questioned "Mauldin's realism" given that he "has never seen the front and probably never will," the editor was quick to mention his service in the Forty-Fifth Infantry Division. Mauldin's experience with the Forty-Fifth sealed his reputation for telling the truth about the front line. As *Time* put it, he "can draw the infantryman truthfully because he has been one himself since he was 18." Don Robinson, the editor of the *45th Division News*, testified that "every chance [Mauldin] gets he wanders out with some outfit that's going into the field and, if the CO will let him, he tosses grenades, goes on patrols and generally participates."[58]

Mauldin saw himself as a veteran of the line. But he never pretended to present the "authentic voice" of the foot soldier, as Stephen Ambrose claimed he did. As for Willie and Joe, they would probably laugh at such an assertion. Instead Mauldin's reputation for realism came from a group of prominent journalists—most importantly, Ernie Pyle, who was also praised for portraying the real war.[59] (General Omar Bradley once said of Mauldin that he "pictured the war Ernie Pyle wrote about."[60]) Pyle characterized *Up Front* as "terribly grim and real," and Willie as "more like a hobo than like your son. He looks, in fact, exactly like a dough foot who has been in the lines for two months. And that isn't pretty." *Time* magazine's Will Lang echoed that opinion, calling Willie and Joe "grimly true to life."[61] Frederick Painton of the *Saturday Evening Post* compared the pair to men of the

Ninety-First Infantry Division he had seen in the Apennines: "Their faces were masks of fatigue, their eyes dull . . . their bodies wet and cold."[62] Asserting Mauldin's realism became an attractive way to bolster one's own status as a journalist. If you knew that *Up Front* was "grimly true to life," you must have witnessed the fire yourself.

Once Mauldin got a reputation for telling the real story, agreeing with that judgment gave you a ticket to an insiders' club. Army officers, often criticized for staying safely in the rear, were eager to join. When British Lieutenant D. Bach wrote to *Stars and Stripes* arguing that Mauldin "truly catches the spirit of the front line soldier," he was also professing his own familiarity with the average Joe. Retired Colonel James P. Barney wrote to Mauldin that after a long career in the army, he could say that *Up Front* was "the finest thing that has come out showing what the REAL GI thinks—and does." "I'm one who has seen plenty of 'Willies' and 'Joes,' " Captain Alfred J. Kelly told Mauldin in March 1945, "and know they look like you portray them."[63]

By the time victory was declared in May 1945, *Up Front* was appearing in seventy-nine daily newspapers back home. Authentic or not, Willie and Joe became heroes. In a cover article about *Up Front*, *Time* reminded its readers that "in any army's vast organization, combat infantrymen are the hundreds of thousands (among the many millions) who are always in the front lines, and who carry the dirtiest, heaviest burden of any war. They are the heroes."[64] Filth had become a sign of heroism. The *Saturday Evening Post* described Willie and Joe as "two hollow-eyed, unshaven infantry characters" who have "immortalized the misery, the grandeur and the godlike patience—as well as the grim humor—of the front-line fighting man."[65] Thanks to Mauldin, the infantryman had shed his disreputable criminal image. If Willie and Joe had tears in their jackets, mud on their boots, and three days' growth on their faces, every smudge, stain, and streak testified to their hardship in combat. If that made them gods, all the better.

One wonders if such a rehabilitation would have been possible if the Allied army had been losing the war. As these dogface bums made their victorious way north, they proved they *could* fight their way out of a piss-soaked paper bag, contrary to what Patton claimed. But if the infantry had been losing, would their muddy, unkempt appearance have become a symbol of defeat? The German case is telling. In April 1945, just before the Russians arrived, a Berlin woman saw a truck pass by with filthy, unshaved German soldiers. She realized the war was lost and she couldn't count on anyone to protect her.[66]

5

Among the Allies, filth became not just an asset but a commodity. Replacement soldiers coming on the line started to pay top dollar for the muddy clothes of the "old-timers." Being dirty was better than revealing yourself as a newcomer. Even men in the rear echelons "tried to look like Bill Mauldin cartoons," one observer noted. They battered their shoes, grew beards, and paid dearly for used infantry clothing.[67] The official army weekly *Yank* began to publish other cartoons in which GIs sported beards.[68] The British also followed the trend. "I had got a new zoot suit at Nijmegen, the right size at last," remembered tankman J. G. Smith. But, he lamented, "despite the rigours of the last few days it was still distressingly clean and noticeable."[69] Mauldin himself mocked the phenomena he had ignited. Of rear-echelon soldiers, he said:

> "Be dirty, be rough, be scuffed," they shouted. If they rode to town on a truck, they hung their faces over the side to get a coat of dust. They let their whiskers grow. They ripped holes in their pants and pounded their shoes with rocks. You could get five fancy officers' shirts for one tattered combat jacket, and if that jacket had a gen-yu-wine bullet hole you could name your own price.[70]

Dirty shirts had become the badge of the manly warrior. But Mauldin only half fell for it. Willie and Joe were hardly virile men. One *Up Front* cartoon features a soldier thrusting his head into a command post tent to deliver a message from the front line (fig. 6). With his bearded face and mud-splotched helmet, the doggie shocks the staff sergeant typing at a desk. The cartoon both derides and

"Eeeeeeek!"

FIGURE 6. *Stars and Stripes*, February 4, 1944. Copyright by Bill Mauldin (1944). Courtesy of Bill Mauldin Estate LLC.

champions the dogface. On the one hand, the infantryman seems to hail from a world beyond the edge of civilization. Unrecognizable as a human, he is a fright. On the other hand, the staff sergeant in his domesticated space seems a little too pristine. Like a girl who has seen a mouse, he declares, "Eeeeeeeek!"[71] Rear-echelon men often appear in Mauldin's cartoons as effeminate ignoramuses. (Infantrymen particularly loathed staff sergeants for being witless and pampered.) While the cartoon evokes the dogface's frightful appearance, it also portrays the staff sergeant as a coward. Crucially, the drawing scrambles the meanings attached to military hygiene: it portrays a dirty body in positive *gendered* rather than negative *moral* terms. The dogface is filthy, but at least he's not a sissy.

But neither is he a manly man. Willie and Joe, in *Time*'s words, endured "mile after mile of tramping, getting just as tired advancing as retreating, sleeping in barns, bathing in icy rivers, scrounging for small comforts."[72] But the pair were hardly willing to stick their necks out; intrepid they were not. Nor do they seem particularly interested in proving themselves *as men*. With their slumped posture, lumpy bodies, and soft features, Willie and Joe don't present as particularly virile. The pair also whine a lot—although in good humor. "Do retreatin' blisters hurt as much as advancin' blisters?" Willie asks Joe.[73] *Up Front* suggests, then, that neither bullet-ridden uniforms nor nonstop complaining have anything to do with being manly. In this way, Mauldin managed to degrade the rear echelon as "girlie" without ascribing to popular conceptions of stoic military masculinity.[74]

6

The dirty bodies of Willie and Joe demarcated the front line just as clean bodies did the rear one. Willie once defined the rear echelon as beginning where "the sojers start shavin.'"[75] Mauldin made no secret of his disdain for soldiers in the rear. As he once commented, "At a time when rifle companies were hacked down to platoon size by casualties, trench foot and pneumonia, there were ten 'support troops' getting fat in Naples and working union hours in the rear."[76] Mud in *Up Front* evokes the often-troubled power relations between frontline men and their rear-line officers. With its power to humiliate, mud became a weapon of the strong against the weak. In one cartoon, three infantrymen working on a road are splashed with mud by a jeep moving too fast. "Damn fine road, men!" derides an officer from the jeep, oblivious to the men's now-filthy uniforms (fig. 7).[77] "If a man barrels past foot troops, splashing mud or squirting dust all over them because he doesn't bother to slow down," wrote Mauldin in 1945, "he doesn't appreciate his job or he's just plain damned stupid."[78]

Officers got away with slinging mud, but not so other GIs. Mauldin recalled an incident much like this cartoon, in which the driver of a big GI truck "splattered the troops pretty thoroughly," then got

bogged down half a mile up the road. When "he had the unbeliev-
able gall" to ask the mud-splashed GIs for help, "they replied as only
long-suffering infantrymen can reply. They shoved his face in the
mud."[79] In one cartoon, a lowly private sits at the wheel of a jeep sunk
deep in the mud. Willie and Joe and a few others stand around as the
driver recites, "I'll never splash mud on a dogface again (999) . . . I'll
never splash mud on a dogface again (1000) . . . Now will ya help us
push?"[80] Mud took the measure of status and power. As if taking his
cues from *Up Front*, medic Robert Franklin captioned a picture of
himself getting a Silver Star from General Alexander Patch: "Patch is
on the platform. I am in the mud"[81] (fig. 8).

"Damn fine road, men!"

FIGURE 7. *Stars and Stripes*, January 15, 1944. Copyright by Bill Mauldin (1944). Courtesy
of Bill Mauldin Estate LLC.

FIGURE 8. Robert J. Franklin and General Alexander Patch. Reproduced from *Medic!: How I Fought World War II with Morphine, Sulfa, and Iodine Swabs*, by Robert J. Franklin. Used by permission of the University of Nebraska Press.

Given Mauldin's delight in using mud to mock the army's much-vaunted pecking order, the run-in with Patton was only a matter of time. In one of Mauldin's well-known cartoons, Willie and Joe run into a sign while delivering rations in a jeep. It warns: "You are entering the Third Army! Fines: No Helmet $25, No Shave $10; No Buttons

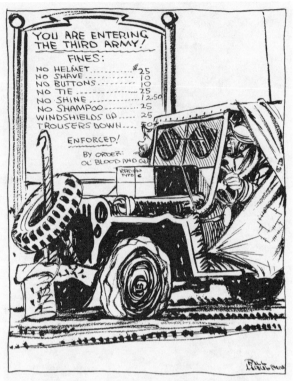

"Radio the ole man we'll be late on account of a thousand mile detour."

FIGURE 9. *Stars and Stripes*, February 21, 1945. Copyright by Bill Mauldin (1945). Courtesy of Bill Mauldin Estate LLC.

$10; No Tie $25; No Shine $12.50; No Shampoo $25 . . . Enforced! By Order: Ol' Blood and Guts" (fig. 9). As Joe catches sight of the sign, he asks Willie to "radio the ole man we'll be late on account of a thousand mile detour." The cartoon is widely considered to be the reason why Patton got so irritated by Mauldin's *Up Front*. According to Mauldin's biographer Todd DePastino, however, Mauldin drew the cartoon about a week before his meeting with Patton, and it had not yet appeared. One can only imagine Patton's reaction when it did. Instead, Mauldin later revealed, the cartoon angering Patton featured townspeople throwing flowers at the troops while the GIs threw fruit at a lieutenant and a colonel. "My, sir, what an enthusiastic welcome," says one officer to the other.[82]

The general was right that discipline was at stake in the battle of Mauldin. But the GIs would have none of it. They were too busy growing beards and trying to muddy their jackets. The unshaven face and dirtied uniform of the frontline man became one of the infantry's most cherished images, one that Mauldin unmistakably shaped. Born of necessity, the dirty, unshaved body became a source of pride and resistance as well as of humiliation. Willie and Joe had transformed filth from a marker of shame into a measure of sacrifice.

WALES

ENGLAND

London •

NORTH

NETHER-
LANDS

Southampton •

Brighton

Plymouth

Portsmouth

English Channel

Dieppe

Lille •

BELGIUM

GREATER
GERMAN
REICH

• Luxembourg
Metz
• Remilly

Brest

Gorron

• Rennes

Orléans

Paris

Seine

VOSGES

• Colmar

Nantes

Tours

FRANCE

Loire

Saône

SWITZER-
LAND

• La Rochelle

• Limoges

Lyon •

Grenoble •

ITALY

Bay of Biscay

100 MILES

100 KILOMETERS

Bordeaux •

Garonne

Rhône

Toulouse •

Montpellier •

Marseille

PROVENCE

SPAIN

ANDORRA

Mediterranean

U.S. & French
Landings
August 15/16

ALLIED LANDINGS ON JUNE 6

25 MILES

25 KILOMETERS

Cherbourg

GUERNSEY

CONTENTIN
PENINSULA

UTAH-U.S.

OMAHA-U.S.

GOLD-Canada

JUNO-U.K.

SWORD-U.K.

Le Havre

Rouen •

JERSEY

N O R M A N D Y

Seine

Saint Lô

Coutances

Caen

• Falaise

Évreux •

BLACKMER MAPS

3

THE FOOT

"He'd thought for a long time . . . that he was going to crack, and trench foot was a more honorable way of doing it than becoming a psycho." So reasoned Michael Patrick, an infantryman in a John Horne Burns story about Naples during the war. When we first see Patrick, he is limping along the Via Roma as fast as he can, trying to reinjure his feet. "The nurses couldn't figure out why his feet healed so slowly." It was a matter of life or death as Patrick saw it. "Tomorrow or the next day his feet would be well," and he would have to return to the front. "Next week, a few hundred miles north of here, there's something waiting for me with my name on it."[1]

Patrick's predicament rested on a contradiction at the heart of army medical services: The moment Patrick arrived at boot camp, the US Army took possession of his body. It did so in a profoundly ambiguous way. On the one hand, his commanding officers assumed moral responsibility to protect Patrick's body. They felt a strong obligation to assure his health, to heal his wounds, and to preserve his life. On the other hand, because the US military wielded the power of sanctioned violence, his superiors could expose Patrick's body to mortal danger. While wounding and death were made to appear accidental, they were, in fact, usually the result of conscious calculation. In short, the US Army sustained Patrick's life to visit death upon him.

British soldiers also felt the jagged underside of military medicine. "All new recruits were given a medical examination, dental treatment, inoculations, vaccination," A. A. Southam said of his training, "presumably to ensure we would be in the best of health if falling on the battlefield." Wounded in the leg, British signaler A. G. Herbert healed enough in a hospital to be "tested" for fitness to serve. In Herbert's words, he and other men were "expected to run along the beach for half a mile, like cattle in a market place, to see if we were fit enough to go to the slaughter-house once more." If Europe was to be freed, men like Patrick had to face death once again. Severely wounded men had less to worry about: their war was over. The distance between healing and death was far shorter for a soldier with trench foot.[2]

There were many men like the fictional Michael Patrick in the two last winter campaigns of war. Trench foot was a serious problem on the front line. For the Allied armies, claims one historian, "the greatest drain upon manpower was not the enemy but disease."[3] In Italy during the winter of 1943–44, there were 5,700 cases of trench foot in the US Army.[4] One year later in Belgium, the condition pulled 12,000 GIs off the line. "A plague" was how General Omar Bradley described it. The French army also had terrible problems in the Vosges, with 3,000 afflicted.[5]

Infantrymen like Patrick contracted trench foot by sleeping in foxholes or standing in the rain or snow. If their feet stood in snow with temperatures below freezing, they could get frostbite. Trench foot derived from cold, wet conditions just above freezing, combined with immobility and a generally lower metabolic rate due to fatigue and malnutrition. All this conspired to slow peripheral circulation in the feet. Deprived of blood and oxygen, the foot turned numb and swollen, then black and gangrenous. Wet socks and leaky, tight boots made it worse.[6] While most men recovered, some lost their feet. A soldier returning to the front after being treated for trench foot told his platoon about "seeing an oil drum full of amputated feet in a military hospital in Liège."[7]

The extent and severity of trench foot in these campaigns begs the question: Why did the US Army sustain so many casualties from an avoidable condition? (British feet fared much better, as we will see.)

At the most superficial level, the phenomenon can be explained as a problem of equipment. Infantrymen, who were by far the worst sufferers of trench foot, lacked good boots and dry socks. The rubber-soled GI boot was not up to the challenge of muddy foxholes in Italy and Belgium. Nor could the infantryman rely on a constant supply of dry socks. Feet got wet, stayed wet, became swollen, and then turned black. In footgear at least, the famously well-supplied US Army was not so well-provisioned after all.

At a more profound level, trench foot emerged as a result of the military logic governing the infantryman's body. By "military logic" I mean the rationales used by army command to justify its power to put men in harm's way. How did generals conceive of the soldier's body and its role in war? How did they rationalize the deployment of men in deadly conditions? Understand their power to both heal and kill? Army commanders at the highest levels negotiated such thorny issues by using the strategy of *abstraction*. In planning and executing battles, they conceived the individual soldier as an abstract unit of violent force. Collectively, such units were known as "manpower." Precisely that abstracted notion of the soldier's body allowed army commanders to understand medical healing as a function of combat. While Army Medical Services were not without compassion, their ultimate goal—to restore manpower to the line—undermined the goodwill at the heart of healing.[8]

1

When a man entered military service, his body became a primary target. Complete mastery over the soldier was necessary if the army was to execute its role as the manager of life and death. To secure that power, training (whether British or American) subjected the recruit to a regime of discipline. The soldier's body and his environment were obsessively controlled. The goal was to break the bond between a soldier and his body. He was taught to choose obedience over anything else, including pain and other signals of physical distress. Trainers looked at the recruit's body as unregulated, disorderly, and incompetent. Their task was to transform it into an effective combat machine.[9] To this end, the Allied army deployed two training regimes: drill and endurance.

Military institutions were among the first institutions, along with prisons and asylums, to impose authority through the disciplining of the human body. The idea was to produce what French philosopher Michel Foucault has called "docile bodies." Beginning in the eighteenth century, regulation of how a soldier marched, ate, slept, and evacuated waste became essential to military training. The strategy rested on an implicit belief that if one could take control of a soldier's body, one could also gain his obedience. As Foucault argued, "By the late eighteenth century, the soldier has become something that can be made: out of a formless clay, an inept body, the machine required can be constructed; posture is gradually corrected; a calculated constraint runs slowly through each part of the body, mastering it, making it pliable, ready at all times, turning silently into the automatism of habit."[10] In describing his own wartime training, British soldier Bill Jardine used the same language of clay being formed: "Individualism long since surrendered, bodies, physically and mentally tired, we were but as lumps of clay in the hands of a potter."[11]

To realize that goal of body-as-machine, infantry trainers had roughly fourteen weeks.[12] One US infantry manual advised recruits to "keep your feet always in good condition" as well as "the four avenues for the escape of wastes (lungs, bowels, kidneys, skin)."[13] The soldier's body was expected to process resources efficiently. Organs were mapped as entrances and exits that must be kept clear. "The understanding and application of simple mechanical principles is a necessary part in the proper handling and correct training of the body," advised one British manual. A soldier was commanded to envision his body as a well-wrought weapon of war: "Under military conditions, where the highest degree of efficiency is often necessary for the preservation of life itself, the full and proper mechanical use of the body becomes of great importance."[14]

Both US and British military training elaborated a regimen of drill and parade.[15] The aim of drill was to lodge obedience in the body in the form of habit. Drill required the soldier to make a series of instantaneous movements in response to a vocal order. In drill, a body's response to military command became not only compliant but automatic.[16] In this process, individual will became inactive, then eventually inert—what British John Guest called "the awful mental constipation that seems to have overtaken us all." David Holbrook described his fellow recruits this way: "None of them felt he was himself any longer. Personality was subdued to the driven life of the body and even the body could barely keep up—all else that was human in them was relinquished."[17] In this way, a soldier's obedience was secured through the body.

Another training method centered on endurance.[18] The goal was to prepare the soldier to expend enormous amounts of energy on the battlefield without ceding to fatigue or mental strain. As one British training manual put it, "Endurance is an essential quality in war. Mechanization has increased the tempo of war and consequently the value of stamina."[19] While endurance training was necessary to modern warmaking, it also had a troublesome side effect: it taught the soldier to ignore the limits of his strength. As he distanced (or abstracted) himself from bodily sensation, he became unthinkingly obedient.[20]

Trainers insisted on long marches or hikes, often in intense heat or cold. Such exercises aimed at producing bodily discomfort, pain, even agony—all of which soldiers were to ignore. In a letter to his parents while in boot camp, Paul Fussell wrote that "the whole object of the training is to become toughened in body and calloused in mind."[21] To endure pain, as recruits did on long marches, was to suffer "like a man." Even apart from the military, manly stoicism was a pervasive norm in American and European cultures. Young boys were taught not to cry "like girls" and not to complain about physical pain. Army commanders used such norms in endurance training as well as in the field. When novelist and World War II veteran James Jones was at the Antietam battlefield, his son asked him, "Why did these young men do it?" Jones responded, "Because they didn't want to appear unmanly in front of their friends."[22] "I firmly believe that the one thing that compels men to do what they have to do, even in the worst hell of battle, is their fear of showing fear," noted GI Bernard Friedenberg.[23]

A soldier developed the mental capacity to face physical pain without tears or complaint. Displays of endurance produced self-respect and garnered the respect of others. "Your self pride gets you thru the combat experience more than any other factor," claimed Rocco Moretto. Recruits who could not endure pain were stigmatized. British Eldred Banfield referred to a man who was scorned because he "went sick everyday." To be sick meant to shirk one's duty. When Edward Arn severely sprained his ankle in training, he refused to go to the dispensary "because I know how the cadet looked with disdain upon gold bricks."[24]

To appear manly, then, soldiers willfully continued a march or other exercise when their bodies told them to stop. British infantrymen often referred to training as a rite of passage from boyhood to manhood. As one soldier observed, it "made men out of boys."[25] Complaints about bodily discomfort became taboo. "Do I dwell on these physical miseries too much, these body aches from cold and wet and chap, and not enough sleep and not enough to eat?" GI Raymond Gantter asked his diary. "It would be more manly, more in the Spartan tradition, to gloss over such complaints, I know." "War creates the necessity to always portray yourself as a tough guy," explained Michael Bilder. "You have to view yourself as tough enough to do your duty in combat and the enemy needs to see you as someone tough enough to fear." Endurance training assured obedience, built stamina, and produced courage.[26]

2

The problem was that a soldier's body could not actually become a mechanical unit of violence. The meticulous ordering of the body during training could not be replicated in the field, where terrible operative conditions rendered that regime impossible. Even the most disciplined body was subject to its internal needs—warmth, food, a dry place to sleep. This was certainly the case of the infantry foot.

Feet were considered to be the most important body part for infantrymen.[27] "The feet of the combat soldier have been one of the prime concerns of his commander from the most remote times," argued military surgeon Edward Churchill. "Marching is the soldier's chief occupation and the foot soldier is no better than his feet," declared a US training manual in 1944.[28] Unlike artillery or armored units, infantrymen moved by marching. Called "foot soldiers" and "dough feet" in the American army and "footsloggers" in the British one, infantrymen were distinguished by their feet. When asked if he had minded being in the infantry, British Eldred Banfield had no regrets. "I have always been fond of walking."[29]

The foot became shorthand for infantry endurance. British tank commanders like Stephen Dyson or gunners like John Majendie pitied "the poor old infantry footsloggers," up to their knees in mud.[30] "Some Tommies felt that they were the poor relations, footslogging for mile after mile," noted British Peter Ryder. "In Italy it was always the slugging, the slugging and more slugging," remembered GI Milo Green. "You're walking, walking, walking," commented Nat Frankel.[31] "Plod, plod, plod," wrote George Biddle in his diary. "We plod on, tired and fed up, planting one foot in front of the other," observed L. C. Pinner of his days in northern Europe. British General Alexander famously described the Italian campaign as a "slogging match" to be won by the army with the most "guts and determination." Replacements arriving at the front were eager to get their "feet wet."[32]

The "leaden" or "dragging" foot symbolized infantry fatigue.[33] British Lieutenant Brian Harpur admired a platoon of exhausted men who went up to the front "with boots as heavy as lead." Ryder viewed the Ardennes offensive in this way: "Many on the verge of collapse lost all sense of time as they dragged their leaden feet through the clinging mud, dodged water-filled shell holes and faced harassing sniper fire." "It did not matter a damn how sick or tired he felt," wrote Harpur of the British foot soldier in Italy. "If he had any life left in him, and was capable of shoving one leaden foot in front of another at less than one minute intervals, he had to take his turn [on watch]." British journalists such as R. W. Thompson romanticized the slogging infantry as "these men on foot, the men with the rifles and the bayonets and the steady slogging courage."[34]

Standing "on your own two feet" symbolized infantry pride. Infantrymen were the prime victims of the "foot" mines left behind by the German army.[35] Walter Bernstein loathed the minefields because they rendered him unable "to walk freely and with dignity again." "It hurt to march tall and proud on cracked and swollen feet, but we did it," proclaimed Donald Burgett on fighting in the Ardennes. "We marched proud with frozen feet on frozen roads." Falling meant you were wounded, but if you could stand again, that meant you were not seriously so. The "walking wounded" knew their lives were not in danger. A veteran of Omaha Beach, the Hürtgen Forest, and the Ardennes, Leroy Stewart understood his odds-off survival in this way: "The wind will blow, the shit will flow, and there will still stand old Stewart." Standing meant *withstanding* the war.[36]

Both practically and symbolically, then, the foot was pivotal. Unfortunately, it was also fragile. Cold, wet weather was its greatest foe. Because infantrymen fought and lived in the open during winter campaigns, they suffered prolonged exposure to cold often just below freezing.[37] For weeks on end, there was no other place to put their feet than in snow, ice, or muddy foxholes. In Italy in 1943–44, a continuous, heavy rain transformed the ground into sludge. "Even England cannot touch Italy for rain," wrote British Sergeant G. F. R. House to his wife. "It comes down in buckets." "Rain pelting down," observed Brit Bill Scully. "I never realized you could fight in such conditions, mud all the way, slopping all over." Scully was under the impression that in such conditions you just canceled war, like a football game. German soldier Hans Bähr described the mountains near Monte Cassino as a "hell" unmatched by any battlefield in history. "The rain trickled down our necks and into our boots," remembered GI Ross Carter. "Our skin commenced to rot. Little patches of fungus formed on our bleached hands and toes."[38] Brit John Clayton wrote home in December that no sooner did he reach the front than his tent was washed away by a storm. "I gathered up my precious blankets and held them while the water swirled around my feet."[39] "The rain came down without mercy even while the sun was shining brightly," noted GI Leonard Dziaba of Cassino. "About the time a body would start to dry off, the rain would come back with a vengeance." A French artilleryman had the same complaint about the snow some months later. It was uncanny, he told his diary, how snow would start to fall every time they moved.[40]

The next winter's fighting was no less difficult. In Holland, Brit Jack Swaab commented in October 1944 that "it's rained all day and been cold and miserable and I've been violently depressed." The same month, German Hubert Gees recorded that he and his comrades fighting in the Hürtgen Forest were exhausted from "wading, lying and fighting in mud." "The roads are completely soaked," he continued in his diary. "The infantrymen look like swine. No rest for over a week and not a dry thread on their bodies."[41]

Then came the terrible cold—the worst, many claimed, in decades. According to the British sapper A. Marshall, it was "not suitable to forming happy smiles or pleasant experiences." Frozen feet were a problem in the French First Army fighting in eastern France. In Holland the British scoured for stoves and made "fireplaces" out of biscuit tins.[42] A German soldier remembered the "grim cold" of that winter, when frostbite harmed "feet, hands, ears, face."[43] "Which God is going to be born in this blood-soaked Christmas?" wrote German Willy Schröder in his diary, complaining of cold and hunger.[44]

The cold felt like an all-out assault on the human body. GI John Coleton said every breath felt "as if our lungs were full of ground glass."[45] "My eye balls would pain from the cold," recalled Robert Gravlin. "I was so cold," recalled John Davis, "I worried that certain appendages might snap clean off, and no needle and thread would be able to fix me up."[46] Raymond Gantter was concerned about damage to his genitals: "You begin to be conscious of cold—biting, searing cold. . . . Your genitals flinch and withdraw and you feel them tightening, drawing up . . . up . . . inside your belly, retreating to the dimly remembered fetal warmth." When the men tried to sleep, they became frozen to their trench walls and needed help to get out.[47] "Fellows had to be picked up and worked on before they could move," recollected GI Mac McMurdie. Cigarettes were a godsend. As British Norman Smith put it, "Even the act of lighting them and holding them in our hands seemed a warming thing to do."[48]

In this weather, the foot suffered terribly. "It seems like there were many miseries because of the wet and the cold but they all seemed to coalesce around misery of the foot," wrote GI Homer Ankrum. In Italy, added Ankrum, "the dreaded trench foot spread like a rampant plague."[49] Exhaustion lowered body metabolism; combat and cold food aggravated stress; blood stopped circulating to the edges of the feet.[50] Trench foot often caught an infantryman off-guard because he did not remove his boots every day, even when he slept. Many men were afraid that if they took off their boots, they would not get them back on again, either because they would shrink or their feet would swell.[51] Plus, the foot soldier was always on the alert for a night attack. Many years after the war, Leroy Coley still had dreams in which he was under attack but couldn't find his boots. "The delay [in putting on boots] might be fatal," warned Dick Jepsen. The vulnerability soldiers felt without their boots was exploited by medic Henry Deloupy of the French First Army. Faced with an arrogant, insulting bunch of German prisoners, he "calm[ed] them down" by taking away their boots.[52]

Because infantrymen tended to keep their boots on, they did not see their feet for days on end.[53] When Roscoe Blunt finally took his boots off, "the sight that greeted me was frightening. My feet had turned almost black and the skin was peeling much worse." "On removing my boots and socks I could see that my feet were in a sorry state," wrote Raymond Walker. "Typical of 'trench feet' I could now peel layers of dead skin from the soles of my feet." A British foot soldier discovered too late that his feet contained "deep raw cracks like crazy-paving, with blood oozing from them."[54] Brit Rodger Lawrence first got a look at his feet in an ambulance on the way to a hospital. He was shocked to discover that they were "covered with large purple blisters." "Blue and frozen" was how Noble Gardner's feet looked when he took off his boots. "I started to rub them but I was too tired and I fell asleep. When I got up the next morning my feet were like balloons, so red and swollen that I couldn't get my shoes on. And when I tried to walk it was like somebody giving me lots of hotfoots and sticking needles in my feet."[55] So well had these infantrymen been trained to ignore bodily distress that their feet could be severely injured before they even noticed.

3

Noble Gardner's blue, frozen feet were a product of the terrible operative conditions in the Hürtgen Forest. But they also resulted from bad boots and a lack of socks. In an army often portrayed as obscenely well-supplied, the American combat boot was a miserable exception. The failure of the boot to keep men's feet warm and dry was no small thing. Infantrymen saw boots as their most important piece of equipment. A story concerning a German soldier in the Ardennes illustrates their singular consequence. As GI Nat Frankel and his buddies approached the German soldier in order to take him prisoner, he had other more important things on his mind:

> Without so much as looking at his captor, the German tried on one pair of shoes, muttered something incoherent, and kicked them off. Then the second pair. His toes protruded and he took those off, too. Finally, the third pair—which seemed all right to me, but what the hell do I know! Once again he took off the shoes, and then collapsed. My comrade peered down at him and returned to the tank. "He's dead," he told me.[56]

The task of the boot was simple: to keep a soldier's foot dry, warm, and comfortable.[57] The GI boot failed on all accounts. "Inadequate" and "extremely bad" were words the GIs later used to describe their boots.[58] If you put on a dry pair of socks, as you were instructed to do, they immediately became wet.[59] In addition, changing socks meant you risked being caught in a German counterattack without your boots on.[60] In Italy the boots absorbed water and sprang leaks, despite frequent "dubbing" or weather-proofing.[61] When they finally dried, they also shrank, transforming a march into an agony.[62] In a letter home from Italy, John Clayton commented that he had so much trouble getting his shrunken boots on in the morning that he was missing breakfast.[63] The problem was particularly bad for soldiers whose feet had swollen to gigantic proportions. Often they resorted to cutting strips in the leather to get the boot back on.[64] GI boots were no more effective in the Belgian fighting a year later. "The footwear was atrocious for such deep snow and cold conditions," complained Rodger Lawrence. By February he was evacuated with severely frostbitten feet.[65]

The front soldier's sacred prerogative was to gripe about his gear. In the case of footwear, there was real cause for complaint. The US Quartermaster Corps later admitted that the combat boots "were not, by themselves, sufficient for foot protection in conditions like those encountered in Europe during the last winter of the war."[66] Bad footgear was not for lack of trying. In fact, the Corps worked fiendishly in 1943 to deliver better footwear.[67] A slowed wartime shoe industry hampered their efforts. The demand for jeep tires and tank tracks led to a scarcity of rubber. By 1944 soldiers were walking on reclaimed rubber soles, already proven unreliable in rain and snow.[68]

Some US commanders dismissed the possibility that any boot could withstand the weather in Italy and Belgium, but the British proved them wrong. The Tommies recalled having "good feet" and "very good boots."[69] The gum sole was a "tap-and-screw" type, considered watertight. "It was an excellent and very versatile item," admitted the US Quartermaster Corps.[70] "They are a great blessing in all this rain and mud," declared British infantry officer Peter Pettit, "when it is difficult to keep any pair of boots dry." Medical officer P. J. Cremin wrote to his wife that even when it rained continually, his boots were "grand— keep me fine and dry." Platoon commander Sydney Jary praised "the excellent all-leather British army boots and pure wool socks" of his men. Jary could not help but feel sorry for the "poor rubber-soled-booted American infantry," whose suffering in the winter was "pathetic to see."[71] The British claimed to have suffered only 443 cases of trench foot during the entire war. Most likely an underestimation, the number is still minuscule compared to the roughly 20,000 cases in the US Army.[72]

The British had learned their lesson from the First World War, when legions of soldiers, mired in the wet, cold trenches on the Western front, were admitted to hospitals with trench foot or frostbite. This time around "feet were washed and fresh socks put on daily," boasted infantry Colonel George Taylor.[73] "Dubbing," or waterproofing the boot leather, was a daily practice. Foot soldiers also benefited from an army of knitters back home. All-wool socks were prized among the men; no other fiber, they swore, could keep feet so warm. Knitting became a patriotic duty for British women. "Go to it and knit. Start at once," urged one instruction manual for "home-knit comforts." "Now is the time for busy needles," commanded another, "if you can knit you can do your bit."[74] Queen Mary sponsored "official" patterns for socks in conjunction with the War Office. The "Army Comforts Committee" laid down strict requirements for "service woolies," which included not only socks but also kneecap warmers, gloves, and balaclava helmets (fig. 10). "I have just received a very thick and well-knitted pair of socks," wrote a grateful infantryman to one knitter. "You can only have a slight idea of how welcome the knitted garments that you and other kind people send."[75]

As for the poor rubber-soled American infantry, the problem lay in supply as well as design. Socks were scarce.[76] The *London Times* claimed that American socks were also too thin.[77] While fighting in Italy in November 1944, General W. M. Livesay of the Ninety-First Infantry Division complained to Fifth Army headquarters concerning the woeful lack of socks in his division. Livesay had initiated a program in which soldiers turned in wet socks for their rations, receiving a dry pair in return. But the effort was failing due to poor supply.[78]

FIGURE 10. *Woolies for the Army: Knit for the Army Comforts Committee* (Weldon Knitting Series, No. 16).

During October 1943, one Fifth Army officer estimated that only 10 percent of the unit's requirement of socks were being fulfilled. On one occasion, the Forty-Fifth Division received only 500 of the 16,000 pairs it had demanded.[79] In Belgium the Quartermaster Corps also fell woefully short in delivering warm clothing and boots.[80] Confident of an early victory, Omar Bradley chose to prioritize gasoline and ammunition over warm clothing in the fall 1944 transports.[81]

Boot supply was at best spasmodic. The Corps began to issue "Arctic boots" once the trench foot epidemic began in Italy. Essentially rubber overshoes with a cloth or leather top, they, too, became a hot topic of complaint.[82] The Fifth Army asked for 208,000 pairs, received only 135,000, and immediately had only 1,000 pairs on hand, all of them in the "child" sizes of 6–8.[83] Sometimes the Corps would send an entire company—several hundred men—two sizes of boots. If your feet were too large or small, you were out of luck.[84] "You could always tell whose boots didn't fit by the man's step," observed Michael Bilder. "Some poor guys had their feet swimming inside oversized boots, while other guys were in agony from jamming their feet into boots that were too small."[85] When Gantter chose overly large boots, they became "like red-hot cases of lead on my aching feet."[86] Too-small boots constricted foot movement and thus encouraged trench foot.

To keep their feet warm, the GIs were left to their own devices. They wrapped their feet in burlap or the toilet paper that came with their C rations.[87] They found blankets abandoned by wounded or dead soldiers, then cut and sewed layers of them to serve as overshoes called "tootsie-warmers."[88] GI Leroy Stewart donned two pair wool socks, then combat boots, then a handmade wool sock *over* the combat boot, and finally four-buckle overshoes tied together with communication wire.[89] Sergeant Dudley refused to wear any boots at all; instead, he wore seven pairs of socks in overshoes.[90]

Boot distribution opened up painful fault lines between front and rear lines. Supply chains favored the rear over the front. In Italy the US Army promised to issue galoshes to infantry enduring wet mud. "The impending arrival of galoshes forms a good part of the conversation in our howitzer crew," journalist Ernie Pyle wrote in his diary in December 1943. "Galoshes have been promised for weeks, actually from day to day, but the rains are two months old and galoshes aren't here yet."[91] If the galoshes did not make it to the front, that was because soldiers in the rear had helped themselves.[92] As Bill Mauldin explained, "The new clothing was being shortstopped by some of the rear echelon soldiers who wanted to look like the combat men they saw in the magazines."[93] The Willie and Joe craze was backfiring on front soldiers.

The Corps then created rules of distribution: All foot soldiers would receive galoshes; 75 percent of Corps and army personnel would get them; and 50 percent of base section troops. But these quotas failed to make a difference.[94] A year later the situation was the same. In response to the Belgian cold, the Corps promised shoepacs. But these, too, were cherry-picked by rear officers and men working in supply.[95] *Yank* estimated that only forty men out of a company of two hundred actually got them. Again the Corps issued rules of distribution. On December 2, 1943, it urged troops at Paris headquarters to cede their shoepacs so they could be shipped to the front lines.[96]

Evacuated to the rear with a fractured foot, George Neill remembered being shocked at how much better everyone's winter clothing was in the rear. "I concluded that those who most needed the army's best winter equipment often did not get it." Even civilians, Neill noted, were better off, having bought equipment on the black market. Mel Richmond was "disgusted" when he saw non-combat soldiers wearing galoshes. Riding in a hospital train, GI Jake Langston couldn't help but notice "all the personnel had insulated rubber boots and some wore fleece-lined tanker clothing." "It was a shock to realize how many cases of frozen feet and trench foot could have been avoided had these shoes gone to the men who really needed them," scolded Jack Capell.[97]

4

At the most superficial level, trench foot resulted from poor equipment that was poorly supplied. If we probe deeper, however, we see other factors at play in the epidemic. Why, for example, did so many men suffer pain in their feet without seeking medical attention? The reasons are complex. Some men were loath to abandon their buddies to the fight on the line.[98] Still others felt guilty occupying hospital beds when other soldiers had serious bullet and artillery wounds. As John Khoury trudged to the hospital to care for his feet, he saw others "who had wounds and ailments that were much worse than mine. . . . I looked fine while others had bandages. I could talk while others mumbled incoherently. I was just too healthy."[99] Most crucially, many infantrymen ignored their physical pain just as they had been taught in training. Any kind of medical assistance, they believed, was a sign of weakness.

Infantry commanders continued to demand manly stoicism. Previously wounded, Peter Ryder went back to his unit with a yellow card from the British Medical Office stipulating he could not yet engage in combat. "They're a sign of weakness," snapped his officer. "In some quarters a yellow card indicated a yellow streak," observed Ryder. Ryder returned to combat, his "whole body racked with pain." Captain Charles MacDonald chastised a complaining soldier for using "every excuse he can to get to the rear." In fact, the soldier was suffering from appendicitis and almost died. The men MacDonald did praise were those who stayed on the line even when sick. "Many men who should be in bed were sticking it out in their holes for 'just one more day' and then 'just one more day.' "[100]

Infantrymen got the message. "Sick again last night so I joined the line of sick, lame and lazy going to the medics," Robert Snyder recorded in his diary as he battled trench foot in Cassino. A soldier fighting in the Bulge was so cold at night, he began to urinate in his sleep. When urged by a buddy to go to the aid station, he refused, saying they would only accuse him of "faking."[101] Infantrymen also pressured each other. GI Dale Lundhigh remembered two Italians in his company, Rocco and Robello, who were "always crying, wailing. Their feet were sore, they couldn't walk, they must have trench foot, they should be evacuated from the platoon and sent to the rear." Everyone dismissed them as simply "nurturing a ticket to the rear," but when they were finally pulled off the line, both had to have their feet amputated. Even when a commander was not there to bark, endurance became a matter of respect. "Leave it alone. It'll be all right," insisted Michael Bilder's buddy, his feet in terrible pain. According to Bilder, "He was repeating that line as a plea when they had to remove his foot."[102]

Many foot soldiers did not even consider medical attention. In the Ardennes, William Fee wrote in his diary that when his commander asked how his feet were doing, "I lied and said, 'Fine.'" William Condon ignored his pain until he was unable to get out of a foxhole in the Ardennes. On his hands and knees, he "hobbled around" with "agonizing cramps and spasms in my legs." Rather than see a doctor, he accepted his unfeeling feet as a fact of life: "From that point on, my feet were totally numb for the next several weeks."[103] Another soldier described trench foot this way: "It was as if a dentist had injected Novocain into my feet causing them to feel as if they were part of me, yet not part of me."[104]

Trench foot inspired numbness of body and soul. A soldier's decision to ignore his condition culminated the process, begun in training, of alienating himself from his body. Silent endurance, praised as heroic by commanders and infantrymen alike, worked in the army's favor. In encouraging silence about pain, officers assured that military obedience would prevail at all costs. Manly stoicism also concealed the full extent of non-combat casualties on the front. In the long run, however, it backfired. Scores of trench foot victims left the line for good.

5

The problem with trench foot culminated in the Belgian winter campaign. By the end of November 1944, trench foot admissions to hospitals in and around Paris had ballooned from 3 to 1,337. In the Third US Army, 1,130 cases were reported during the second week of November alone.[105] "Trench Foot Peril Rises," warned a *Stars and Stripes* headline on November 29, claiming that the affliction represented 37 percent of casualties in some areas. Between October 1944 and April 1945, a total of 46,000 GIs were admitted to the hospital with trench foot—a number equivalent to three infantry divisions.[106]

By mid-November, Commander in Chief Dwight D. Eisenhower and his generals had really started to worry. On November 18, Omar Bradley (Twelfth Army Group) wrote to Courtney Hodges (First Army) that "trench foot is producing a serious loss of manpower in the combat units."[107] Hodges then wrote about the problem to his unit commanders.[108] Once Paul Hawley, the command surgeon of the European theater of operations, was informed that "trench foot, particularly in Third Army, has increased markedly in recent weeks," he wrote to the Third Army's surgeon that "the ratio of trench foot to battle casualties is so high that, by failing to solve this problem, we are doing practically as much damage to our own troops as the enemy."[109] By the end of the month, the command surgeon's office had provided a detailed report of trench foot based on Hawley's visits to Third and Seventh Army headquarters. According to the report, the real problem lay in the infantry. Units not directly on the front line, such as artillery and engineers, were scarcely affected.[110] By the first week of December, the bad news had reached the War Department in Washington, which expressed alarm concerning the "excessive number of cases of trench foot in our armies."[111]

Key to understanding these commanders' view of trench foot is the word "manpower," used frequently in their flurry of missives. Bradley worried about the "serious loss of manpower in the combat units."[112] Hodges also fretted about a "serious loss of manpower" due to trench foot.[113] In Italy the Surgeon General made it clear to his medical officers that "the primary mission of the Medical Department" was "to conserve manpower."[114] Originally used in relationship to horsepower, manpower meant "the power or agency of a person expending energy" measured in quantifiable terms.[115] The generals used manpower to refer to a collective force of soldiers weaponized to do violence.

When the generals talked about manpower, they abstracted a soldier's body into a quantifiable unit. Bradley, for example, wrote that, given trends in hospital admissions, "1,000 soldiers a day may be rendered non-effective in the Twelfth Army Group."[116] In Italy the surgeon for the Fifth Army also phrased the problem of trench foot in terms of the erosion of collective physical strength. "Trench foot is militarily important," he argued in October 1944, "because four out of five men who get trench foot are lost to the unit for an indefinite period and those who do return cannot be used satisfactorily in the cold and wet."[117] In a memo, George Patton (Third Army) elaborated on this view:

> At this point we have practically eliminated trench foot from this army, but I think we must seriously consider the rapid replacement of able-bodied soldiers in the ETO [European theater of operations] by those who have suffered from this disease. It seems to me highly probable that many of these men could do duties as MP's or truck drivers under conditions where they are not exposed to cold or wet. As you know, the situation as to replacements is desperate, and we must get more men. It is also important that the maximum number of non-battle casualties be returned to their units in the minimum of time. This applies with equal force to any battle casualty capable of service. Other battle casualties, not suitable for full-time service should and must replace able-bodied men in the rear areas, who in turn must come to the front.[118]

Patton referred to his men in terms of bodily capacity: they were "battle casualties" or "non-battle casualties," "able-bodied" or "capable of service." The goal was strength of force. As in training, soldiers' bodies were understood as machines to be used as efficiently as possible.

Of course neither Bradley nor Patton was indifferent to the suffering of their soldiers. But they—and other Allied generals—had been trained to think of soldiers in terms of manpower. The aim of such thinking was to enable officers to strategize a battle or campaign. It also allowed them to send men to their death in a calculated manner. How else not to be overcome by the moral burden inherent in their power over life and death? How else to decide who would live and who would die, or when a death was justifiable? The answers to such questions required a strategy of mental disavowal. The ultimate goal of war was to destroy the enemy, not to spare one's men. And so it must be.

For a soldier, trench foot meant pain, fear, and weakness; for a commander, it meant an obstacle to the effective use of bodies. The difference in these two views explains why commanders did not see their double imperative—to heal and to harm—as troubling. The infantryman was the most valuable weapon on the line. For generals such as Bradley or Patton, healing trench foot was fixing a machine, not mending a suffering body.[119] In other words, healing was not opposed to harming; the first was rather a function of the second. Sending men back to face death was part of the job.

6

Trench foot was a screwup for command. Officers at every level had been entrusted with the responsibility of keeping a soldier's body healthy. Trench foot evidenced their failure to do this. Unwilling to admit fault, both publicly and to their superiors, army commanders blamed the problem on the soldiers themselves. At fault was poor infantry discipline, they claimed. In explaining to the American public why trench foot was rampant in Belgium, the Supreme Headquarters Allied Expeditionary Force did not say a word about shoddy boots and poor supply.[120] While Eisenhower recognized the terrible operative conditions, he also claimed after the war that "effective prevention was merely a matter of discipline—making sure that no one neglected the prescribed procedure."[121]

Even as infantry commanders at all levels sought to find Arctic overshoes, waterproof boots, galoshes, ski socks, shoepacs, and warm winter clothing for their men, Army Medical Services complained about poor foot discipline in the infantry.[122] Everyone knew the problem was not discipline, at least not completely. French army surgeon George Arnulf laughed at the idea that "constant and vigilant" care could eliminate trench foot. Instead, he pointed his finger at the American boots he and other French soldiers had been supplied.[123]

Commanding the Ninety-First Infantry Division in Italy, Major General W. M. Livesay begged Fifth Army headquarters for dry, clean socks on November 29, 1944. This plea, however, did not prevent him from attributing trench foot to infantry "negligence" in a memo to his officers the next day.[124] Command surgeon Hawley defined trench foot as chiefly "a disciplinary problem" that merited "strict discipline" and, if necessary, "the use of disciplinary action." "The long arm of discipline and training," advised a Fifth Army medical circular, "should reach into every fox-hole and dugout to insure that the preventive measures are carried out."[125] "Poor soldiers and poorly-led soldiers develop the greatest amount of trench foot," wrote one colonel to Hawley.[126]

Infantrymen were made to think that the affliction was no one's fault but their own. A *Stars and Stripes* editorial claimed that soldiers suffered trench foot due to "carelessness" (fig. 11). The soldier was instructed to cut out the two pinups, or "lallapaloozas," featured on the page in order to put them inside the bottoms of his boots. Soldiers would take their boots off more frequently, the editorial implied, if they could "feast" their eyes on the two women. The piece then instructed the soldier to massage his feet. The language unmistakably referenced masturbation. (GIs were known to masturbate using pinups.) "Rub them and drub them until your dogs begin to bark. Don't stop looking—and rubbing—until your blood pressure bulges and your corns call quits." Not only was trench foot preventable with discipline, the editorial implied, but also that soldiers found their only motivation in sexual pleasure.[127]

Blaming trench foot on "poor foot discipline" was attractive to the military for several reasons. It reasserted discipline as a fundamental value; it exonerated US Army commanders of responsibility for the outbreak; and it displaced attention away from the fact that the army had lost control over the health of its men. Poor discipline remained the primary cause of trench foot in a postwar study by the Army Medical Services Board. While the board admitted to the poor quality of infantry boots, it also stated that ignorance and poor self-care were

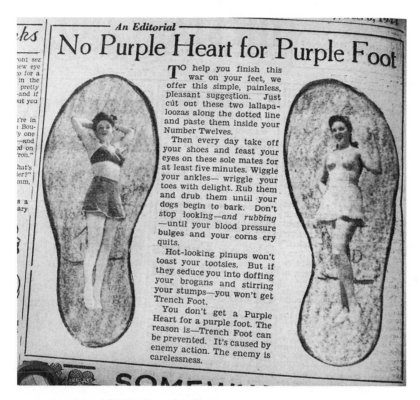

An Editorial

No Purple Heart for Purple Foot

TO help you finish this war on your feet, we offer this simple, painless, pleasant suggestion. Just cut out these two lallapaloozas along the dotted line and paste them inside your Number Twelves.

Then every day take off your shoes and feast your eyes on these sole mates for at least five minutes. Wiggle your ankles— wriggle your toes with delight. Rub them and drub them until your dogs begin to bark. Don't stop looking—*and rubbing* —until your blood pressure bulges and your corns cry quits.

Hot-looking pinups won't toast your tootsies. But if they seduce you into doffing your brogans and stirring your stumps—you won't get Trench Foot.

You don't get a Purple Heart for a purple foot. The reason is—Trench Foot can be prevented. It's caused by enemy action. The enemy is carelessness.

FIGURE 11. *Stars and Stripes*, December 6, 1944.

equally important factors in the outbreak of trench foot. Control of cold injuries "was found to be directly dependent on the state of discipline in the unit." If soldiers had only changed their socks and massaged each other's feet once a day, the board concluded, they would not have contracted trench foot. Furthermore, they pathologized trench foot by including it on a list of scurrilous behaviors. A high rate of the condition, they argued, occurred in units where there was also "a high venereal disease rate, a high court-martial trial rate, and a high absent without leave rate."[128] "Trench foot is similar to the venereal problem," claimed one army surgeon. "Both of them depend on the education of the individual soldier."[129] Grouped with promiscuity, crime, and desertion, trench foot became not a physical injury but a moral failure.

7

The decision that US Army officials made to blame the "careless" infantry for their trench foot infuriated foot soldiers. The irony, of course, was that the army had taught its soldiers to ignore their pain, then called it poor discipline when they did just that. His feet "swollen and purplish black," William Condon waited for medical help until after the Ardennes battle. At a Parisian hospital, a doctor told him his injured feet were a result of "negligence." Condon tried to be tolerant. "The doctor could afford to be judgmental because he slept in a warm, dry bed in Paris with his spare clothes in the closet."[130]

Other soldiers had no such patience. When trench foot broke out in the Thirty-Fourth Infantry Division, the men who had been forced to cross the Volturno River three times were blamed for not carrying a pair of dry socks in their helmet. Even if these helmet-stored socks didn't end up soaking wet, one sergeant protested, "who in the hell wanted to change socks in a mine field with machine gun bullets whistling around you?"[131] When Noble Gardner sought help for his blue, frozen feet after the Battle of Hürtgen Forest, a doctor told him, "You get that from not changing your socks when your feet are wet." Gardner exploded: "Christ, what the hell you gonna do when you're living in a hole for two weeks and the water's up to here and Jerries are shooting at you and you can't go no place!"[132] Army Medical Services half acknowledged how operative conditions rendered foot care impossible. "Uncontrollable situations will arise that may result in trench feet casualties," admitted a Fifth Army medical bulletin, "but of these cases that have already appeared this cause has been the exception and not the rule."[133]

Anger on the line escalated when, in January 1945, *Time* explained that trench foot had reached epidemic proportions because "the Americans did not attend to dry socks or foot massages." In this failure, the magazine argued, the GIs contrasted badly with the Russians who enjoyed regular massages, and the British who kept their boots waxed and frequently changed socks.[134] When infantrymen read such articles, sent to them from home, they were outraged. Roscoe Blunt had this to say in response:

> Soldiers in combat, the article stated, should replace their wet socks everyday with clean, dry ones. Also, a soldier should remove his boots at least once every hour and massage his feet for 10 minutes. Furthermore, a soldier should never put his feet in water if temperatures were going to drop below freezing. And lastly, he should wear overshoes with no holes in them and buckled up at the top at all times. The article forgot to mention that GIs should also take a break at 3:00 every afternoon for milk and cookies and brush after every meal.[135]

Anger fueled not only ridicule but also insubordination. It soon dawned on infantrymen that their feet could be a ticket to the rear.[136] The narrator in William Wharton's novel *A Midnight Clear* considered "losing a few toes a small price to pay if we get to snuggle into a warm cozy hospital bed, miles away from this insane scheme, and more importantly, have a chance to live." His comrades, he noted, "start sleeping in their wet socks and boots, hoping and praying...." One night in the Ardennes, an exhausted Nat Frankel said he "got down on my hands and knees and pleaded with God to give me trench foot.... I had seen one too many severed heads and far too many frozen, dangling blood vessels." He was jubilant the next morning when he could not walk. "Who knows, I may have induced trench foot myself by simply wanting it so awfully badly."[137]

However, it was not always so easy to contract. Lester Atwell described another private's frustration about the condition: "And there I was, leavin' my feet out, stickin' them in ice water, trying everything.... *They wouldn't freeze!*"[138] Once in the hospital, an infantryman like J. H. Burns's fictional Michael Patrick could prolong his stay by intentionally reinjuring his feet. Charles Swann had another trick. Before the doctor arrived every morning, he would hang his foot over the edge of the bed until his toes turned purple.[139]

In fact, the feet already had a long history of malingering. While the infantry foot stood for endurance, it could also symbolize cowardice. "Always dragging their feet" and "pussy footing around" was how the Americans described the British in the Italian campaign.[140] "On the trot" meant to desert the front line.[141] A time-tested means of getting off the line was to shoot oneself in the foot. According to a GI medic, shots in the foot increased during periods of waiting, when fear had time to build up.[142] In the Ardennes, surgeon Jesse Caldwell recorded in his journal on December 17 that three men had shot themselves in the foot within the space of fifteen minutes.[143] The common excuse was that it was an accident. Soldiers would fire at their feet through a loaf of bread to avoid the telltale black powder burn.[144]

But no one was fooled. GI James Fry once saw a boy use the gun-cleaning excuse, "then his eyes met mine and shame flooded into his features. His eyes fell to his lap and tears ran down his cheeks." British Charles Whitehouse remembered a luckless soldier who shot himself in the foot only to graze the area between his big and second toe.[145] Because authorities usually could not prove the wound was self-inflicted, they convicted such soldiers for carelessness, a six-month sentence. An entire company could suffer bad morale from one soldier's self-inflicted wound.[146] Shots to the foot forced others to draw on their last resources of courage. Because the foot stood for endurance, its mutilation could cause a crisis of morale.

While wounds to the foot were seen as telltale signs of weakness, trench foot offered a more discreet way to exit the line. As Burns's GI put it, "He'd thought for a long time . . . that he was going to crack, and trench foot was a more honorable way of doing it than becoming a psycho."[147] Trench foot as a form of malingering was less readable as cowardice and therefore more "honorable." In early 1943, soldiers could receive a Purple Heart citation for the condition, at that point still officially considered a "wound" received in action. But when cases began to escalate in late fall that year, army commanders became suspicious. At issue was the thorny question of "deliberate intent."[148] It was one thing to get off the line with a self-imposed injury, and quite another to earn a medal for it. By the onset of the Battle of the Bulge in December 1944, military commanders were threatening soldiers with court-martials if they contracted trench foot. This tactic was hardly effective. As GI John Khoury pointed out, "A sick and miserable GI at the front could use a court-martial to ease his suffering. If he was a private, what could he lose in rank and pay? How unhappy would he be in a stockade, miles from the front and served hot food and given a clean bed and a roof over his head?"[149] At the same time, few malingerers felt joy at their escape from the line. For one, it brought the shame of unmanliness. "Of his trench foot," Patrick thought, "perhaps it was some subconscious cowardice that had broken out in his feet."[150] To mutilate one's own body countered a deep human instinct for self-protection; it took a strange kind of courage. "Maybe I lacked a special kind of nerve to carry on my own shameful temptations to a conclusion," admitted Edward Arn after witnessing a lieutenant shoot himself in the foot.[151]

For infantrymen, trench foot carried an ever-more complex register of meanings. It signaled the army's failure to take care of soldiers' bodies. In addition, the condition sharpened divisions of class and rank, front and rear echelons. The rear men and officers who least needed good boots and dry socks were the ones who got them. And to top that off, infantry soldiers were faulted for their own misery, described as lazy and careless. For the men on the front line, then, trench foot served as a reminder of their plebian status in the army. Finally, how you handled your numb feet determined what kind of man you were. Enduring trench foot quietly demonstrated your manliness. Seeking medical help stigmatized you as "yellow." But it was almost never that clear-cut. Who could tell when trench foot was deliberate and when it was a result of manly stoicism? Who was a "real" man and who just appeared to be? Malingerers counted on that ambiguity; infantrymen despaired at the dilemma it produced. For how could you be both manly and take care of your body? How bad did your feet need to be before your manhood was no longer in question?

For generals, trench foot meant weakness of another sort. The injury rendered ineffective human units of violent force. It ate away at a division's core strength and threatened the successful prosecution of the war. Like the men they oversaw, generals also considered trench foot to be a command failure. But they defined that failure differently: as inadequate training of proper foot discipline. Such an explanation sidestepped the problem of bad equipment and terrible operative conditions. It also implied that infantrymen were too stupid to take care of their bodies. At the heart of the trench foot epidemic was a class condescension with deep roots in American, French, and British cultures. Lower-class men were stereotyped as lazy, careless children.[152] One US Army manual claimed that the average Joe "will not care for himself properly without the direction of authority. He has a contempt for things he does not understand."[153]

Trench foot was probably unavoidable in the miserable conditions of the two winter campaigns. At the same time, thinking about the body in the abstract terms of manpower did not do a soldier any favors. Donald Burgett of the 101st Airborne told a relevant story about the Ardennes. Because his company commander felt that the men's bulky winter wear would hinder their combat efficiency, he forced them to leave it all behind in a field. "We could come back and pick up our heavy winter clothing the next day," Burgett related, "after we'd whipped the Germans back to where they'd come from." Burgett knew enough about the Eastern front to know that "the Russians did quite well in winter wearing overcoats, but evidently someone up at headquarters didn't think we could handle it." Despite the penetrating cold, the entire company stripped down to their summertime clothing. The men never got back to the field. When the weather dipped below zero, Burgett bitterly remembered, he didn't have his "warm overshoes and warm overcoat with its pockets stuffed with K rations that I had been ordered to leave in a field outside Noville before our attack." It did not take long for his feet to freeze: "We watched each step to keep from stumbling and falling. It was as though I were floating. I could see my legs stride forward and hear the sound of my footfalls, but there was no feeling of contact with the ground. . . . There's not a damned thing you can do about it but grin and bear it."[154] Burgett's commander was probably exceptional in his stupidity, but if commanders had thought less about their soldiers as manpower and more about them as sensate beings, fewer men would have lost their feet.

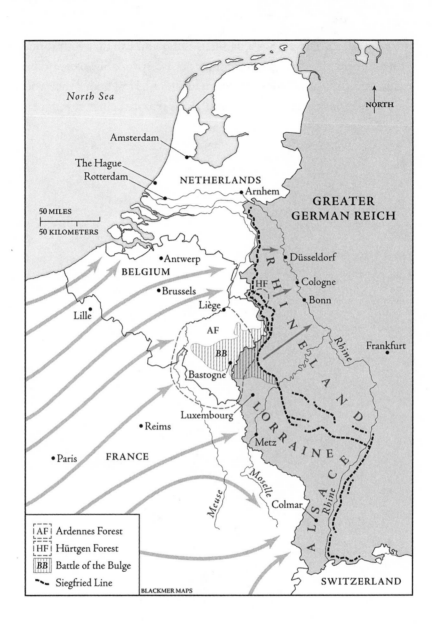

North Sea

NORTH

Amsterdam

The Hague
Rotterdam

NETHERLANDS

Arnhem

GREATER
GERMAN REICH

50 MILES
50 KILOMETERS

Antwerp

BELGIUM

R H I N E L A N D

Düsseldorf

HF

Cologne

Brussels

Bonn

Liège

Lille

AF

Rhine

Frankfurt

BB

Bastogne

L O R R A I N E

Luxembourg

Reims

Metz

Paris

FRANCE

Moselle

Meuse

A L S A C E

Colmar

Rhine

AF   Ardennes Forest
HF   Hürtgen Forest
BB   Battle of the Bulge
      Siegfried Line

BLACKMER MAPS

SWITZERLAND

4

THE WOUND

With his face wounded from eyes to mouth, British soldier John Thorpe found himself on an ambulance train going to an English hospital in October 1944. The train was set to arrive in "the dead of night." When Thorpe asked why, he was told that transporting the wounded after dark was standard procedure in order "to prevent public concern over the high number of casualties being observed during the day."[1] The practice typified how wounded men were hidden from view. They appeared to the British public mostly as names on a casualty list.[2] Stretcher bearers hurried wounded men off the battlefield not only to tend to their injuries but also to hide them from soldiers moving forward. As GI Keith Wheeler put it, "In war one lives with the unbroken living and with the dead. One sees little of the wounded, except to see them hit and carried away, bloodied and usually silent burdens on bloody stretchers."[3] Once wounded, British soldiers were confined to stations and hospitals far from public view. Only medical personnel saw them.

Popular military historians have also often erased the wounded from view.[4] Narratives of the Battle of Normandy are a case in point. In these texts, wounded soldiers are numbered rather than described. They appear as they did in casualty reports or memoirs of military commanders—as the numerical "cost" of victory or the "price" of conquest.[5] Few soldiers would describe their own wounding in this way. Historians of Normandy also obscure wounding through redescription. Divisions, not individual soldiers, get battered, mauled, and chopped to pieces.[6] A battle is a "monstrous blood mill," not a massacre of humans.[7] When a man's wounds *are* described, they are often so gory or bizarre as to seem unreal. An upper torso is crushed by a jeep, an eyeball falls out of its socket, a boot is found with a foot still inside it. Men have their heads blown off, their intestines trail on the ground, and their brains are held together by a helmet.[8]

In fact, such catastrophic wounds were uncommon among casualties. Sixty to seventy percent of wounds suffered by British were considered "light," and thus too banal to be included in popular historical narratives.[9] But what did they mean to those who suffered them, assessed them, bandaged them, or operated on them?[10] What did it feel like to be hit by a bullet or artillery piece? Among soldiers, wounds were classified according to their location on the body and the context in which they occurred. Some were welcomed and some were feared. In aid stations, ambulances, and hospitals, wounds altered dramatically in meaning, becoming objects of medical diagnosis and procedure. Despite the differences between how soldiers and doctors perceived the same wounds, both saw in them the sad scrawl of what war can do to a human body.

An enormous historical field, war medicine is best reviewed through a national focus. My attention here is on British soldiers and medical personnel involved in the Italian and northern European campaigns, 1943 to 1945. In all theaters of the Second World War, one out of every ten British soldiers was wounded in action, for a total of almost 250,000 casualties. Taking the case only of Europe, we can ask how did these men classify and rank different kinds of wounds? How did they later remember their wounding? How did the same wounds change in meaning as the injured moved from the battlefield to the surgeon's table? Why were the wounded, as Thorpe discovered, hidden from the light of day?

1

Soldiers talked about wounding all the time. What limb was better to lose: a leg or an arm?[11] Every infantryman knew the effect artillery could have on the human body. "Scab and matter pie" was the name soldiers gave to a badly wounded arm or leg.[12] The sight of such wounds reminded them that the war could turn them into matter.[13] To survive that thought, soldiers lived in a state of half-denial. "Friends would have their feet blown off and their balls mutilated by 'bouncing Bettys,'" remembered Douglas Allanbrook of Italy. "Habitual horror does not dim the sight; the soul grows scar tissue."[14] Losing friends was the exception. When Rex Wingfield's mate Ted got wounded and taken away, he would lose sleep thinking about whether or not Ted was dead. "Did he try to break his fall? If he did it probably meant that he was only wounded, but if he seemed to sag at the neck, knee or ankle you knew what that meant."[15]

The best wound to receive was the "Blighty," also called the "Blighty touch."[16] Named after the slang word for London, the Blighty was a wound that got you out of the fighting and back home without permanently disabling you. (For GIs, it was the "million-dollar wound.")[17] Before a battle, the men would call out to one another, "Cheer up, we might get a Blighty."[18] The Blighty was nothing if not a piece of good luck. Being hit in the arms, hands, and feet, preferably by a bullet, was optimal. Such wounds tended to be less severe—that is, they didn't incapacitate you in some "vital part." When James Allen took stock of his chest wound, he was happy to discover that "no vital parts, limbs or appendages" were missing. "It might," he declared, "have earned the title of a 'Good Blighty One.'" E. J. Rooke-Matthews also described his Blighty in terms of "no bones, no vital parts effected." When W. S. Scull felt pain in his foot, he was hoping he had been hit there. Alas, it had only been bruised by a stone. "All I got was a sore foot for a week, it wasn't a Blighty one after all."[19]

A Blighty, then, was serious but not too serious. Optimally it secured a trip home. In this sense, a wound could ironically offer safety. It was "the way out," as Wingfield put it.[20] While many wounded would rather have rejoined their comrades on the battlefield, others were all too happy to "be out of it."[21] According to one account, the "walking wounded," as they were called, were the most cheerful men on the battlefield.[22] One of the first questions the wounded Welsh fusilier Peter Ryder asked his medical officer was "Will I be going home?"

Rooke-Matthews remembered how the doctors would first examine a wounded man in bed, then nod to the orderly. "A huge grin on the face of the patient would indicate that he would be going home." Nurse Mary Morris wrote in her diary one day that the soldiers in the ward were "chatting cheerfully, relieved to be away from the fighting."[23]

For men who simply could not stand another day of combat, a Blighty was an exit ticket with none of the stigma attached to a self-inflicted wound. What kind of wound you suffered took the measure of your manliness. Context was everything: How and why were you shot? Men who shot themselves in the foot or hand claimed it to be an "accident." But such wounds were immediately recognizable to medics and other soldiers as attempts to malinger, and they became markers of shame. By contrast, the Blighty was respectable. It made you a hero at a reasonable cost.

All wounds were feared, but some more than others. Armored crews dreaded the terrible burns men suffered when their tanks were struck by artillery.[24] French tanker Jean Navard told his diary that while it was difficult to see "wounded ripped open and screaming," this sight was "nothing in comparison to the men who, mad with pain, jump out of their tanks with their bodies in flames." Infantrymen also dreaded wounds to their eyes. "We always used to talk about it," remembered one soldier, "arms, legs—ok–but eyes? That would be worse than anything. . . . You didn't mind being killed, but you didn't want to be blinded."[25] Unlike the Blighty, a wound causing blindness demanded too much of your future. You became a war waste product for the rest of your life.

Men also feared wounds to the core of the body. A bullet in the heart or the stomach meant you were probably a goner, not only because the injury affected "vital parts," but also because such wounds required immediate surgery. You could bleed to death before you got help. Then there were the humiliating wounds. No one wanted to go home without their genitals.[26] Many soldiers slept with their helmets protecting their "meat and two veg" rather than their heads. They joked that while a head wound would kill them, the loss of their manhood would make them want to be dead.[27]

Wounds to the butt cheeks were also humbling. In the Italian mountain campaign, Thorpe remembered seeing soldiers hauled down on the back of mules "placed posterior upwards." "You've got a hole in your arse," a medic informed Scull when he got hit there. "I hope I have," he replied. When David Evans came under fire in a street battle, it occurred to him "that my backside was above the kerb level and that it would be a little ignominious to be 'shot in the arse'; not something to boast about at all." When Evans later landed in the hospital with ruptured eardrums, he recalled one patient who was wounded by a bullet passing through both cheeks of his buttocks. One day as Evans and others were watching a nurse dress the man's wounds, "a Geordie lad spoke up. 'D'ye know, from where I'm standing, it looks as though Mike has got five arseholes.' A roar of laughter greeted this sally."[28]

2

During the war, then, soldiers made sense of wounds by classifying them according to severity, debilitation, and humiliation. These meanings also emerged in retrospect from a soldier's memory. Memoirs performed significant emotional work for their authors. By reconstructing the time, scene, and course of their injury, including moments of unconsciousness, a soldier brought coherence and closure to his wounding experience. In addition, he regained the authority over his body lost at the moment of wounding.[29]

Soldiers usually began their wounding stories with a combat scene. Often the battle is vicious and the odds of survival unfavorable. For example, tank engineer Robert Boscawen's narrative opened in full battle with his unit badly outnumbered. From inside his tank, Boscawen saw many men dying as they tried to get across a bridge, as well as having four German 150 mm guns pointed at him.[30] Setting the scene for his wounding in Belgium, Peter Ryder described "almost impossible conditions, with a raging blizzard, and hilly, wooded terrain that hid fanatical enemy machine-gun nests." Presenting the battle as desperate was an act of self-forgiveness. If a man got wounded, it was because the situation was out of control. "Why the hell were our gunners not dealing with the German heavies? Why were we being left to die in such a one-sided contest?" asked a soon-to-be-wounded H. W. Freeman-Attwood.[31]

The moment of wounding was pivotal. As a form of weaponry penetrated a soldier's body, it breached a psychic barrier between himself and the world. When Ryder was wounded in the Ardennes, he felt like his "whole world dissipated." A wound had the power to break the boundaries of the self—to reveal the inside to the outside. Some men remembered the moment as being out of their own body. "There was a blinding flash and I found myself staring blankly at a small, smoking crater straight in front of my feet," observed Walter Elliott, "although my body must have hit the ground, I found myself in the curious position of thinking that I was looking down on myself." "Then suddenly I was seeing every light and hearing every bell in Italy," recalled Bill Scully, wounded at Cassino. "I just remember falling back to earth again."[32]

To normalize the moment of impact, soldiers used everyday metaphors. A bullet hit a "mighty blow," "a nasty blow," or "heavy blow."[33] David Evans remembered a "blast of hot air and the feeling that I had been smacked very hard indeed, all over my body at the same time."[34] "I felt a great smack on my left arm, buttock and shoulder. A big wham," recounted Peter Hall.[35] Alternatively, it was a "thump" or a "kick" or an "electric shock."[36] "One is often asked what it feels like to be shot," wrote James Allen. "The best I can say is that one minute you are up and the next you are down having been kicked by a horse."[37] When John Thorpe was hit by a mortar, "it was as if I had been hit in the face with a red-hot cricket ball."[38] The soldier was socked, smacked, kicked, hit by a hot ball, with the instance evoking the loss of control. The next moments in the narrative dramatize trying to regain it.

A wounded soldier's first impulse was to examine his injury. Where had he been hit? How badly? It was hard to judge: neither pain nor bleeding were reliable indicators of a wound's severity. The absence of pain could mean either a grave injury or no injury at all. A severely wounded soldier often went right into shock; sometimes he was distracted by combat; sometimes his body was numb with cold.[39] "The shock seems to anaesthetize the system till it wears off, then it hurts!" noted Allen. Raymond Walker did not feel pain in his arm until he began to warm up at the hospital. Shock's deceit left infantrymen in a state of agonizing uncertainty. When W. S. Scull was hit, he thought "my leg was off, as I had heard somewhere that you felt no pain for a while until feeling came back." However, he had only a minor wound in his foot. Rex Wingfield was "disappointed" when he felt "no mortal agony, no frenzied writhing and no shattering pain churning my body." In fact, he was seriously wounded.[40]

Blood was no more of a reliable indicator than pain. Stewart Montgomery thought he had escaped an artillery attack until he discovered himself bleeding. "My God, I must be absolutely riddled," thought Elliott as he noticed "blood beginning to flow down my left side." Observing blood on their person often led a soldier to think the worst. "I felt a thump in the back, good old me who was always going to be alright," recollected Edward Horrell. "I slipped a hand inside my back pocket, which came out covered in blood and told me otherwise."[41] Bleeding from the mouth was particularly feared, as it signaled internal injuries.[42] Blood could pour from superficial wounds, making them look worse than they really were. P. G. Thres was alarmed when "blood spurted out" of a bullet wound to his face. Despite the fact that he was "profusely losing blood," a simple head bandage was all he needed to get back to the line.[43] "It looks so much worse than it really is," noted Montgomery of his wound. John Hall felt a heavy blow to his chest and thought "for a split second, on seeing blood, that I had been seriously wounded." He later realized a red-hot shell fragment had landed on him.[44]

And yet blood was the most common metonym of wounding. "Splattered everywhere was blood," recalled one soldier of an aid post; "it lay in pools in the rooms, it covered the smocks of the defenders and ran in small rivulets down the stairs."[45] Being "showered" with blood is how Evans described one of his most intense battles; he also retained a vision of a tank floor "covered in blood and bits of torn

flesh." "Blood spurted" from the head stump of a replacement soldier, observed A. G. Herbert. "Frank was very badly injured," wrote A.
Marr of his commander. "He was in an awful state with blood coming
through his uniform in many places." Cecil Newton noticed red marks
on a tank turret. He did not believe his commander when he told him
it was rust.[46] The American GIs also weighted blood with symbol-
ism.[47] Nat Frankel explained how, during the Battle of the Bulge, his
armored division was in such a hurry to get to the front lines that the
men pissed off the side of the tank rather than stop to do their business along the road. Once the deadly fighting began, recalled Frankel,
"blood, not piss, was running down the sides of our machines. When
I remember the Bulge I remember that the color of movement was
yellow, while red was the hue of all immobility."[48]

Because wounded men commonly fell in and out of consciousness
as they were rescued, they went days without knowing where they
were. Creating a coherent story of "what happened" became a challenge. After he was wounded in the leg, Peter Holyhead recollected
only "flashes": being put on a stretcher, traveling in a boat, lying in
a hospital. Newton vomited over the side of a lorry, woke up on a
stretcher in the grass, looked up to see a surgeon, then regained consciousness between clean sheets. Separated from his unit, signalman
L. F. Roker called out to the stretcher bearers, heard men marching
down a road, covered himself with foliage, and was carried out spread
over an armored car.[49] Allen's story was also typically broken. Someone
came to tend to his wounds, then died on top of him. He awoke in an
aid post where someone gave him a cigarette, then again on a stretcher
perched on a jeep, then once more in the operating theater, and finally
in a crowded hospital corridor. Walker remembers only being cleaned
by a nun bending over him. He thought he was in heaven.[50]

In reconstructing their wounding stories, then, many men did not
possess a cohesive narrative. At the same time, connecting the dots
was a vital need. Veterans went to great lengths to understand what
happened to them. Roker, for example, did extensive research in unit
histories and personal correspondence. He also returned in 1984 to
the spot where he was wounded and drew a detailed map (fig. 12).

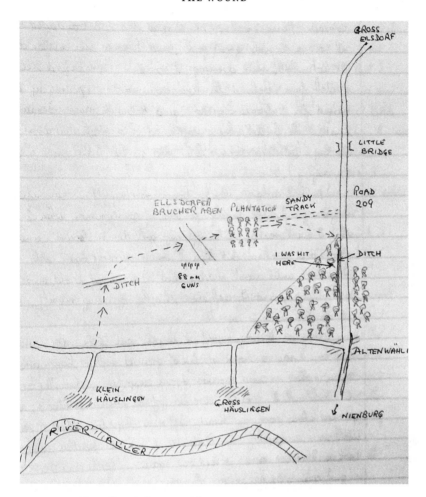

FIGURE 12. Diary of L. F. Roker, Imperial War Museum.

Allen regretted not dating a letter penned to his mother "since that might have put a time scale on my move from battlefield on the 10th of February till consciousness."[51]

Wounded men relied on others to help them fill in the blanks. When Evans burst an eardrum, he suffered amnesia, so he asked his buddy Dave to help him remember. "The remainder of the night is still a blank and it was morning when, so Dave told me later, I was noticed as being 'a bit queer.'" "I was very angry and noisy about being sent home," claimed Padre Leslie Skinner on the evidence of two friends' testimony. Ryder recounted how three buddies claimed to have made "the long dangerous journey" back to where he lay in the snow.[52]

Fashioning a continuous account with a beginning, middle, and end enabled these men to mend a traumatic break they experienced when wounded. A central driving force moved the action forward. Sometimes it was intuition. Brian Harpur was riding in a jeep when he decided to take off his helmet. But "something made me stay my hand." A minute later he received a blow from a shell fragment. When he awoke, he found a huge dent in his helmet and concluded it had saved his life. Because the shell knocked him off the jeep, he lay by the side of the road in the dark. Again, he recounted, some unknown force saved him. Against all odds, the jeep behind him stopped to pick him up. "Normally he would have ignored a body on the road," reasoned Harpur. "But on this occasion he told me something made him do it." The wondrous unknown was another driving force. As Wingfield was lying in the field awaiting the stretcher bearers, he recalled someone telling him that "in moments of danger, psychic messages could be sent to dear ones. I concentrated very hard and tried to tell my mother that I had been hit. She heard me. There is no explanation."[53]

Luck was another agent driving the story. When Scull was injured in his buttocks, his doctor told him that "another half inch higher the bullet would have lodged at the base of my spine and I would have [been] paralyzed for life." "You were lucky," a medical officer told Ryder when he received a head wound. "A fraction the other way and you wouldn't be here asking questions." Montgomery was also told by his surgeon that he was fortunate the shrapnel in his back did not tear into his lungs. And Captain D. H. Clark would have received shrapnel in his belly had it not hit his leather belt in just the right way.[54] The "almost but not quite" wound suggested benevolent forces at work on the battlefield—an idea many soldiers embraced as a psychic tool of survival.

Some soldier authors gave their wounding stories a larger "historical" significance by integrating them into established military narratives. Using eyewitness German accounts, photographs, and weaponry manuals as well as letters from his mother and comrades, Robert Boscawen wrote his wounding into the story of the Battle of Arnhem. Arriving at some "truth" of the battle seemed emotionally crucial to him. Similarly, the map created by Roker joined together personal and operational narratives (see fig. 12). "I was hit here," Roker noted, locating his wounding within a certain topography and a specific military operation. The map visualizes ditches, trees, a "sandy track," and a "little bridge," but also gun positions and troop movements. Roker even sought to correct the historical record by arguing that he was not "hit by Panzerfaust fragments as had been claimed."[55]

Roker's narrative centers on his attempt to control the wounding experience. The agent in his story is himself. As he fell in and out of consciousness, Roker found a water bottle to answer his thirst; he ate an emergency ration of chocolate for energy; he dressed his own leg wound, and finally, by ordering himself "by numbers" to do it, he managed to remove his wet boots. The "stretcher-bearers later told me that I had done a good job of bandaging." Determined to reach the British lines, he dragged his body along a path, "expecting to be hit by a burst of machine-gun fire at any moment."[56] Personal courage and endurance formed the threads of Roker's account. By presenting himself as a hero, he regained a sense of control lost in the trauma of wounding.

Newton also used his war story to recover lost authority. Despite suffering a serious chest wound, Newton portrayed himself as always on top of things. Crawling into a nearby house, he had the presence of mind to put his German Browning pistol under the bed. "The Germans were not very kind to prisoners who had any of their equipment." Although he was bleeding heavily from the mouth, Newton remembered remaining calm and collected. "At no time did I believe that I would not be able to get out of my predicament."[57] One may doubt that Newton's sense of control was as complete as he claimed. But while the truth of his wounding experience can never be known, how he chose to recollect it is equally important. Wounding was—consciously or unconsciously—experienced as a loss of power. Its recovery was crucial to psychic healing.

The wounding story was restorative as well as redemptive. The narrative moved from chaos to order, from misery to comfort, and from danger to safety. Many wounded men noted "the life-saving cup of tea" they were given at the aid post.[58] Regular hospital meals gave the day a rhythm and routine much appreciated by veterans of the front line.[59] Wounding also meant women. "We were nursed by some very pretty charming Canadian ladies," observed E. J. Rooke-Matthews. Thorpe described his nurses as "fresh, crisp English girls . . . marvelous to see." As Evans was stretchered off the line with a light wound, his buddies advised him not to "go screwing all the nurses too soon, give yourself chance to do justice to the job."[60]

The cleanliness of bedding symbolized safety.[61] Ryder was relieved to wake up "lying between clean sheets of a hospital bed." After going in and out of consciousness for days, Newton woke up "between clean crisp sheets." Thorpe similarly awoke in a hospital where "starched white aprons revive my childhood memories, comfort and security from squalor."[62] The hospital bed was the opposite of the slit trench. As wounded men felt the touch of sheets on their bodies, they knew they were saved.

3

As a soldier sought care for his injury in the British military medical system, his wound underwent a radical change in meaning.[63] On the battlefield, a wound had been a source of sensation and pain. In the British military medical system (Royal Army Medical Corps, or RAMC), the wound became the object of a diagnosis. Attention focused not on the patient but on the wound, which was subjected to a set of medical and surgical procedures. "You were no longer master of your destiny," noted Stewart Montgomery of his time in the system.[64] While medical benevolence lay at the heart of the RAMC, its goal was to send soldiers back to their fighting units as quickly as possible.[65] We have already seen how healing meant confronting death once more.

The RAMC treatment for wounds revolved around two procedures: assessment and evacuation. Stretcher bearers carried the wounded off the battlefield (unless these men were able to walk on their own) and brought them to an aid post or dressing station. In these stations, placed close behind the front lines, medical personnel determined how badly you were wounded. The decision determined *where* you would be evacuated to and *how soon* you would be treated. Priority was given to the most seriously wounded. Here medical officers also gave you emergency treatment, including bandaging and blood transfusions. Soldiers in shock or otherwise too unstable to be evacuated remained at these stations, while those who needed surgery or were more mobile went farther back from the line to a casualty clearing station. At a CCS, the wounded were once again evaluated. If they needed an operation, they were sent on to a surgical center; if their wounds were not life-threatening, they were evacuated to a hospital.

Triage transformed a wound into a difficult choice. At every level of the medical system, a decision had to be made about who would be treated first. Instituted in the Napoleonic army, this system was named "triage" after the French verb *trier*, meaning to sort. Triage began on the battlefield. From the moment the soldier was found injured, his wound was assessed for relative severity. All wounds were judged in relation to each other. As first-aid men traversed the battlefield, often under fire, they had to make rapid decisions concerning priority of treatment. How serious was the wound? How close to death was the wounded? Could he be moved? Was he a hopeless case or worth the investment of medical care? The fact that neither pain nor blood took an accurate measure of severity made the decision all the more difficult. Superficial wounds could bleed profusely; shock sealed the worst injured into silence. Stretcher bearers had to develop their own criteria. One medic based his decision on the sounds of the wounded. If a soldier was crying out for his mother, it meant he was grievously wounded and probably dying. If he was calling for a medic, his wounds were not serious.[66]

Beginning in June 1940, medical practitioners were conscripted into the Army Medical Services. Medics and stretcher bearers were drawn from the general population and were usually without professional medical qualifications. In training they learned how to use medical equipment, arrest bleeding, improvise splints for fractures, and safely collect the wounded.[67] These first responders developed sharp eyes. When a medic came over and took "a quick look" at E. J. Rooke-Matthews's wound, he "gave me one of these reassuring looks that 'medics' are noted for and gave me a field dressing which he told me to hold tightly to the side of my chest." Medics could be tough. When P. G. Thres discovered blood spurting from his cheek and ear, he tried to get the attention of a medic moving from man to man on the field. According to Thres, the medic "dismissed my call by shouting that he had to 'attend wounded not s . . . of b. . . . . .s like me' and to use my field dressing." When Michael Hunter received a shrapnel wound in his arm, he went to the aid post thinking it was a Blighty. "The bloke cut off my shirt, put a bit of sticking plaster on it and said 'Bugger off.' "[68]

As a soldier began the long journey to the hospital, doctors and nurses set out to decipher his wound. Where did the foreign agent enter? What path in the body did it take? How much damage did it render to flesh and bone? The wounded were classified as "dying," "in desperate situation," "in serious condition," or in "satisfactory condition."[69] A patient's color, pulse rate, and blood pressure factored into his classification.[70] "We had to sort them out, bandage their wounds and pack them into ambulances to go back to the main dressing station," recollected D. H. Clark of his work at an aid post.[71] A doctor explained, "In reception . . . there was scarcely room to move. The task was one of sorting: sorting out which patient was to go where for what treatment and with what degree of urgency."[72] The wounded soldier tried to glean the truth about his injuries by reading a doctor's facial expression. One surgeon recalled "that peculiar, quick piercing scrutiny" a soldier would give him when examined.[73]

Triaging wounds was highly stressful for those who did it.[74] Abdominal wounds were almost always a priority as they had to be operated on in less than twelve hours for the patient to have any chance of survival.[75] Sorting was never routine. If a soldier's condition changed as he waited for surgery, the evacuation/surgical lists would shift.[76] If soldiers needed blood transfusions before the operation, they would be put further down the surgery list.[77] Triage transformed wounding into a game in which the winners were the losers: those given first priority were closest to death. "Most difficult of all" for surgeon Stanley Aylett were the "poor men mangled by many gross wounds, whom the surgeon knew very well to be beyond all aid . . . for if he were not put on the operation list his death warrant was sealed."[78] Many surgeons, however, moved the dying down the list. Faced with a body gravely wounded in the abdomen, surgeon J. C. Watts "despondently" refused the case in order to operate on ten men with much better chances.[79]

Since both the German and British medical systems practiced triage, prisoners of war were customarily "sorted" in the same way.[80] Although it is impossible to know in every case, evidence exists that strict rules were followed on both sides. Captured in the Battle of Arnhem and forced to work in a German hospital, physician T. Redman reported that the selection for surgery was "quite impartial, nationality never being considered."[81] "They are all patients, rank and nationality do not count," Nurse Mary Morris wrote in her diary. British nurse Rachel Millet reassured her reader that the Germans "were treated exactly the same as all the other wounded and given the best possible treatment under difficult conditions." "A nurses' training of caring cannot be switched on and off like a light," insisted Brenda McBryde. But when an SS soldier spit in McBryde's face and called her a "British pig," the attending surgeon announced he would be the last man treated.[82] In fact, British medics welcomed the escalation of injured Germans. Such wounds were good news in terms of the war.[83]

Wounds were subject to a complex calculus that balanced the amount of surgical time against chances for survival. "One of our most difficult tasks," noted surgeon J. A. Ross, "was to sort out the casualties and to decide on the order in which they should proceed to the [operating] theatre. An abdominal case takes at least an hour to operate on, during which time three or four men with limb wounds can be done, with a certainty of good results, whilst an 'abdomen' has about a fifty-fifty chance only."[84] By Ross's math, one abdominal case was equal to three limb cases in surgical time, with the latter having a better chance of survival. While such a calculation may seem callous, wounds presented surgeons with a torturous set of obligations: to heal every one that could be healed and to heal as many as possible. As another surgeon, Charles Donald, put it: "It is not heartless because the idea in a rush was to get to as many bodies as possible rather than those who are going to die."[85]

To make matters worse, mistakes were made. According to Ross, a man deemed beyond hope nevertheless remained conscious, asking, "What about me?" whenever a doctor entered the pre-op room. When the surgeon grudgingly gave him X-rays to confirm his poor prognosis, it turned out that his wounds were only superficial. Mistakes remained everyone's worst fear. "It was our one dread that we would miss an urgent case and be responsible for another man's death," admitted Nurse Millet. Doctors also wondered about the morality of healing men who had lost their genitals or were blinded in both eyes. "Were we right to fight so very hard to save them?" asked Aylett. "Sometimes we wondered."[86]

As a soldier moved through the system, he literally *became* his wound. On his body hung a field tag describing his injury. If he was given morphine, the dose and time were written on his forehead. Physicians denoted patients by the type and severity of their wounds. Ross, for example, referred to wounded men as "limb cases" or "abdomens." Watts described them as "abdominal cases."[87] "Compound fracture of the femur" was how another soldier was labeled.[88] Mostyn Thomas designated two Germans as "a right thorax wound" and a "gunshot wound through the shinbone." According to Nurse McBryde, the head injury ward was called simply "Heads."[89] Ross described the men in his pre-operative room in this way:

Some unconscious, these chiefly head wounds, whose loud snoring breathing distinguished them. Some (too many—far too many) were carried in dying, with gross combinations of shattered limbs, protrusions of intestines and brain from great holes in their poor frames torn by 88-mm, shells, mortars, and anti-personnel bombs. Some lying quiet and still, with legs drawn up—the penetrating wounds of the abdomen. Some carried in sitting up on the stretchers, gasping and coughing, shot through the lungs.[90]

A soldier's wrecked body, not his personhood, became the singular focus of medical personnel. A primary concern was capacity for movement. G. Cowell, who unloaded men from trains and ambulances, described the injured as "stretcher cases" or "walking wounded."[91] Doctors designated their patients as "sitters," "sitting cases," or "stretchers."[92] Surgeon Stuart Mawson went into action when "three walking wounded arrived; two with superficial wounds but the third with a smashed arm." He also referred to soldiers as "abdomens, heads and major amps [amputations]."[93] This synecdochic vision of the wounded body was by no means limited to war surgery. Even in peacetime, doctors were trained to distance themselves from their patients, that is, to treat them primarily (but not exclusively) as a "case." Surgeons in particular were taught to view the body in a technical manner. No less than generals, surgeons abstracted a body in order to sanction the violence they visited upon it. But while the army saw that body as a unit of deadly force, RAMC saw it as the object of a medical assessment.

Wounding erased differences of nationality. There were many types of wounds but no real differences between men with the same wound. A German abdominal wound and a British abdominal wound looked much the same. Aylett recalled the men's faces changing, but "still there were the same dreadful heart-rending wounds. Despite the different shoulder badges of various units, the clothes were equally caked with drying blood and torn and ripped open by high explosives." "Again and again they came," lamented McBryde, "through day and night, men with different faces, different names, but the same terrible injuries." McBryde also had to burn uniforms worn by the wounded. "Hard-won stripes and pips and crowns, sewn on by proud Mums, wives and girlfriends; the leaping black boar of XXX Corps, the blue and red flash of 21 Army Group. It was all the same now. The field incinerator smoked all night."[94]

Wounded soldiers became numbers.[95] Diaries of medical personnel are filled to bursting with numbers. Stretcher bearer J. A. Garrett recorded a plane attack as 12 wounded, 22 killed in a nearby infantry unit. The day after D-Day, Cowell reported transporting "150 this time; 90 stretcher cases, including six deaths, and 60 walking wounded." A few days later, he told his diary that he was taken to a railway depot at 3:30 a.m. to unload wounded "and had 180 patients to deal with. 140 stretcher cases and 40 walking wounded." (Cowell's schedule, which mostly entailed working late at night, confirms what John Thorpe was told: the wounded were transported at this time to prevent public exposure). "Never saw anything like it," reported medical officer P. J. Cremin to his wife, "terrific stuff coming in . . . 64 cases; it certainly kept me busy all night." In October he wrote her that he had seen 782 cases in 26 hours at Bayeux. "Suffering considerable casualties," Dr. E. H. P. Lassen recorded in his diary shortly after D-Day, "108 cases passed through in 8 hours. . . . During the night about 165 cases passed through the A.D.S. A large proportion of them required surgical interference."[96] Surgeons were also counting. On September 13 in Italy, surgeon George Feggetter recalled operating "on 22 men until midnight and on another 25 in the next two days." "The surgical work was easing off rapidly; in the first week we did 80 operations, in the second week 24, in the third week 21," said surgeon Watts about the Normandy campaign.[97]

Medical personnel had good reasons for enumerating the wounded. Army Medical Services set quotas for them. In field dressing stations, 250 soldiers were to be treated every twenty-four hours. Surgical centers were to operate at a rate of one man every hour.[98] Considerable pressure was placed on surgeons to treat wounded men as efficiently as possible. When Watts treated a German soldier with an old infected leg wound, he categorized him as "sick" rather than wounded "in order not to spoil our figures for the interval between wounding and admission."[99] The surgeon's need to reach a quota inspired this ditty by a medic:

> We worked like slaves in those days
> And tried out our medical skill
> We patched up the mangled bodies
> After they had been through the mill
> The patients came in by the dozen
> Whip 'em in! Whip 'em out was our creed
> And the Commander in Chief admitted
> That he'd never seen such speed.
> The Surgeon worked up such a tempo
> That he nearly made a mistake
> and carved up a stretcher bearer
> To make up his twenty eight![100]

Designating soldiers as numbers and types of wounds conforms to the format of medical reporting. The two things doctors needed to record were the type of wound and the number of cases treated. Even in the chaos of Arnhem, G. M. Warrick managed to report that he had treated approximately 700 soldiers from the First Airborne Division on September 25 and another 650 admitted the next day.[101] A. W. Lipmann-Kessel's medical post was so chaotic in Arnhem that he lost his documents and case notes. Nevertheless, he was able to record from memory that he had performed 7 surgeries of the abdomen, 1 of the head, 2 of the urethra and bladder, 3 of the thorax, 2 of the jaw, 14 of the femur, and 70 "miscellaneous fractures and flesh wounds."[102] Similarly, S. M. Frazer, captured by the Germans to take care of British POWs, still remembered his 17 amputations, 5 abdominal wounds, 12 fractures of the femur, and 7 fractures of the tibia and fibula.[103] Medical accountability came in the form of numbers.

The quantification of wounds served yet another purpose. Medical personnel used numbers to emphasize their exhaustion and need for personnel. When Lassen recorded in his diary on June 9, 1944, that 108 cases had passed through his field dressing station in eight hours, he was expressing his utter fatigue. "There were 118 of them in 36 hours," noted Clark as he read the dressing station records from one night. "By the end, my hands and clothes were stiff with blood and I was dizzy and exhausted." The medical rhythm of healing (following the battle rhythm of wounding) was spasmodic. From a casualty clearing station in Normandy, Cremin wrote his wife that he was either "slack" or doing "a rush job."[104] There would be long lulls in which soldiers rested and prepared for battle, but once it started, medical personnel would be quickly overwhelmed.[105] The sheer number of wounded demanded everything you had—and then some.

A soldier's wounds sped up the world around him. There was a race against time, a race against blood loss, a race against bacteria, and a race against the pressing needs of others. You were consumed by the human need for water, plasma, morphine, and a surgeon's knife. "There was only one way to cope with all these cases and that was to work and work until it was impossible to go on any longer and we had to go away for a few hours to rest and sleep," remembered Aylett. "We were tired, incredibly tired, for the days and nights wore on and still the pre-operative wards were always full." Clark described the twenty-four hours after a battle as "a blur of demanding, exhausting medical work, transfusing, bandaging, estimating degrees of shock. . . . I slept and toiled again. Gradually things slackened." "I struggled through the list," recalled Ross, "working all the time mechanically, like a boxer who has been down for a count but has got up again and is carrying on automatically." D. G. Aitken met other medical officers "who look very tired and played up. I think we have all aged about forty years." "It was like a nightmare," Millet recorded in her diary. "I kept repeating to myself 'this can't continue.' Stretchers filled the passages, the balconies and all the small rooms on the second and third floor." McBryde recollected a day when the ward was so overloaded with wounded, she couldn't put a foot or a knee between the stretchers. Afterward, Morris wrote, there was "the nauseating job of clearing up the blood-stained theatre" and "carrying away the legs to an incinerator and watching until they were completely burned."[106]

Sleep was golden. "It was a purely animal existence," noted surgeon Ross, "work, sleep, work. I found I could turn in at any time and get a ration of sleep—sleep, more precious than food and drink in these conditions." Aylett would work up to seventeen hours, then snatch "a brief and exhausted sleep," then work again another seventeen hours. This would go on for several days and nights. When doctors finally slept, they were often too tired to take their clothes off. Surgeon Feggetter realized one day that he had been in North Africa for several weeks without taking off his uniform. During the Battle of Arnhem, physician Warrick reported the "M.O.s [medical officers] and orderlies were almost out on their feet but kept going." Also at Arnhem, Mawson had no trouble falling asleep on the hard floor with his boots on. Ross and his anesthesiologist both fell asleep standing up.[107]

Caring for wounded men in the Italian mountain campaign was particularly demanding. Medical officer E. Grey Turner complained of "life in holes in the ground at 3000 feet." The result, he claimed was "(a) exhaustion; (b) exposure; (c) nervous strain."[108] Having to evacuate wounded down rugged terrain, often under a cold rain, took every ounce of the stretcher bearers' strength. In the Battle of Monte Cassino, medics worked for seventy-two hours straight. "Towards the end they worked like robots," noted one witness, "their limbs moving only from an unbreakable sense of duty." One private helped carry a wounded officer down the mountain, a task taking sixteen hours. When he reached the advanced dressing station, the private collapsed and died. He was forty-two years old.[109]

4

The surgeon, of course, had the most visceral, intimate relation to a soldier's wound. Only a surgeon could cut open a soldier's body. Only he could fully assess the wound's damage by tracing its path inside the body. There were two types of surgeons: field and rear. Field surgeons treated wounds quite close to the front with the aim of saving lives. Rear surgeons were miles from the front or back home in London. Their job was to complete operations still needed after the initial field surgery. Rear surgeons sniffed that field procedures were so hasty that many wounds were not sutured until they could be treated in rear hospitals.[110] Field surgeons told them they should be happy the soldiers were alive at all.

As increasingly destructive explosives were deployed on the battlefield, wounds changed in nature and severity. In contrast to a bullet, which created a small hole when it entered the human body, a shell fragment left a large jagged edge. By lacerating human tissue in an irregular manner, and by bringing bits of clothing, dirt, and other foreign agents into the wound, a shell fragment imposed a greater threat of infection.[111] Surgical reports from field hospitals, including case studies and new protocols, dominated British medical journals during the war. Taken together, they testify to the appalling effect of the new weaponry on the human body.

The new wounds presented field surgeons with new challenges but also new opportunities. On the one hand, they were frontline witnesses to the war's filth and suffering, forced to work to exhaustion. On the other hand, treating enormous numbers of patients enabled them to gather research data on wounding, some of which they used to further knowledge and also to advance their careers. Surgeons like Captain Archibald Stewart carried a small notebook in which he recorded data on "cases of interest" including transfusions, operations, and medications.[112]

To the surgeon, the wound was first and foremost an object for medical explanation. Only the surgical eye had the power to fully decipher the wound and render its truth—that is, the damage it caused and its chances for healing. To do so, the surgeon brought the wound into full view, making incisions and inserting retractors under surgical lights.[113] His aim was to discover the path of the foreign agent in the soldier's body and the devastation it caused. The surgeon described this path as he would write a travelogue. We learn where the agent entered, its direction in the body, and where it stopped or exited. "The shell fragment appears to have taken an upward and outward path, entering the left side of the neck at the junction of the upper two-thirds and lower third of the interior border of the sterno-mastoid," reported surgeon B. Reese in the *Bulletin of War Medicine*. He then recorded the impact of the wound's journey in terms of tissue damage. "The fragment fractured the left superior cornu of the thyroid cartilage, passing between the external branch of the left superior laryngeal nerve and left recurrent laryngeal nerve."[114]

Wounds could be deceptive. Feggetter described an injured soldier at the Battle of Arnhem: "The shirt was lifted up, displaying that small, gory hole where the main fragment had entered, and the wound was revealed, a small circular red mark in the skin of the abdomen oozing blood slightly—so small, but pregnant with fatal possibilities."[115] While the wound appeared unassuming, it was, in fact, rife with danger. The worst of these "fatal possibilities" was infection. In infection, the body turned against itself, defiling its own flesh, causing it to smell, rot. In one way or another, every aspect of surgery aimed to prevent a wound's infection. In the case of gas gangrene, infection led to the loss of arms and legs. In the case of sepsis, it led to death. And there was little at the time to fight infection. Doctors began using penicillin in 1942, but it could not be produced in large enough quantities to save the tens of thousands of wounded men who needed it.[116] Until the very end of the war, the epic battle was largely fought with much less effective antimicrobial sulfa drugs.

The idea was to make a fresh start. Nurse McBryde explained the logic: "to transform the dirty pulpy mess left by shell explosion into a clean area where what remained of the structures could be repaired."[117] The surgeon used a scalpel to cut away damaged flesh.[118] Lacerated flesh was fodder for bacteria. Ross described this process of debridement: "Then with knife and scissors, those ragged holes, torn by steel and bomb in the flesh of these gallant fellows in that hell of mud and torrent and rocky crag which blocked the road to Rome, were opened up, their edges trimmed, and all devitalized tissue cut away."[119] Debridement, sometimes also called "wound toilet," removed the war from the wound.[120] The surgeon could not unblock the road to Rome, but he could "widen tracks to avoid subsequent pocketing" in the wound's internal pathways.[121] To drive infection from the body, you had to give it no place to hide. "All nooks and crannies in which pus may collect are laid open," reported another surgeon.[122] Foreign agents driven inside the body by the force of the bullet or fragment were also excised. They consisted of dirt and pieces of uniform, but also bits of leather and webbing equipment or even items from the soldier's uniform pocket.[123] The outside had to be excised from the inside. Finally, the surgeon sprinkled "a good frosting" or a "hoar-frost" of sulfa drugs on the wound, protecting it as if with a blanketing of snow.[124]

When wounds healed, doctors were able to proclaim progress. They inserted the wound into a heroic story of saving lives. New drugs and procedures played a key role in the drama.[125] Wartime medical journals were filled with such narratives. No surgeon wanted to admit he was in it to advance his reputation. Nevertheless, reports on "cases of interest" often smacked of careerism. "I have removed many large missiles from the human body in treating war wounds," surgeon Richard Charles assured his reader in a near-boasting tone. He went on to showcase his skill in fixing a shrapnel wound. Like the wounding narrative, the medical narrative began with catastrophe and moved toward restoration. According to Charles, a downed RAF pilot arrived in the hospital "greatly shocked, restless, in great pain, cyanosed and suffering from dyspoenia." A large shell fragment lay lodged in his eighth rib. Charles was able to save his life by operating twice, once to remove the fragment and once to debride "the entire tract of the missile with all layers." The story ends in triumph, with the pilot writing Charles to say he was "fit and well" and once again flying.[126] Also in the *British Medical Journal*, surgeon Donald congratulated himself on developing a procedure for testing the extent of an abdominal wound. His technique, "introduced by me in the Desert Campaign," had been "designated, not unkindly but with some lack of euphony, 'Donald's explorotomy.'"[127]

Reporting on war wounds this way, Charles and Donald took possession of them. The soldiers who suffered these wounds became mere markers of an individual surgeon's achievement. Wartime medical journals served as repositories for wounds now exploited by surgeons to showcase their skill. Not everyone was impressed. "Have just seen a perfectly fatuous article in the BMJ [*British Medical Journal*]," complained medical officer R. Barer in a letter to his wife. It "suggests that an estimate of volume of blood lost should always be made and Hb done before and after transfusion! I should have liked to see [the author] do it the night I had to transfuse four men in a stable with badly wounded people arriving every moment!"[128]

As in the army itself, there was a front and a rear in medical services. And like the case for trench foot, a chasm opened up between the meticulous medical protocols of the rear and the inability to follow them in the desperate conditions of the front lines. "How very different this rough-and-ready work was to the skillfully planned operations in hospitals far away in Blighty!" observed Ross. While field surgeons, too, harbored ambitions, these were tempered by the sight of the war's suffering. "Once again," observed Aylett, "we surveyed the all-too-familiar scene of shattered bodies, guts spewed out, legs and arms blown off, broken bones protruding and faces disfigured." Such scenes reminded doctors that a soldier's wounds were not theirs to possess. "The suffering of the wounded caused me more anxiety than anything else," Turner confided to his diary. As Ross put it, "Any despondency one felt at the present waste of precious years when, instead of being initiated into the technicalities of modern surgery, one was restricted to the monotonous repetition of trimming and cleaning and removal of projectiles, vanished at the sight of these men."[129]

As was the case in 1914–18, the wounded body stood in for the horror of war. Wounds were the essence of war and yet its greatest secret. Beyond the soldiers fighting, only stretcher bearers, ambulance drivers, medics, and field surgeons knew the full truth of the squalor, the suffering, the death hovering over all of it. Artillery could render your body unrecognizable in a sheer instant. Ross described one wounded man as "a frightful, legless, bleeding fragment . . . a monstrous bit of mangled flesh."[130] Ambulance driver Jim Wisewell remembered one day in his ambulance unit this way:

Hour after hour we worked and evacuated, and still the flow continued. Ghastly wounds, there were, of every type and state of severity. Heads with skulls so badly smashed the bone and brain and pillow were almost indivisible; faces with horrible lacerations; jaws blown completely away leaving only two sad eyes to plead for relief from pain. Chests pierced through with shrapnel and lungs that spouted blood from gushing holes. Arms were mangled into shapeless masses left hanging by muscle alone and waiting the amputation knife. There were abdomens perforated by shell splinters and displaying coils of intestine, deadly wounds. Buttocks were torn and in some cases spinal injury had followed bringing paralysis. But the leg wounds! Thigh-bones splintered knees without kneecaps; legs without feet; red, mangled flesh and blood flooding the stretcher.[131]

This horror was largely kept from the public in an effort to maintain morale. Wounding was the dirty secret of the war.

The RAMC complied with the concealment in two ways. First, they evacuated injured men away from the front and placed them in surgical centers, hospitals, and rehabilitation facilities where they saw only each other and the medics, doctors, and nurses who treated them. The wounded were then moved to London hospitals in "the dead of night," as John Thorpe and G. Cowell discovered. Second, the aim of healing itself was to seal or set a wound, ultimately removing its traces. Through physical therapy, men learned to walk or move their arms and hands again. Plastic surgeons reconstructed faces devastated by wounds to the jaw, nose, or eyes. Scarring was minimized. By the time the wounded were reunited with their families, they were bandaged, clean, and relatively free of pain.

Being wounded did bring some comfort. At every level of the RAMC, extreme efforts were made to lessen pain by medical personnel. Barer wrote his wife: "It's impossible to over-emphasize the importance of making the man comfortable." Morphia and anesthesia were considered godsends. Aylett remembered that no wounded man was stripped of his clothing until anesthetized because "it would have been too excruciatingly painful to do this while he was conscious."

McBryde described in detail one wounded man she and another nurse attended to. After gently easing him out of his clothing, they rolled him onto his unwounded side to softly soap and sponge his back. They then dressed him in clean pajamas, and rolled him over. "Swiftly now, because he was lying on his injured leg," they pulled out the dirty blanket from underneath him and exchanged it for a clean one. "Then we cleaned his furred tongue and crusted lips so that the sips of water that followed tasted sweet and good. We combed his dusty hair . . . gave him an injection of penicillin and left him to slide back into restorative sleep. It took forty minutes to make just one man comfortable."[132]

Perhaps most importantly, wounds brought renewal. David Holbrook told the story of a lightly wounded soldier named Paul in the hospital, who saw an infantryman opposite him with multiple back wounds. So disgusting was the dressing on his back—"a mass of dried blood and pus, green in places"—that the nurses had put off changing it. Paul decided to do it himself. When "the filthy thing lay on the floor . . . the marvel was revealed of the white healed flesh, the creature come whole again by itself." In a moment of rare intimacy, Paul gazed at the soldier's body, "a marvelous thing like some great wild flower in its own tissue-growing life."[133] Under the filth that had become the soldier's back, new white flesh emerged. In their healing, wounds evoked the mysterious power of a body to make itself whole again.

5

THE CORPSE

Is it morbid to study the history of the dead body? Historians have largely averted their eyes, as if the corpse stood beyond time and place, beyond life itself.[1] With its stench and decay, the human corpse inspires revulsion and fear; it compels us to look away. Yet the corpse is central to understanding the Second World War. The war was about heroism, yes, but ultimately the war was about death. It was the dead body that took the measure of the war's sacrifice. Our victories were counted in lives lost as well as territories gained.

The starved corpse, the carbonized corpse, the corpses said to be "stacked like cord wood" in Polish and German extermination camps—these bodies came to stand for the war's unique atrocities, the insanity of the Nazi state, the Frankenstein of modern mechanized warfare.[2] In places like Dachau and Ohrdruf after the war, German civilians were forced to parade in front of dead bodies, to come to terms with their own complicity in genocide (fig. 13). The corpse bore the weight of German shame.

The dead body may have inspired revulsion, but it also commanded attention (fig. 14). "One came upon them and wanted to stare hard," wrote one US Navy lieutenant, "but there was that feeling that staring was rude." "My eyes were drawn irresistibly towards them," remembered Charles B. MacDonald. "but I forced myself to turn away." The body became the object of morbid fascination. "Many of the men went over to look at the bodies, drawn by a horrible

FIGURE 13. German civilians forced to look at bodies at Ohrdruf.

FIGURE 14. Dead German soldier.

fascination," noted Raymond Gantter.[3] What made the corpse so compelling? Perhaps because it suspended our sense of place, disrupting the relation between here and nowhere. The soldier's corpse represented a person, but the person was no longer present. He was there but not there; nor was he anywhere else.[4] "We believe that a certain aura pertains to physical remains," claims Thomas W. Laqueur, "even if we believe these remains are, in their essence, of no significance; we act as if the dead are somewhere even if we claim to believe they are nowhere."[5]

The corpse was above all a stench, a sweet and sickening smell of decay, which became all too familiar, yet never ceased to repel. The corpse revealed the fault line, concealed in life, between subject and object, flesh and "soul." He was flesh without consciousness, will, or agency.[6] The soldier as corpse refused to be an "it" but yet could not be a person. The dead bodies remained after the soldiers were gone. It was who they had been and yet external to them. As such, the corpse represented the opposite of active, virile manhood. It reminded soldiers just how close they were to losing all manliness and control.

As such an absent presence as well as symbol of the abject, the dead body arrested the attention of everybody engaged in warfare—the officers, the gravediggers, the civilians, the infantrymen, and the grieving families. Despite aggressive efforts on the part of the army to erase the corpse from view, to deny its very existence, the participants in this war remained witnesses to it. Their journals, memoirs, and letters reveal a preoccupation with the corpse—its positioning on the battlefield, its shattered limbs, its dignity (or lack of dignity) in death. At the sight or the stench of a soldier's dead body, these witnesses did not fail to feel revulsion. But they were also startled into witnessing, recording, and recalling the corpse in their mind's eye.[7] The testimony that resulted is pervasive and significant. In this witnessing, the dead body came to symbolize not only the war's effects, but the war itself. It operated as a framework for understanding the war.

To understand the corpse as a complex symbol, let us look at how two commanders viewed the same spectacle of human carnage at the

Falaise "gap" or "pocket." The time is 1944 and the place is Normandy, France. In Falaise, south of Caen, the German Seventh Army, about fifty thousand men, was surrounded by the Allies. Tens of thousands of Germans were killed outright. Here, first, is how Dwight D. Eisenhower, commander in chief of the Allied forces, experienced the dead at Falaise:

> The battlefield at Falaise was unquestionably one of the greatest "killing grounds" of any of the war areas. Roads, highways, and fields were so choked with destroyed equipment and with dead men that passage through the area was extremely difficult. Forty-eight hours after the closing of the gap I was conducted through it on foot, to encounter scenes that could be described only by Dante. It was literally possible to walk for hundreds of yards, stepping on nothing but dead and decaying flesh.[8]

For Eisenhower, the scene had a macabre Dantesque quality. But the corpse itself he saw primarily in strategic terms. The corpse posed a strategic problem because it hindered the passage of his army. Dead bodies were choking roads and highways; one could not walk without stepping on them. Eisenhower's view of the body was also his view of the war—as a set of obstacles to be overcome in a march toward Berlin and victory.

In stark contrast to Eisenhower's strategic view of the dead was the testimony of Hans Eric Braun, Oberfeldwebel (German army master sergeant), who also witnessed the slaughter:

> The never-ending detonations—soldiers waving to us, begging for help, the dead, their faces screwed up but still in agony, a soldier stumbling, holding back the intestines which were oozing from his abdomen. . . . But also there were civilians lying by the roadside, loaded with personal belongings . . . and still clinging to them in death. Close by a crossroads, caught by gunfire, lay a group of men, women, and children. Unforgettable, the staring gaze of their broken eyes and the grimaces of their pain-distorted faces.[9]

Death signaled the chaos the war had become. The German body, like the German army, had been vivisected. Its entrails were hanging out. Braun's description was as much an indictment as a lament. He casts the battle as a slaughter of innocents. By focusing on civilians, his eye was able to sketch a scene of atrocity. French civilian corpses, with their broken eyes and their efforts, even in death, to cling to their personal belongings, transformed a German defeat into a war crime. The French corpse articulated, in his view, an inhumane war fought by the Allied forces.

The dead body was made to do the work of the living: to condemn an enemy, to lament a defeat. This human tendency to make the dead body *speak* merits our historical attention because, in speaking, the corpse tells us much about what the war meant to those who fought it. Let us, then, explore how the body came to symbolize the war for its participants—US military officials, gravediggers, French civilians, and, last but not least, American soldiers.

1

We begin with the Graves Registration Service, the official US military organization charged with identifying and burying dead soldiers. Graves Registration was initially deployed in the First World War in France. In American wars before that, such as the Civil War, the work of burying dead soldiers fell largely to those who had survived the battle.[10] This practice changed during the First World War because modern industrialized warfare so dramatically increased the scale of death. At the same time, what persisted into the twentieth century was the expectation that a dead soldier deserved a decent burial.[11] With that goal in mind, Graves Registration returned 233,181 bodies to the United States for burial after the war. Another 93,242 bodies remained abroad in overseas American cemeteries.[12]

At heart, Graves Registration struggled with the paradox of modern American warfare: that it was conducted in the name of individual freedoms, and yet created a style of death that was increasingly impersonal in scale. As a result, Graves Registration viewed the dead

soldier primarily as a logistical problem. Despite the highly mechanized, mobile warfare that formed the backdrop to their efforts, they
claimed to attend to a body in individual terms. There were collective
German graves, but no collective American graves. Each soldier was
buried separately even if he remained anonymous.[13] At the end of the
war, every effort was made to identify the estimated 150,000 bodies
whose names remained unknown.[14]

The name "Graves Registration" was intentionally anodyne. When
the organization was conceived, one assistant chief of staff suggested
the designation "Mortuary Service." Others insisted on "Graves Registration" because "to the public mind, the word 'grave' is far less re-
pugnant—if not gruesome—than the word 'mortuary.'"[15]

Despite extensive planning, the Graves Registration (GR) units
assigned to Normandy in June 1944 were quickly overwhelmed.[16]
It became clear that the US military had seriously underestimated
how much death would be produced by the invasion.[17] Those who
were killed in action were reported as "dead stock" on personnel
lists.[18] Hours after the landings began on June 6, the GR units began to arrive. Their view of Omaha Beach was quite different from
that presented to the American public (fig. 15). The beaches were
littered with thousands of bodies. So numerous were the corpses
that they clogged the harbor and beach, preventing men and supplies from moving forward. At first burying bodies was impossible
because the beaches were not secure.[19] Because no American soldiers
were returned home until after the war, the dead had to be buried in
nearby fields. British bodies were buried in "Allied Plots," and German
ones in "Enemy Plots."[20] GR units were first able to establish operations in Blosville and St.-Laurent-sur-Mer.[21] Because caskets were too
cumbersome to send into a theater of war, the dead were wrapped in
white mattress covers or blankets.[22] Some were buried naked; others
in their uniform.[23]

So many dead bodies raised urgent health concerns among the living. Sheer numbers also made it impossible for Grave Registration
to meet their object of rendering the corpse invisible. As officers led
soldiers onto the shore the day after D-Day, they commanded them

FIGURE 15. Dead on Omaha Beach. National Archives.

to keep their heads down, not to shelter them from bullets but to prevent them from seeing so many bodies.[24] GR private Tom Dowling was struck dumb by the sight of the dead at Omaha Beach. But his sergeant jolted him out of his stupor by screaming, "Every day, new troops pour into here, land on the beach and move up. We've got to get these bodies out of their sight. They'll see enough as they move forward."[25] A GR commander wrote that "there were Colonels coming in every day saying to get the bodies buried. Get them buried. 'We don't care how you do it, but get them buried.'"[26]

Dowling and his GR unit did what they could to "evacuate" the bodies from the beach. Their work was described in hygienic terms as in to "clear," to "clean," or to "sweep" the battlefield of bodies. "Our job," noted one commander, "was to sweep the battle areas for all dead, pick them up or disinter them, and transport all remains to the nearest U.S. military cemetery."[27] When Raymond Gantter arrived on Omaha Beach several weeks after the landings, he noted that "attempts had been made to clean it up, discipline it into some kind of order."[28] Similarly, graves were put in precise symmetrical patterns,

FIGURE 16. Cemetery at St.-Laurent-sur-Mer, Normandy, France. © Tristan Nitot/ Wikimedia Commons, CC BY SA 3.0 (unported).

as you now find them at St.-Laurent-sur-Mer (fig. 16).[29] Orderly lines and clean geometric shapes implied that the chaos of war was temporary, and that the world could and would be made right again.[30] In a postwar *Saturday Evening Post* article raising the question "Shall We Bring Home the Dead of World War II?" Blake Ehrlich reassured the American public that the overseas cemeteries "look wonderful. . . . Those who have seen [them] marvel at their beauty."[31] In these war cemeteries, the dead were still forced to serve the nation—as emblems of patriotism.[32] Wounding erased differences of nationality, as we have seen. All injured men were to be treated equally by medical personnel. But death reinscribed such differences. Corpses became symbols of national sacrifice.

The dead body was kept from the American public. Journalists were allowed to print photographs of dead soldiers only when officials felt it was necessary in order to raise money for war bonds.[33] After the war, the family of the deceased could choose to bury their loved one permanently abroad or bring the body home. Even when the bodies of the deceased were rejoined with their families, however, a military guard accompanied the casket to prevent the loved ones from seeing the body. Sometimes the guards had to forcibly prevent relatives from opening the casket.[34]

2

While family could not see or touch their loved one's remains, they could have his so-called "effects" or possessions—the watches, money, pictures, and souvenirs found on his person. These items were stripped from the body at collecting points near where the soldier would be buried (fig. 17). A soldier's effects, when sent to his family, again transformed him into an absent presence; his family received him only through his possessions. To safeguard them, "effects" were sent to an Effects Bureau established in Kansas City, Missouri, a city with good access to railway networks. Millions of objects were inventoried and processed in Kansas City. Workers identified a

FIGURE 17. "Collecting Effects on the Battlefield," from Edward Steere, *The Graves Registration Service in World War II* (Washington, DC: Office of the Quartermaster General, Historical Section, 1951).

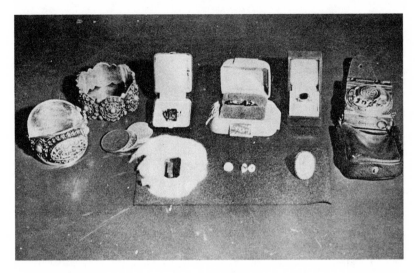

FIGURE 18. "Valuables That Came Home through Kansas City," from Edward Steere, *The Graves Registration Service in World War II* (Washington, DC: Office of the Quartermaster General, Historical Section, 1951).

soldier's property using brand names: Ronson chrome-finish lighters, Parker and Sheaffer fountain pens, Remo wristwatches, Elgin pocket watches, Oxford mechanical pencils, and Burgess flashlights.[35] The grieving relative would receive a package and a list. Dominic Giovvinazzo's wife, for example, got the following: "wallet, leather cigarette case, pocket knife, Unk fountain pen, Oxford Mechanical Pencil, wooden cigarette case, pipe, souvenir note, 14 K wedding ring, souvenir ring, holy card, religious medals, rosaries, address book, photos, social security card, driver's license"[36] (fig. 18).

Infantrymen on the front line had considerably fewer belongings than those who worked in bases. "There isn't much left to send home when an infantryman is killed," one soldier remarked, looking at "the pitiful little array of possessions" a friend left behind.[37] Souvenirs like Italian lire and cameos distinguished those who had fought in other theaters. In Kansas City, foreign currency was converted to dollars; soiled garments were cleaned of dirt and blood. Still other possessions were judged too filthy or bloodstained to go home. Lieutenant Robert D. Kellett had in his possession "one letter water-soaked, dirty grewsome [*sic*]," which was removed from articles sent home.[38] Also taken away were objects "deleterious to the . . . owner's character" or "injurious to the owner or the soldier's reputation," according to an official manual.[39] In other words, pornography or anything that might upset the family was removed. Rolls of film were also taken, perhaps for security purposes.[40]

Families waited months for their loved one's personal belongings. Mrs. Elaine Zatko, whose husband George was killed on November 29, 1944, wrote the Effects Bureau at the end of May that "it has been over six months and I understood that I would receive his things by then. . . . I have been waiting patiently every day for them as of course that's the only remembrance we have of him." Dickie Kramer was dead almost a year before his mother, Pearl, received his Parker pen and two coins. When she complained about how long it had taken, she received a form letter from the Quartermaster office. The value of the effects was personal not monetary. When the army wrote to Gilbert Smith's wife, Beulah, to ask if she still wanted a rusted pocket knife and a damaged pen, she insisted she did. When she received these items, she wrote to the Quartermaster: "No doubt this, like many others, is just property to you but to me it means deffinatly [*sic*] that my loved one has left us." To receive a soldier's belongings became the final proof that he was gone. Families were also hungry for any details about the soldier's death, even the smallest ones. Arnold Schmall's father wrote: "What I would like to know now where [*sic*] there any last words before his death if so let me know." "Would there be anyplace I could write for an eyewitness account of my husband's death?" asked Ernest Schultz's wife. "I am very anxious for any information about the details surrounding my dear husband's death."[41]

When the effects finally arrived, they could be a disappointment. Theft of a dead soldier's possessions was common, occurring on the battlefield as well as during the burial process.[42] The thief could be German or American.[43] Family members complained bitterly that watches, cameras, rings, and wallets did not return home. Eugene Fidler, father of Elmer Fidler, killed November 4, 1944, wrote the Effects Bureau complaining that he had received only an Old

Testament and a class ring. Where was his son's billfold with money and photos? James Kurz's mother wrote two years after her son had died in May 1945: "It would give me great solace and satisfaction if I knew that I had received all of my son's personal belongings. I received only a few, and I believe that much of them are still in U.S. government warehouses." "All I got back that was send [sic] to me was a small stone and a rosery [sic] that all," complained Lilliam Pepke, the mother of Gilbert Hinrichs, who died January 23, 1945. "He had many things with him that I send [sic] him and that he was going to have when he come home." The Effects Bureau could only express its regret "that more property was not received here. No other items were listed on your son's inventory of effects, apparently no other items were recovered."[44]

Putting a soldier's property in good order was meant as a gesture of respect, but sanitizing the possessions made them strangely impersonal. Consider how journalist Ernie Pyle approached the matter. A few days after the fighting at Omaha had stopped, Pyle had the idea of going down to see the beaches. By now the bodies had been removed. What remained, he noted, were "toothbrushes and razors, and snapshots of families staring up at you from the sand. Here are pocketbooks, metal mirrors, extra trousers, and bloody, abandoned shoes. I picked up a pocket Bible with a soldier's name in it, and put it in my jacket. I carried it half a mile or so and then put it back down on the beach. I don't know why."[45] Unlike GR effects, these belongings were permitted to bear the dignified traces of their former owners. Pyle felt the pull of the individual so much that, without knowing why, he felt obligated to give back the Bible. He looked upon these jackets and shoes as beloved things left behind in the rush to survive. In giving them integrity and respect, Pyle did the same for their owners. By contrast, the Effects Bureau saw toothbrushes and snapshots in grammatical terms—as the effects of an absent subject.

3

The military brass had concerns about Graves Registration. The unit's inability to keep up with the demand for countless burials during the Battle of Normandy drew critical responses. Robert McGowan Littlejohn, who commanded GR units beginning in 1945, characterized them as badly trained or untrained. In a postwar report, he urged the system be revamped with "key people who are in the mortuary business in civilian life and know what they are doing."[46] Although GR grew more competent as the American army made its way across northern France, the collection of bodies was still a problem. Here is how the official military historian Edward Steere viewed the dead at the Battle of the Bulge:

> New problems of evacuation arose during the Ardennes break-through and Allied counterattack. Although there was a marked increase in the number of casualties, the additional load on collecting points was offset by a diminishing distance from the front to Henri-Chapelle. Then, as the Allies struck back and reduced the enemy salient, the distance of evacuation increased. Moreover, a deep blanket of snow impeded collection. Many bodies which had been left as they fell during the German advance could not be recovered until the snow melted and a force composed of two graves registration platoons ... detailed to sweep the area.[47]

For Steere, the dead body formed a calculus of labor whose efficiency was measured in number of bodies evacuated over the distance between place of death and place of burial. Such a calculus took into account several variables: the movement of the front line, the geography of battlefield and cemetery, the relative concentration of bodies, and the weather. In the summer, bodies bloated and decomposed more quickly. GR units sometimes had to remove gas from bloated bodies by putting their knee on the corpse's back and applying pressure. In the winter, bodies froze but were not easily moved because of snow.[48] For Graves Registration planners, then, the dead body was heavy, uncertain work. It posed unexpected challenges, as did the war.

GR units—the men who actually carried the bodies and dug the graves—shared that view of the dead body as a gruesome logistical labor. One member of the 603rd GR Company remembered June 9,

1944, in this way: "Bodies were piling up and somebody got the idea that a bulldozer was just the thing. Got one and started to dig a plot with it. It did not work. Had to cover it up and start digging the separate holes again."[49] But for the gravedigger, the most important quality of a body was its degree of fragmentation or decomposition. Crucial as well was the extent to which the body was determined to be "recoverable," in Steere's words, that is, "chargeable to the field forces for purposes of evacuation."[50] In plain language, a "recoverable" body could be picked up and carried. Some could not. "Picked up bodies," one gravedigger observed. "The first body was a GI lying on his face. He had been shot in the back of the head. The next body was a German killed sitting in his foxhole. The third one we could not pick up. He had been killed by a mine."[51]

Graves Registration was tough work. "Not a very nice job," as Ralph Schaps put it.[52] It could also be dangerous. The Germans often mined the fields where American corpses were discovered—or they booby-trapped the body itself. To avoid explosions, GR units were instructed to remove the body by a rope at least 200 feet long. A soldier's "dog tags" could also be attached to a grenade set to go off as they were torn from the body. The GR General Board considered such practices "sickening." "Our men hated such a despicable trick," noted GR soldier Joseph Shomon.[53] Handling the dead bodies was difficult enough as it was. GR men often vomited as they worked. They dealt with the stench of decaying flesh by smoking one or even two cigarettes at a time. Many stayed drunk to get the job done.[54] Still others somehow managed to shut off their feelings. As Roscoe Blunt put it, "Mental sensitivities were totally turned off as we numbly went about our job—find them, load them, and get rid of them."[55]

Graves Registration work, though crucial, was tainted. Only those who worked at the collecting points were envied because the gathering of effects was, in the words of one gravedigger, "the glamorous and exciting part of the work."[56] There were two reasons for the negative attitude toward GR work. First, African American soldiers made up a large proportion of GR units. Gravedigging was typical of the degrading, non-combat tasks assigned to black men during the war.[57] And once GR became known as a black man's job, no white man wanted to do it.[58] Second, GR soldiers were not allowed to engage in combat. To be concerned with only the "waste" of war was demeaning for them.

In the corpse, GR men saw their own degraded status. As Tom Dowling's company made their way across the channel toward Normandy, they saw their first body float by. "The eyes of everyone in my barge turned to the body. Under their helmets, the eyes seemed frightened and disgusted as they watched the body with its arms bobbing gently in unison with the legs, big torso acting like a cork, legs and arms dangling like strings from the four corners."[59] Dowling describes his own work as a gravedigger in similar terms: "During the first two months, none of us did very much talking. We seemed to be robots doing a job we never could quite understand."[60] Like the dead bodies of soldiers, Dowling's soldiers were dummies or robots. In this way, the dead body materialized their own abjection as soldiers.

4

Despite the best efforts of Graves Registration to erase the dead body from view, it lay everywhere in Normandy during the summer of 1944. French civilians encountered dead bodies along the road, in their fields and front yards. Eleven-year-old Louis Blaise and his family tried to leave their house when the battle grew too near, only to trip on the dead bodies outside their front door.[61] Civilians with houses along main roads peeked out their windows to see American trucks passing loaded with bodies, sometimes with the leg of a fallen soldier protruding from the back.[62] "Everyday we discovered new corpses in the fields," observed Marcelle Hamel. "It was often the smell which led us to them."[63] The sight and smell of bodies was particularly traumatic for French children. Little Christian Letourneur recalled having to walk past hundreds of corpses at Carquebut: "Never has a field seemed to me so big! It was so hard and I wanted so much to leave!"[64]

Civilians took part in burying the dead. During the first few days of the invasion, the overwhelming number of bodies commanded the work of German prisoners of war and French civilians.[65] Norman men, described by one GR soldier as "very old or crippled in some way," were put to work removing bodies from the beach and digging graves. They drank cider and wine and refused water. The US Army paid them with canned meat and other rations.[66] Even when Graves Registration was nowhere to be found, Normans found a way to pay their respects to the American dead, sometimes digging graves on their own. In Rémilly, Madame Le Bourg recalled a pilot crashing to his death in a plane called "Ladylou" near her house. Before the Germans took the pilot's papers, she and her family discovered he had been a Catholic. Without his papers, they were unable to inform his family, but they did say words in his honor as they buried him in the town cemetery.[67]

Normans treated the bodies of German and American soldiers differently. German corpses lay exposed and were often mutilated (fig. 19).[68] Children robbed them of boots and other valuables. While a German body was left faceup and bereft of belongings, an American one remained facedown, a bouquet of flowers on his back.[69] Although the village of Gorron was still under Nazi control, an unmarked grave of an American soldier was heaped with flowers, a crown of laurel leaves, and a tricolor ribbon. The Gorronnais had risked imprisonment to pay their respects.[70] On June 6, Marcelle Hamel observed a young peasant kneeling near a dead paratrooper, gathering up papers and photographs scattered near his body, putting them safely into his uniform pocket, and covering him with the silk of his parachute.[71]

The bodies of Americans stirred the gratitude of French civilians. In the American corpse, they saw the realization of the war's highest goals and ideals. One civilian remembered the sight of a dead American soldier "having come to the Norman earth to pay with his life for the freedom of others."[72] Upon seeing a long line of body bags at St.-Laurent-sur-Mer, a nineteen-year-old Frenchman had this thought: "These young soldiers have come from distant American lands where they could have very well lived in peace. By hundreds and thousands they have lost and continue to lose their lives in the name of freedom."[73] The dead body evoked the purpose of the war for the French: to free them from the Germans. Freedom was not

FIGURE 19. Dead German soldier in Normandy.

abstract: it meant the freedom to speak, to gather, and to protest for the first time in four years.

Freedom was also ideological. Long before a foot made a print on Omaha Beach, the American Office of War Information was engaged in what they called "psychological warfare" against the Nazis. Beginning in 1943, civilians read propaganda air-dropped by Allied planes, defining US war ambitions as the opportunity "to see our flag recognized throughout the world as a symbol of liberty and irresistible force consecrated to the defense of freedom."[74] Not surprisingly, then, these words echoed in the French construction of the American dead.

5

Concepts such as "liberation" played no part in how American soldiers saw dead bodies. Like French civilians, American soldiers were subjected to the sight of corpses every day. No doubt some GIs saw the dead bodies of their comrades as representing a necessary sacrifice for freedom. Some even envied the dead because for them the war was over.[75] Much more common among infantrymen, however, was an anxious identification with a corpse, even a German one. In the dead body, foot soldiers saw the precarity of their own lives.

The army's dogged attempts to keep death out of sight became the butt of jokes among infantrymen. Enormous was their contempt for anyone who believed they had not yet come to terms with the reality of death.[76] "Each day in combat," noted Blunt, "I witnessed every face of death imaginable." "I hated the dead, but there was no escaping them. They were everywhere we went," recounted Donald Burgett. "Just so many dead," recalled George Biddle of the Italian campaign. "You stir them with your foot, lying in the grass; in ditches, hanging out of cars; carbonized under burnt vehicles." Even sixty years after the war, the sight of dead American soldiers at Hürtgen Forest "remains vivid and traumatic" in Spencer Wurst's mind.[77]

To see a corpse for the first time was a reckoning. It forced you to confront the unmistakable possibility of your being killed. Michael Bilder was "stunned into disbelief" when he turned a dead man over. "Forget it[,] Mike, he's gone," someone said. Bilder replied, "But I was just talking to him a minute ago." Roscoe Blunt gently kicked a man lying on the ground. At first Blunt thought the man was sleeping but then realized his error: "It took a few moments before it sunk in—I was looking at my first dead American. . . . Without looking back, I continue[d] on, but having now actually touched death, I was even less confident of my own abilities."[78]

Death's relentless presence made you realize there was no magic shield to protect you. Upon seeing his first corpse, Paul Fussell lost his "adolescent illusions": "I suddenly knew I was not and never would be in a world that was reasonable or just." "It was quite against logic to suppose that you were destined to survive the war," wrote Andrew Wilson. "You saw a pair of boots sticking out from a blanket, and they looked exactly like your own; there was no ground for thinking that the thing that had come to the owner of these boots was not going to come just as casually to you."[79] Jim Gavin recalled one of his men who, upon seeing his first dead body, turned white, then green. "I knew his state of mind. Every young soldier first entering combat is horrified by the sight of dead bodies. . . . They always equate themselves with the dead they see and think that it could happen to them." Mac McMurdie had the same response upon seeing his first dead person, in this case a German soldier: "He looked so small and insignificant, even though his body was bloated from lying there for some days. I could not help but ask myself if each one of us was so small and so insignificant as this? It was a very sobering moment."[80]

No wonder commanders wanted to hurry bodies off the battlefield. As the famous GI Audie Murphy once remarked, the corpse "makes a man reflect upon what his own life may come to." Walter Brown watched as bodies were thrown on trucks "like back-home cordwood. I wondered if some day they might be picking me up the same way. It gives you the willeys [sic] to think of it." Upon seeing a mass of very young dead, Robert Bowen asked: "How much more of this could we go through before we might be the ones stacked like poles ready to be loaded on a truck?" As Paul Boesch and his unit were en route to an attack, they came upon "a ghastly column of dead Jerries . . . sprawled over the road in various frantic postures of violent death." Despite the command to pass by and not look, several men vomited, and several others had to be physically prodded in order to move forward. Some men coped with their anxiety by ignoring the dead. "I resolved never to really look at a dead body," recalled Morris Courington; "they were 'noticed' hundreds of time, but never really 'seen.'"[81]

It both did and did not matter if the dead were German. Soldiers felt a mixed set of emotions upon seeing German dead. On the one hand, they could be callous. German bodies provided opportunities to steal Nazi souvenirs and watches. So prized were German pistols and helmets that the Germans booby-trapped their corpses, hoping to make the looter pay with his life. German bodies could also stir anger and revenge among infantrymen, particularly if the dead had served in the elite SS troops, infamous for their savagery. After witnessing SS atrocities inflicted upon Belgian civilians, Blunt came upon a hacked-up SS corpse. "Without reason or provocation," he separated the head from the body with a savage kick, then continued to play with it like a soccer ball. "I felt nothing but macabre elation," he recalled.[82]

On the other hand, infantrymen saw in the German corpse their own abjection.[83] French soldier Henry Deloupy was distressed to see German prisoners unceremoniously throwing the bodies of their former comrades into a ditch. Jean Navard's French armored unit came across the dead body of a highly decorated German officer. "To see him dead in front of us," he recorded in his diary, "it seems idiotic but we were all moved. We kept silent and arranged his body so that it was positioned in a more dignified manner." The French armored felt an "idiotic" kinship to the German infantry because both were the war's dead meat. Fussell remembered observing some very young German soldiers: "They were losing for one thing, and their deaths meant nothing, though they had been persuaded that resistance might 'win the war.'" Bowen had a similar response upon seeing dead teenage German boys: "Now they lay dead in the snow, freezing and lost forever to their families and friends. I felt sorry for them. I became horribly depressed. They had been struggling for survival the same as us." "It was a terrible thing to see them," recalled Rex Flower, "young men in the prime of their life." Bloated German corpses reminded Robert Humphrey of dead cows back home in Texas. It bothered him "to see human beings, even Germans, lying there unattended, like some dead animals." Upon seeing a dead German body in the rain, French writer André Chamson observed how "the water streamed gently down the corpse's cheeks so he looked like he was crying."[84]

For infantrymen, the corpse symbolized a loss of self. They saw a soldier's body at once through two contradictory optics. On the one hand, foot soldiers looked at the dead as mere bodies—without personhood or manhood. On the other hand, they viewed the corpse through the personal, individual lens of family. In this view, he was Joe, Bill, Lester, David—someone's brother, boyfriend, husband, or son. When Orval Faubus was grieving his friend Cull, he learned that Cull's body had been abandoned by Graves Registration to be evacuated at a later date. That night he wrote in his journal about Cull's wife: "If she could have really known, that her true love was no more, and that his body was lying in the wet fields of No-Man's Land in far-away Normandy, perhaps even her life would have bled away."[85] For Faubus, Cull's body represented both a beloved husband and an object abandoned to the wet fields of Normandy. In the contrast between these two views lay Faubus's deep distrust not only of Graves Registration, but the army in general, with its anonymity and disregard. Faubus's war was played out in a no-man's-land between his own sense of himself and the army's indifference toward him.

The dead body also reminded the soldier that it was impossible to remain the person he had been back home. Once a brother, a son, a sweetheart, or a husband, the soldier had been transformed into a mere body. Like the corpse, the living soldier had left a self and a spirit behind, and was now nowhere—neither here nor somewhere else. The dirty, cracked pictures of loved ones carried by soldiers like Faubus evinced their desire to cling to a fragile personhood. A young GI from Michigan had this vision of dead bodies: "The living are complicated but the dead have been stripped of all meaning. We saw them coifed in crab-shaped helmets, dressed in gray uniforms, mouth agape, gray teeth, gray hands, worn boots, no identities, indistinguishable one from the other, dead meat, nothing to grieve. We were stupefied by the death we'd breathed, and stumbled toward combat clutched by the fear that we, too, could be made simple."[86] The army, like death, took away the person. The soldier's body had become rigged into a unit of violent force. Now as a corpse, it would be processed by Graves Registration.[87] "It wasn't long before I could articulate for myself the message the war was sending the infantry soldier," wrote Fussell: "*You* are expendable. Don't imagine that your family's good opinion of you will cut any ice here. You are just another body to be used."[88]

Death clarified the logic of military command. To see a dead man and think of his family not only rendered *him* a person but salvaged your *own* personhood. Watching corpses being "piled into trucks like debris," Bilder used to think "if only the mothers of these poor boys could see how their sons were being treated what hell there would be to pay." "If his mama could only see him now," commented a foot soldier upon seeing the body of a lieutenant, "frost glistening on his uniform." When Lester Atwell saw the body of Lieutenant McGrath looking "like a log wrapped in a frozen, snowy shelter-half, tied with a rope," he remembered how McGrath used to give classroom lectures on the philosophy of St. Thomas Aquinas. When a GI threatened to cut off the finger of a dead German to get a ring off, his corporal was deeply upset because it was Mother's Day. "Think of that mother with the ring being cut off the Jerry."[89] British Bob Sheldrake dragged the body of a German gunner off the road where it had been repeatedly run over. "I thought of his mother and his wife," he explained.[90] German soldiers had the same impulses. When Hubert Gees saw his first dead American soldier, his eyes open and staring at the sky, he wondered, "Where in far off America will a mother grieve over him?" And then: "How would my mother cry over me if I had met the same fate?"[91] In the corpse, infantrymen saw the meaning of their war. Forced to leave their selves behind, they fought and died as nothing more than a body, a living corpse.

6

I want to end with a story told by medic Brendan Phibbs that in my mind captures how the infantryman understood the dead body. Phibbs was a surgeon in the US Army, and so he saw a great deal of death. One day in the spring of 1945, Phibbs and his unit were in Germany. That morning a spray of burp gun fire had killed a man named Wally. As the company readied for a German counterattack, they were forced to leave Wally's body behind on the road. Abandoning a body was something they had done countless times before. "In our world," wrote Phibbs, "a dead man simply had to lie there, naked to the snow or the rain, dying over again anytime anybody looked at him or came into the range of his staring eyes. Our dead had to be dumped like rubbish and ignored."[92] Wally had been a close friend of many in the company; he was liked by all the men. Now Phibbs and the team had to watch Wally's body get splattered with mud as the army moved their machinery forward. A battery of giant guns nearly crushed him as they passed by.

When an angry German spit on Wally's body, one of the medics, Sergeant Feehan, snapped. He picked up a stretcher and put Wally on it, covering him with a gray blanket. He explained what he intended to do: "We ain't gonna let Wally lie there in the street with them goddamn tanks runnin' over him and maybe squashin' him, and them goddamn Krauts pissin' on him. We're gonna put him somewhere, goddamit."[93] As Feehan went to pick up the body, he was joined by the other men. The procession for Wally began, and as it did, a crowd of infantrymen gathered around the stretcher. The group gained force as it moved down the street. As Phibbs told it, "Men were jumping down from half-tracks, walking quietly up to us, asking who the dead man was, calling out his identity to the man ahead, and starting to walk behind us. Many took off their helmets." At the same time, Phibbs felt anxious: "I had an uneasy presentiment that this natural, kind, human procedure was going to be regarded as somehow improper or even subversive by those dedicated to organizations and chains of command."[94]

He was right. The procession was soon stopped by an angry colonel. When the soldiers refused to disband, the colonel threatened to arrest them. One infantryman, Falcone, emerged from the group to tell the colonel he would welcome arrest. Turning to the men, he said, "What can they do to us worse than they done? We're gonna die, you goddamn fools. . . . You dead men: you gonna die in the dirt while this prick sticks pins in maps." At that point, Phibbs saw a "shattering" truth dawning on the men's faces: "They were the ultimate sacrifice of the whole war, the point platoon of an infantry company, and all that kept them there was their pride in their own manhood and their friendship for each other."[95] Phibbs described these men in the same terms he used for Wally's corpse: both were bodies disregarded in their sacrifice.

To take control of Wally's body, to give it a proper burial, was to embrace a common selfhood. Despite meddling officers, the group was soon allowed to do that. A small distance down the road, the unit found a field with a high, dense, beautiful bank of red and blue flowers. "As we lowered Wally's body into them, they bent over the old gray blanket; he disappeared in starry red and blue." Each of the men said their goodbyes to Wally while performing some final act—straightening the blanket, pulling over the flowers to cover him. "I know the others felt the same grateful peace that I did as we watched the innocent flowers sprinkle the stiffening limbs with loveliness," wrote Phibbs. "I had an irrational feeling that we had beaten the system: before long the ghouls of the Graves Registration Units would come along with their mattress sacks, their stapling tools, and their stencils, and Wally's mortal parts would be dumped into the returning chain of the vast assembly line that had brought him here, but none of that would matter. Wally had escaped into the flowers."[96]

For Phibbs, Graves Registration represented the vast assembly line of modern warfare into which he and Wally had unceremoniously been dumped. Phibbs's men cared about Wally's body not because he had died for freedom but because, like them, he was a person who deserved attention and respect. Wally's body became the gate through which Phibbs's unit escaped the war into a world of beauty. A gesture of respect, protecting Wally's corpse also became an act of resistance.[97] As such a site of rebellion, Wally's body tells us much about what the war meant to the infantrymen who fought it. When faced with a corpse, then, historians should try not to look away. For in the history of the dead, we can learn much about how the living, despite everything, lived on.

ACKNOWLEDGMENTS

With profound pleasure, I thank the many institutions and people who have helped to make *Sheer Misery*. My greatest institutional debt is to the Graduate School at the University of Wisconsin, Madison, so ably led by Lea Jacobs. The Graduate School provided several funding awards that enabled the many research trips necessary to write *Sheer Misery*. In this regard, I am also very grateful to Jim Sweet and Laird Boswell, the two most recent history department chairs. These two colleagues had my back personally as well as professionally. With generosity and good humor, they have done so much for me.

My research for *Sheer Misery* took me to archives in both the United States and Europe. I would like to thank the staffs of the Imperial War Museum, the Wellcome Library, and the British Library in London; and the Museumsstiftung Post und Telekommunikation in Berlin. In France, my thanks go to Stéphane Simmonet at the Mémorial de Caen, Alan Talon at Les Archives départmentales et du patrimoine de la Manche, and Anne-Marie Pathé at the Institut d'histoire du temps présent. In the United States, I am very grateful to the staffs of the Military History Institute at Carlisle Barracks, Pennsylvania; the National Archives and Records Administration in Maryland; and the Library of Congress in Washington, DC. Finally I want to thank the Interlibrary Loan staff at the UW's Memorial Library. Against all odds, they managed to track down and obtain hundreds of infantry memoirs, some incredibly obscure. *Sheer Misery* owes a great deal to them.

It has been a privilege to work with Susan Bielstein at the University of Chicago Press. I am so honored by the time and attention she has given my work. With great skill and gentle good humor, Susan has taught me how to write in a new way. Kate Blackmer dazzled me with her skills as a mapmaker. I particularly appreciated her willingness to work cooperatively on the maps. She made the task so much fun. Erin DeWitt was a copy editor extraordinaire, combining a razor-sharp editorial eye with great kindness and enthusiasm. Working with these three consummate professionals has been one of the great pleasures of making *Sheer Misery*. I also am profoundly grateful to James Toftness for his guidance, patience, and efficiency.

Books generate from networks of scholars, and mine did much to contribute to *Sheer Misery*. For their guidance and friendship, and for hosting me at their own universities, I thank Bruno Cabanes, Holly Grout, Anna Krylova, Emma Kuby, Elissa Mailänder, Lucy Noakes, Kevin Passmore, Javier Samper-Vendrell, David Sorkin, Joan Scott, Laura Smoller, Lisa Tetrault, and Garthine Walker. A special note of gratitude to Regina Mülhäuser and the research group "Sexual Violence and Armed Conflict" for their 2015 conference in Hamburg honoring Susan Brownmiller. At this highly stimulating gathering, the idea of exploring the somatic body of war first occurred to me.

Sheer Misery has grown enormously thanks to the support and expertise of my wonderful colleagues at the University of Wisconsin. With love and gratitude, I thank Kelley Conway, Skye Doney, Nan Enstad, Susan Friedman, April Haynes, David McDonald, and Daniel Ussishkin. I am particularly grateful to the four colleagues who took the time to read the entire manuscript and give me their invaluable comments: Laird Boswell, John Hall, Fran Hirsch, and Elissa Mailänder. Of course, all errors in the text are their fault, not mine. John Hall, in particular, has been generous with his skills as an historian and his knowledge of the United States military.

The center of my intellectual life continues to be the graduate students with whom I have the privilege of working. In my "Gender and War" seminar, these young scholars shaped my thinking of many central issues in *Sheer Misery*. Our War in Society and Culture Program at

Madison has been particularly important in this regard. I thank the students who invited me to their workshop and gave me excellent feedback on chapter 2: Denis Alfin, Kate Alfin, Conrad Allen, Sam Cabusora, Chad Gibbs, and Robert Mueller-Stahl. I have learned so much from all of them. Brian North, in particular, has given me excellent criticism, relevant readings, and necessary citations. He has also taught me so much about how the US Army "works."

Sheer Misery has also thrived because of a loving web of friends and family. In particular, I thank Kathy Baus, Jennifer Burian, Pat Hanson, Jeff Liggon, Katharine Lyall, Katy Nelson, Paul Rynders, Simone Schweber, and John Tortorice. My sister Katherine has kept me laughing by reminding me of our happy childhood. May Fraydas has been an unstinting source of support through difficult times, as has my sister Pam. They are the two kindest persons I know. Megan Williamson has given me her love and strength and humor. I am so grateful to her and to the entire Williamson family for welcoming me so warmly into their lives.

It is with great love and admiration that I dedicate this book to my sister Elizabeth Baer. Ever since I can remember, Beth has guided my intellectual life. When I was a child, she put me to sleep by reading Golden Books. When I was thirteen, she put into my hands Henry James's *The Portrait of a Lady*. When I was twenty-two, she invited me to attend a National Women's Studies Association meeting. I decided at that conference to become a women's historian. When I received tenure at Stanford University in 1997, Beth got the first call. I was so moved when she cried with joy. When I took my first trip to Berlin, she sent me a hotel recommendation, Brian Ladd's *Ghosts of Berlin*, and a handmade tote for my knitting. A highly regarded scholar of the Holocaust and the Herero genocide, Beth has indelibly shaped how I think about the Second World War. I am so grateful for her loving presence in my life.

NOTES

Introduction

1. Private Papers of Leroy Stewart, "Hurry Up and Wait," 44, World War Two Survey Collection, 1st Infantry Division, US Army Military History Institute, Carlisle Barracks, PA.

2. Ernest Harmon, with Milton MacKaye and William Ross MacKaye, *Combat Commander: Autobiography of a Soldier* (Englewood Cliffs, NJ: Prentice, 1970), 243; Bill Bellamy, *Troop Leader: A Tank Commander's Story* (Phoenix Mill, UK: Sutton, 2005), 152.

3. Kenneth T. MacLeish has described the soldier's body as "simultaneously a sensate, feeling organism and an abstract object produced by systems of discipline and regulation." See MacLeish, "Armor and Anesthesia: Exposure, Feeling, and the Soldier's Body," *Medical Anthropology Quarterly* 26, no. 1 (2012): 55.

4. Patton, quoted in Carlo d'Este, *Patton: A Genius for War* (New York: HarperCollins, 1995), 539, 544.

5. George W. Neill, *Infantry Soldier: Holding the Line at the Battle of the Bulge* (Norman: University of Oklahoma Press, 2000), 95. For historians who have looked closely at the lives of infantrymen, see Lloyd Clark, *Blitzkrieg: Myth, Reality and Hitler's Lightning War: France, 1940* (New York: Atlantic Monthly, 2016); Stephen G. Fritz, *Frontsoldaten: The German Soldier in World War II* (Lexington: University Press of Kentucky, 1995); and John Ellis, *On the Front Lines: The Experience of War through the Eyes of the Allied Soldiers in World War II* (New York: John Wiley and Sons, 1990).

6. A particularly thoughtful conversation on the use of personal sources in twentieth-century history can be found in Konrad Jaurausch, *Broken Lives: How Ordinary Germans Experienced the Twentieth Century* (Princeton, NJ: Princeton University Press, 2018), 5–14.

7. Elaine Scarry, *The Body in Pain: The Making and Unmaking of the World* (New York: Oxford University Press, 1985), 110.

8. S. Agulnick, W. R. Condon, R. G. Conroy, and A. L. Bogardus, eds., *In Their Own Words: The Battle of the Bulge as Recorded by Members of Company C* (self-pub., 1996), i–ii.

9. Martin Jay, "In the Realm of the Senses: An Introduction," *American Historical Review* 116, no. 2 (April 2011): 307–15.

10. The best account of these campaigns from the perspective of US infantry operations remains Peter R. Mansoor, *The GI Offensive in Europe: The Triumph of American Infantry Divisions, 1941–1945* (Lawrence: University Press of Kansas, 1999), chaps. 5, 8, 9.

11. William B. Foster, Ida Levin Hellman, Douglas Hesford, and Darrell G. McPherson, *Physical Standards in World War II* (Washington, DC: Office of the Surgeon General, Department of the Army, 1967), 132.

12. Foster et al., 69–79, 129–57. The best secondary source on the process of selective service is William A. Taylor, *Military Service and American Democracy: From World War II to the Iraq and Afghanistan Wars* (Lawrence: University Press of Kansas, 2016), chap. 2. See also Robert R. Palmer, Bell I. Wiley, and William R. Keast, *The Procurement and Training of Ground Combat Troops: The United States in World War II* (Washington, DC: Center for Military History, United States Army, 1948); and Christina S. Jarvis, *The Male Body at War: American Masculinity during World War II* (DeKalb: Northern Illinois University Press, 2004), 58–61. For bodily requirements in the Soviet Red Army in the Second World War, see Brandon M. Schechter, *The Stuff of Soldiers: A History of the Red Army in World War II through Objects* (Ithaca, NY: Cornell University Press, 2019), 27.

13. Corinna Peniston-Bird, "Classifying the Body in the Second World War: British Men in and out of Uniform," *Body & Society* 9, no. 4 (December 2003): 33.

14. Private Papers of E. J. Rooke-Matthews, Imperial War Museum, London. On this point, see Emma Reilly, "Civilians into Soldiers: The British Male Military Body in the Second World War" (PhD thesis, University of Strathclyde, 2010), 30–31. As Reilly points out, this induction method derived from industrial health research and Taylorist practices of rationalizing the body in factories.

15. Peniston-Bird, "Classifying the Body," 34–35; Reilly, "Civilians into Soldiers," 33.

16. Cummins, quoted in Reilly, "Civilians into Soldiers," 41.

17. David Holbrook, *Flesh Wounds* (London: Methuen, 1966), 51.

18. Scarry, *The Body in Pain*, 71. On this point, see also Kevin McSorley, "War and the Body," in *War and the Body: Militarisation, Practice and Experience*, ed. Kevin McSorley (London: Routledge, 2015), 160; and John M. Kinder, "The Embodiment of War: Bodies for, in, and after War," in *At War: The Military and American Culture in the Twentieth Century and Beyond*, ed. David Kieran and Edwin A. Martini (New Brunswick, NJ: Rutgers University Press, 2018), 217: "The human body has been—and continues to be—the defining feature of armed conflict." Kinder also notes that "the field of military history has shied away from the bodily dimensions of the war (eating and sleeping, sickness and injury, hunger and health)" (219).

19. George H. Roeder Jr. *The Censored War: American Visual Experience during World War II* (New Haven, CT: Yale University Press, 1993), 14.

20. For some of the measures the British took to prevent dysentery, see Brian Harpur, *Impossible Victory: A Personal Account of the Battle for the River Po* (New York: Hippocrene Books, 1980), 98–100.

21. Testimony of William Condon in *In Their Own Words*, ed. Agulnick et al., 21.

22. Paul Fussell, *Doing Battle: The Making of a Skeptic* (Boston: Little, Brown, 1996), 114. See also Lester Atwell, *Private* (New York: Simon and Schuster, 1958), 125.

23. Rachel Woodward and K. Neil Jenkins, "Soldiers' Bodies and the Contemporary British Military Memoir," in *War and the Body*, ed. McSorley, 160.

24. Sean Longden, *To the Victor the Spoils: Soldiers' Lives from D-Day to VE-Day* (London: Robinson, 2007), 229; Paul Fussell, *Wartime: Understanding and Behavior in the Second World War* (New York: Oxford University Press, 1989), 254.

25. Charles Whiting, *The Battle of Hurtgen Forest: The Untold Story of a Disastrous Campaign* (New York: Orion Books, 1989), 257; Nat Frankel and Larry Smith, *Patton's Best: An Informal History of the 4th Armored Division* (New York: Hawthorn Books, 1978), 12.

26. Walter L. Brown, *Up Front with U.S.: Day by Day in the Life of a Combat Infantryman in General Patton's Third Army* (self-pub., 1979), 414–15. On urination as a symbol of power in the contemporary US Army, see Aaron Belkin, "Spoiling for a Fight: Filth, Cleanliness and Normative Masculinity," in *Bring Me Men: Military Masculinity and the Benign Façade of American Empire, 1898–2001* (New York: Columbia University Press, 2012), 125–50.

27. Neil McCallum, *Journey with a Pistol* (London: Victor Gollancz, 1961), 45. McCallum was in North Africa, not Europe, at the time he wrote this sentence.

Chapter One

1. Martin Shaw, "Strategy and Slaughter," *Review of International Studies* 29, no. 2 (April 2003): 269–77.

2. G. W. Target, *Scenes from a War* (New Malden, UK: Fellowship of Reconciliation, [1976]), 7; Donald R. Burgett, *Seven Roads to Hell: A Screaming Eagle at Bastogne* (Novato, CA: Presidio Press, 1999), 65.

3. Sight was the most important sense, and the most noted sight of the battlefield, the dead body, demands separate treatment. See chapter 5. The sense of touch is rarely talked about in these soldiers' memoirs, perhaps because of taboos on same-sex touching. When soldiers do mention touch, it concerns its absence—a numbing in their feet due to trench foot. See chapter 3.

4. Lena Groeger, "Making Sense of the World, Several Senses at a Time," *Scientific America*, February 28, 2012, https://www.scientificamerican.com/article/making-sense-world-sveral-senses-at-time/.

5. Private Papers of A. G. Herbert, Imperial War Museum (hereafter IWM), London, 12. On this point see also Sydney Jary, *18 Platoon* (Surrey, UK: Sydney Jary Ltd., 1987), 132; and Private Papers of D. Evans, 77, IWM.

6. Peter White, *With the Jocks: A Soldier's Struggle for Europe 1944–45* (Phoenix Mill, UK: Sutton, 2001), 177; Brian Harpur, *Impossible Victory: A Personal Account of the Battle for the River Po* (New York: Hippocrene Books, 1980), 165. On the immediacy of infantry life, see also Richard Flemming, 88th ID Survey, World War Two Survey Collection (hereafter WWII Survey), US Army Military History Institute (hereafter MHI), Carlisle Barracks, PA; and testimony of William Condon in *In Their Own Words: The Battle of the Bulge as Recorded by Members of Company C*, ed. S. Agulnick, W. R. Condon, R. G. Conroy, and A. L. Bogardus (self-pub., 1996), 27.

7. Harpur, *Impossible Victory*, 165. See also the testimony of Richard Root in *In Their Own Words*, ed. Agulnick et al., 129; and Stanley Smith, "When the Rubber Meets the Road," 3, WWII Survey, 3rd ID, MHI.

8. R. M. Wingfield, *The Only Way Out: An Infantryman's Autobiography of the North-West Europe Campaign, August 1944–February 1945* (London: Hutchinson, 1955), 160; White, *With the Jocks*, 177–78; Arnold Whittaker, *Foxhole Promises: Stories from WWII Foxholes* (Marietta, GA: Deeds, 2011), 37; Frank Denison, "Soldiering On," 11, WWII Survey, 101st Airborne Division, MHI.

9. Roger Guillaume, *Larmes du Bois d'Arsol: récit d'une bataille* (Strasbourg: self-pub., 1989), 84, and see also 144, 154.

10. Roscoe C. Blunt Jr., *Inside the Battle of the Bulge: A Private Comes of Age* (Westport, CT: Praeger, 1994), 14. See also the diary of Robert Strong Snyder in Italy, November 10, 1943: *And When My Task on Earth Is Done: The Day by Day Experiences of a Christian Written in His Diary Which Was Sent Home by the War Department* (Kansas City, MO: Graphic Laboratory, 1950), 78: "It is surely difficult to know what's going on (we don't get any newspapers up here); and maybe the GIs aren't supposed to know."

11. Morrisey, quoted in Robert E. Humphrey, *Once upon a Time in War: The 99th Division in World War II* (Norman: University of Oklahoma Press, 2008), 196, and see also 139.

12. As one of Patton's foot soldiers put it, "Strategy and tactics and the personalities of the men who render them, are only important insofar as they make for more or less sweat" for the infantryman. See Nat Frankel and Larry Smith, *Patton's Best: An Informal History of the 4th Armored Division* (New York: Hawthorn Books, 1978), 92.

13. Kenneth T. MacLeish, *Making War at Fort Hood: Life and Uncertainty in a Military Community* (Princeton, NJ: Princeton University Press, 2013), 11.

14. Kenneth T. MacLeish, "Armor and Anesthesia: Exposure, Feeling, and the Soldier's Body, *Medical Anthropology Quarterly* 26, no. 1 (2012): 55.

15. On the history of sound, see Daniel Morat, ed., *Sounds of Modern History: Auditory Cultures in 19th- and 20th-Century Europe* (New York: Berghahn Books, 2014). The classic work is by Alain Corbin, *Village Bells: Sound and Meaning in the 19th-Century French Countryside*, trans. Martin Thom (New York: Columbia University Press, 1998).

16. This was also true of the First World War. See Axel Volmar, "In Storms of Steel: The Soundscape of World War I and Its Impact on Auditory Media Culture during the Weimar Period," in *Sounds of Modern History*, ed. Morat, 229.

17. For a thorough historical analysis of a "soundscape," see Carolyn Birdsall, *Nazi Soundscapes: Sound, Technology and Urban Space in Germany, 1933–1945* (Amsterdam: Amsterdam University Press, 2012).

18. Tom Perry, quoted in Patrick Delaforce, *The Fighting Wessex Wyverns: From Normandy to Bremerhaven with the 43rd Wessex Division* (Stroud, UK: Sutton, 1994), 27; Walter Bahr, *Kriegsbriefe, Gefallener Studenten, 1939–1945* (Tübingen: Rainer Wunderlich Verlag, 1952), 430–31, letter dated February 29, 1944.

19. Gordon John Scriven, *Regimental Stretcher Bearers in Action!* (1951; repr., Weymouth: self-pub., 1972), 8–9.

20. Mack Bloom, WWII Survey, 3rd ID, MHI; Private Papers of Major H. W. Freeman-Attwood, 17, IWM; Hans Stock to his family, January 27, 1944, Museumsstiftung Post und Telekommunikation, Briefsammlung, Feldpost Zweiter Weltkrieg.

21. Maurice Piboule, *Du Maroc au Voralberg via Roma, 1942–1945: Journal de guerre d'un artilleur* ([Montluçon?]: self-pub., [1995?]), entry of December 20, 1943, 27. This was a "carnet de route" written by a French artilleryman, which Piboule found in a German canteen and eventually published. The author is not known.

22. Eric Codling, quoted in Delaforce, *Fighting Wessex Wyverns*, 77; US infantry- man, quoted in Charles Whiting, *The Battle of Hurtgen Forest: The Untold Story of a Disastrous Campaign* (New York: Orion Books, 1989), 24; Jary, *18 Platoon*, 131; Stuart Mawson, *Arnhem Doctor* (Gloucester, UK: Spellmount, 1981), 58; Raymond Gantter, *Roll Me Over: An Infantryman's World War II* (New York: Ivy Books, 1997), 37.

23. Gordon Gammack, *Columns from Three Wars* (Ames: Iowa State University Press, 1979), n.p. Gammack was an American journalist with the troops in Italy. The ma- terial here originally appeared in the *Iowa Register*, November 19, 1943.

24. Scriven, *Stretcher Bearers*, 28, 8; soldier, quoted in Whiting, *Battle of Hurtgen Forest*, 24–25.

25. Dominick Graham and Ian Hogg, "Artillery," in *The Oxford Guide to World War Two*, ed. I. C. B. Dear and M. R. D. Foot (Oxford: Oxford University Press, 1995), 44.

26. Eighty-Fourth Division Sergeant Ed Steward, *Battle of the Bulge: The American Ex- perience*, directed by Thomas Lennon (Los Angeles: Lennon Documentary Group, WGBH, November 9, 1994), quoted in Frank Lavin, *Home Front to Battlefront: An Ohio Teenager in World War II* (Athens: Ohio University Press, 2016), 145.

27. Robert Kotlowitz, *Before Their Time: A Memoir* (New York: Alfred A. Knopf, 1997), 117.

28. In his diary, Maurice Boverat mentions a buddy who did this. See his *Du Cotentin à Colmar avec les chars de Leclerc* (Paris: Éditions Berger-Levrault, 1947), 41.

29. John Clayton, letter dated January 4, 1945, WWII Survey, 3rd ID, MHI; Boverat, *Du Cotentin à Colmar*, 91.

30. Patrick Delaforce, *Red Crown and Dragon: 53rd Welsh Division in North-West Europe, 1944–1945* (Brighton, UK: Tom Donovan, 1996), 105.

31. Bill Mauldin, *Up Front* (New York: W. W. Norton, 2000), 94–95; Leroy Coley, *A Little Bit of War: The Battle of the Bulge* (Centralia, WA: self-pub., 2003). 18. See also Clayton, letter dated January 4, 1944, MHI.

32. Geoffrey Picot, *Accidental Warrior* (London: Penguin, 1994), 30; Lester Atwell, *Private* (New York: Simon and Schuster, 1958), 49.

33. Harpur, *Impossible Victory*, 37.

34. Private Papers of Captain R. Barer, MC, 38, IWM.

35. Private Papers of Captain D. G. Aitken, IWM. Another common night sound was the roar of planes flying overhead, sometimes hundreds at a time. On this point, see Piboule, *Du Maroc*, 36.

36. Gammack, *Columns*, n.p., originally in *Iowa Register*, November 19, 1943.

37. Private Papers of Captain P. J. Cremin, letter dated June 14, 1944, IWM.

38. Graham and Hogg, "Artillery," 44.

39. Piboule, *Du Maroc*, diary entry of May 11, 1944, 42; Jean Navard, *La Libération avec les chars: du débarquement en Provence jusqu'à Ulm, 15 août 1944–8 mai 1945 avec la 1re Armée française* (Paris: Nouvelles éditions latines, 1980), 231; Hans Bähr, *Die Stimmen des Menschen: Briefe und Augzeichnungen aus der ganzen Welt, 1939–1945*

(München: R. Piper, 1966), entry dated March 22, 1944, 501. The entry of March 15 is much the same. For another soldier who deemed the Western Front worse than the Russian one, see Willy Schröder, *Nur ein Kriegstagebuch: Rein menschliche Reflektionen* (Baden-Baden: Verlag Presse Informations Agentur, 1982), 133. See also Ralph B. Schaps, *500 Days of Front Line Combat: The WWII Memoir of Ralph B. Schaps* (New York: iUniverse, 2003), 105; and Franz Kurowski, *Ich Kam Durch! Kriegsschicksale in Dokumenten* (Herrsching: Pawlak, 1985), 16–17. For a German dealing with the overwhelming noise of artillery in the French campaign, see Erich Kuby, *Mein Krieg: Aufzeichnungen, 1939–1944* (München: Knesebeck u. Schuler, 1989), 308, 311.

40. Stuart Hills, *By Tank into Normandy* (London: Cassell, 2004), 131.

41. Wingfield, *Only Way Out*, 142; Byers, quoted in Humphrey, *Once upon a Time*, 82.

42. Mauldin, *Up Front*, 94–95. A "doggie" was a nickname for the GI, a variant of "dog-face." In the Italian mountains, soldiers grew beards and got their faces very dirty, hence the nickname.

43. White, *With the Jocks*, 155; Trevor Greenwood, *D-Day to Victory: The Diaries of a British Tank Commander* (London: Simon and Schuster, 2012), 248. Greenwood's book is a series of original notebooks that have been edited for publication; Louis-Christian Michelet, *La flamme de la revanche: Témoignage d'un combattant* (Paris: Godefroy de Bouillon, 2002), 324.

44. White, *With the Jocks*, 157; Blunt, *Inside the Battle of the Bulge*, 12; Malraux, quoted in André Chamson, *La Reconquête, 1944–1945* (Paris: Éditions Plon, 1975), 113. Chamson and Malraux were fighting side-by-side in the First French Army during the last winter of the war.

45. Steward, quoted in Lavin, *Home Front to Battlefront*, 145.

46. Sean Longden, *To the Victor the Spoils: Soldiers' Lives from D-Day to VE-Day* (London: Robinson, 2007), 9.

47. Mauldin, *Up Front*, 95–95.

48. Donald Lavender, *Nudge Blue: A 9th Infantry Division Rifleman's Memoir of World War II* (Bennington, VT: Merriam Press, 1998), 29–30.

49. Testimony of Mel Lowry, in *War on the Ground, 1939–1945*, ed. Colin John Bruce (London: Constable, 1995), 130; Burgett, *Seven Roads to Hell*, 66; Arthur Reddish, *Normandy 1944: From the Hull of a Sherman* (Wanganui, NZ: Battlefield Associates, 1995), 35; Captain Jesse Caldwell, "Combat Diary," WWII Survey, 87th ID, MHI.

50. William F. McMurdie, *Hey, Mac! This Is Serious Business! A Guy Could Get Killed!* (Gig Harbor, WA: Red Apple, 2000), 99–100.

51. E. A. Reitan, "A Rifleman in World War II," 59, WWII Survey, 3rd ID, MHI.

52. Ross S. Carter, *Those Devils in Baggy Pants* (New York: Appleton-Century-Crofts, 1951), 81.

53. Freeman-Attwood, 15, IWM; Francis L. Ware, "Family Doctor to 2nd Battalion 12th Infantry, 4th Infantry Division," 53, 4th ID, WWII Survey, MHI; Private Papers of Lieutenant E. A. Brown, 31, IWM.

54. Testimony of Bill Scully, in *War on the Ground*, ed. Bruce, 155, 163; Michelet, *La flamme de la revanche*, 336.

55. Testimony of Noel Bell, in *The War on Land: The British Army in World War II: An Anthology of Personal Experience*, ed. Ronald Lewin (New York: William Morrow, 1970), 255.

56. Frankel and Smith, *Patton's Best*, 83.

57. James Hagan, WWII Survey, 1st Armored Division (hereafter AD), MHI.

58. Bert Damsky, 26, WWII Survey, 1st ID, MHI.

59. John Khoury, *Love Company, L Company, 399th Infantry Regiment, of the 100th Infantry Division during World War II and Beyond* (Maywood, NJ: Chi Chi Press, 2003), 87. See also Morris Courington, *Cruel Was the Way* (Park Forest, IL: Velletri Books, 2000), 22–23, 118.

60. Fernand Pistor, *Correspondances de guerre: de Tunis à Marseille avec les troupes françaises d'Afrique du Nord, mai 1943–aôut 1944* (Pau: Les amis de Fernand Pistor, 1978), 92; testimony of Chester Wilmot, in *The War on Land*, ed. Lewin, 259.

61. Harpur, *Impossible Victory*, 57–58; Carter, *Those Devils*, 252; Schaps, *500 Days*, 98–99; Clayton, letter dated January 4, 1945, MHI; Mauldin, *Up Front*, 98. See also William McConahey, *Battalion Surgeon* (Rochester, MN: self-pub., 1966), 110.

62. Jary, *18 Platoon*, 131.

63. Greenwood, *D-Day to Victory*, 248. See also Michael Bilder, *Foot Soldier for Patton: The Story of a "Red Diamond" Infantryman with the U.S. Third Army* (Philadelphia: Casemate, 2008), 111.

64. Rocco Moretto, WWII Survey, 1st ID, MHI.

65. Leroy Stewart, "Hurry Up and Wait," 73, WWII Survey, 1st ID, MHI.

66. The US Army claimed, however, that the American machine gun, although slower, was more accurate. See F.B. No. 181, "Automatic Weapons: American v. German," https://www.youtube.com/watch?v=Oyj-ZHXFKQI.

67. Clayton, letter dated January 4, 1945, WWII Survey, 3rd ID, MHI. See also Russell Cloer, WWII Survey, 3rd ID, MHI; and testimony of George Taylor in Delaforce, *Fighting Wessex Wyverns*, 117.

68. John Davis, *Up Close: A Scout's Story: From the Battle of the Bulge to the Siegfried Line* (Bennington, VT: Merriam Press, 2008), 92.

69. Gammack, *Columns*, n.p., originally in *Iowa Register*, November 19, 1943.

70. Peter Ryder, *Guns Have Eyes: One Man's Story of the Normandy Landings* (London: Robert Hale, 1984), 105, 123. Peter Ryder is a pseudonym for a man who did indeed experience all the things in this book. His friend George B. Bennett helped him tell his story under this anonymous name. See also testimony of Mary Morris in Marcus Cowper, *The Words of War: British Forces' Personal Letters and Diaries during the Second World War* (Edinburgh: Mainstream, 2009), 382–83.

71. Milo Green and Paul Gauthier, *Brickbats from F Company, and Other Choice Memorabilia Selections* (Corning, IA: Gauthier, 1982), 174. See also Humphrey, *Once upon a Time*, 80.

72. L. C. Pinner, *A Conscript at War* (Salisbury, UK: self-pub., 1998), 116; Chamson, *La Reconquête*, 113.

73. Carter, *Those Devils*, 81. On this point, see also Coley, *A Little Bit of War*, 31; and Scriven, *Regimental Stretcher Bearers*, 23, 27–28.

74. Freeman-Attwood, 16, IWM; Evans, 45, 104, IWM; Peter Bepulsi, *A GI's View of World War II* (Salem, MO: Globe, 1997), 29.

75. Henry Deloupy, *Les blindés de la Libération* (Paris: Service Historique de l'Armée de Terre, 1991), 52.

76. Bepulsi, *A GI's View*, 171, 254; Kotlowitz, *Before Their Time*, 137, 140. On this point, see also Delaforce, *Red Crown and Dragon*, 38; and Sean Longden, *To the Victor the Spoils*, 9–10.

77. Navard, *La Libération*, 65, see also 233.

78. Schröder, *Nur ein Kriegstagebuch*, 158.

79. Frankel and Smith, *Patton's Best*, 87, 99, 112; Deloupy, *Les blindés de la Libération*, 120.

80. Robert T. Gravlin, "World War II as a Combat Engineer with the Third Armored Division," 8, WWII Survey, 3rd AD, MHI; Burgett, *Seven Roads to Hell*, 2, 138; Longden, *To the Victor*, 7–8.

81. Scriven, *Regimental Stretcher Bearers*, 8–9.

82. Testimony of Bill Scully, in *War on the Ground*, ed. Bruce, 155–56; Freeman-Attwood, 26, IWM.

83. Isherwood, quoted in Delaforce, *Red Crown and Dragon*, 161; Jary, *18 Platoon*, 131; Robin Cross, *True Stories of WWII* (London: Michael O'Mara Books, 1994), 187.

84. Testimony of Robert C. Conroy in *In Their Own Words*, ed. Agulnick et al., 47; Dale Lundhigh, *Show Me the Hero: An Iowa Draftee Joins the 90th Infantry Division during WW II in Europe* (Bloomington, IN: AuthorHouse, 2009), 109; Knappe, quoted in Stephen G. Fritz, *Frontsoldaten: The German Soldier in World War II* (Lexington: University Press of Kentucky, 1995), 34.

85. On this issue in Italy, see "The Diarrheal Diseases," *Preventive Medicine Bulletin* #2 (July 14, 1944), 700–823, Record Group 338, Records of Army Commands, Fifth Army, Adjutant General Section, General Correspondence, National Archives and Records Administration. See also William McConahey, *Battalion Surgeon* (Rochester, MN: self-pub., 1966), 109; and Bernard Friedenberg, *Of Being Numerous: World War II as I Saw It: Medical Detachment, 1st Battalion, 16th Regiment, 1st U.S. Infantry Division* (Pomona, NJ: Holocaust Resource Center, Richard Stockton College of New Jersey, 2008), 70, where Friedenberg remembers: "For utensils all we were given was a small spoon that we stuck in one of our boots. After we used the spoon, we would clean it by taking a handful of earth and rubbing this over the spoon to remove the grease. Is it any wonder that many of us suffered from dysentery?"

86. Fussell, *Wartime*, 254.

87. Richard M. Stannard, *Infantry: An Oral History of a World War II American Infantry Battalion* (New York: Twayne, 1993), 65; Graham A. Cosmas and Albert E. Cowdry, *The Medical Department: Medical Service in the European Theater of Operations* (Washington, DC: Center of Military History, US Army, 1992), 235, 543. See also Jack Welch's diary, dated January 17, 1945, in Welch, *Battalion Surgeon: A Combat Journal* (Fresno, CA: self-pub., 1996), 213.

88. Jack Capell, *Surviving the Odds: From D-Day to VE-Day with the 4th Division in Europe* (Claremont, CA: Regina Books, 2007), 162. On the same situation in Normandy, see Longden, *To the Victor*, 159.

89. Testimony of Harry Jubelirer and testimony of William Condon, in *In Their Own Words*, ed. Agulnick et al., 71, 22; Whiting, *Battle of Hurtgen Forest*, 6. See also Charles Whiting, *Poor Bloody Infantry* (Staplehurst, UK: Spellmount, 2007), 233.

90. Longden, *To the Victor*, 229.

91. William Wharton, *A Midnight Clear* (New York: HarperCollins, 1982), 112.

92. George W. Neill, *Infantry Soldier: Holding the Line at the Battle of the Bulge* (Norman: University of Oklahoma Press, 2000), 112. On this point, see also the case of a British gunner, Private Papers of P. G. Thres, "Memoirs, 1940–1946," 28, IWM.

93. Whittaker, *Foxhole Promises*, 38; Lundhigh, *Show Me the Hero*, 116; Paul E. Cunningham, ed., *Freezing in Hell: World War II, Ardennes: Battle of the Bulge, December 16, 1944–January 25, 1945* (Salisbury, MD: P. E. Cunningham, 1998), 136.

94. Testimony of Robert Conroy, in *In Their Own Words*, ed. Agulnick et al., 41. See also Bill Jardine, *Number, Rank and Name* (Suffolk, UK: Fine Publishing, 1990), 100; and the testimony of Nick Cutcliffe, in Delaforce, *Red Crown and Dragon*, 62.

95. Coley, *A Little Bit of War*, 36; Kotlowitz, *Before Their Time*, 120.

96. George Biddle, *Artist at War* (New York: Viking, 1944), 240; Wharton, *Midnight Clear*, 35, 112; testimony of Robert Conroy, in *In Their Own Words*, ed. Agulnick et al., 41, 46; Lewin, *The War on Land*, 176; Bilder, *Foot Soldier for Patton*, 176; Stephen W. Dyson, *Twins in Tanks: East End Brothers-in-Arms, 1943–1945* (London: Imperial War Museum, 1994), 65.

97. Reddish, *Normandy 1944*, 69–70.

98. Quoted in Longden, *To the Victor*, 153.

99. Evans, 104, IWM. A few days later, Frank got showered with cow intestines when a tank ran over a dead cow; once again his buddies cleaned him off. Later around the fire, remembered Evans, "Frank came in for some ribbing about his episode with the cow's intestines, but no-one reminded him of the other affair, when he messed up his pants."

100. Pearce, quoted in Delaforce, *Fighting Wessex Wyverns*, 46. See also Green and Gauthier, *Brickbats from F Company*, 197.

101. Official, quoted in Whiting, *Poor Bloody Infantry*, 201; *Stars and Stripes*, November 1944, quoted in Whiting, 200.

102. Quoted in Whiting, 201.

103. Pistor, *Correspondances de guerre*, 60; Michelet, *La flamme de la revanche*, 329; Herbert, 29, IWM; Private Papers of R. Walker, "The Devil of a War," 17, IWM (this is a memoir of Normandy, not the Bulge).

104. Charles B. MacDonald, *Company Commander* (Washington, DC: Infantry Journal Press, 1947), 34; Rick Atkinson, *The Guns at Last Light: The War in Western Europe, 1944–1945* (New York: Henry Holt, 2013), 170; Walker, "The Devil of a War," 17, IWM.

105. On the cultural meanings linked to taste, see Jeffrey M. Pilcher, "The Embodied Imagination in Recent Writings on Food History," *American Historical Review* 121, no. 3 (October 2016): 861–87; David Howes, "Introduction: Empires of the Senses," in *Empire of the Senses: The Sensual Culture Reader*, ed. David Howes (Oxford: Oxford University Press, 2005), 11; and Priscilla Parkhurst Ferguson, "The Senses of Taste," *American Historical Review* 116, no. 2 (April 2011): 371–84.

106. Paul Fussell, "My War," in *The Boy Scout Handbook and Other Observations* (New York: Oxford University Press, 1982), 46. This was true for the Germans as well. Their letters home often described good meals in considerable detail. See, for example, Hans Joachim-S to his wife, July 9, 1944, and Hans Stock to his family, January 17, 1944, Museumsstiftung Post und Telekommunikation, Briefsammlung, Feldpost Zweiter Weltkrieg.

107. "Chow," *Red Bulletin*, May 26, 1945.

108. *45th Division News*, October 21 and November 6, 1943.

109. Navard, *La Libération*, 91.

110. Piboule, *Du Maroc*, 27; Private Papers of J. A. Garrett, diary entry of December 25, 1944, IWM.

111. Private Papers of Lieutenant Colonel W. S. Brownlie, letter dated December 25, 1944, IWM; Atwell, *Private*, 101; Private Papers of L. F. Roker, IWM; James Graff,

Reflections of a Combat Infantryman: A Soldier's Story of C. Co. 134th Inf. 35th Div. (self-pub., 1977), 21.

112. See, for example, *45th Division News*, December 11, 1943; G. D. Sheffield, *Leadership in the Trenches: Officer-Man Relations, Morale and Discipline in the British Army in the Era of the First World War* (London: Macmillan, 2000), 142.

113. McIlroy, quoted in Humphrey, *Once upon a Time*, 108; Bill Mauldin Papers, undated speech, Speeches, box 8, Library of Congress; Honey, quoted in Humphrey, 109.

114. Stewart, "Hurry Up and Wait," 82, MHI; Davis, *Up Close*, 68; Gantter, *Roll Me Over*, 13.

115. Bahr, *Kriegsbriefe, Gefallener Studenten*, letter dated December 22, 1944, 430–31.

116. Hubert Gees, "Recollections of the Huertgen Forest: A German Soldier's View-point," unpublished ms. excerpted in Huey E. Tyra, *Love Always, Ben: The Story of a Young World War II Soldier Who Gave His Life for God, Family and Country* (Gastonia, NC: P & H Publications, 2002), 174; diary entry of Erich Nies, in Hans Dollinger, *Kain, wo ist dein Brüder? Was der Mensch im Zweiten Weltkrieg erleiden Mußte—dokumentiert in Tagebüchern und Briefen* (München: List Verlag München, 1983), 296–97.

117. Longden, *To the Victors the Spoils*, 299.

118. Testimony of Scully in *War on the Ground*, ed. Bruce, 164–65.

119. Harpur, *Impossible Victory*, 96.

120. Private Papers of A. Glasspool, 7, IWM; Harpur, *Impossible Victory*, 96.

121. Roker, diary entry of November 6, 1944, IWM; Longden, *To the Victor*, 304.

122. Popeye, quoted in Stanley Whitehouse and George B. Bennett, *Fear Is the Foe: A Footslogger from Normandy to the Rhine* (London: Robert Hale, 1995), 95; Freeman-Attwood, 10, IWM.

123. Quoted in Longden, *To the Victor*, 303.

124. Jarvis, quoted in Longden, *To the Victor*, 299–300; testimony of Scully, in *War on the Ground*, ed. Bruce, 164–65; Ryder, *Guns Have Eyes*, 81.

125. Bill Buemi, WWII Survey, 3rd ID, MHI; see also Bloom, MHI; and Blunt, *Inside the Battle of the Bulge*, 11.

126. Friedenberg, *Of Being Numerous*, 69.

127. Erna Risch, *The Quartermaster Corps: Organization, Supply and Services*, vol. 1, *United States Army in World War II: The Technical Services* (Washington, DC: Office of the Chief of Military History, Department of the Army, 1953), 130. For good explanations of C rations, see Whiting, *Battle of Hurtgen Forest*, 52; and Smith, "When the Rubber Meets the Road," 3, MHI.

128. Kline and Reagler, quoted in Humphrey, *Once upon a Time*, 64; Lawrence Collins, *The 56th Evac Hospital* (Denton: University of North Texas Press, 1995), 114–15. As for the British, Peter Ryder remembered that "only the men's extreme hunger and the uncertainty surrounding the arrival of the next meal prompted them to tackle anything." See Ryder, *Guns Have Eyes*, 91. See also Thomas Bleyler, WWII Survey, 45th ID, MHI.

129. Atwell, *Private*, 119; Risch, *Quartermaster Corps*, 131; Collins, *The 56th Evac Hospital*, 114.

130. Biddle, *Artist at War*, 172. See also the Bill Mauldin cartoon in *Stars and Stripes*, August 29, 1944.

131. See Jean Raspaud, *Chronique et itinéraires de mes campagnes, 1942–1945* (Paris: Éditions des écrivains, 2000), diary entry of December 28, 1944, 129; Piboule, *Du Maroc*, 30; Deloupy, *Les blindés de la Libération*, 116; Henri Savournin, *Parachutiste avec la France combattante, 1939–1945* (Paris: Barre & Dayez, 1985), 236; and Boverat, *Du Cotentin à Colmar*, 176.

132. John C. Fisher and Carol Fisher, *Food in the American Military: A History* (Jefferson, NC: McFarland, 2011), 150.

133. McMurdie, *Hey Mac!*, 115.

134. Atwell, *Private*, 29; Julian Richard Jacobs, WWII Survey, 34th ID, MHI.

135. Bloom, MHI; Snyder, *And When My Task*, diary entry of November 10, 1943, 77; Bepulsi, *A GI's View*, 241. See also Kellen Backer, "World War II and the Triumph of Industrialized Food" (PhD diss., University of Wisconsin–Madison, 2012), 59–60. Standardization was achieved by creating "specifications" for each food, so that even if it was made by different factories it would be exactly the same.

136. Courington, *Cruel Was the Way*, 40; Mauldin, *Up Front*, 172.

137. US Army, *Basic Field Manual, Soldier's Handbook* (Washington, DC: War Office, 1941), 228.

138. Fisher and Fisher, *Food in the American Military*, 148. See also Backer, "World War II and the Triumph of Industrialized Food," 68.

139. Testimony of Gerald Creehan in Courington, *Cruel Was the Way*, 119; McDaniel, quoted in Humphrey, *Once upon a Time*, 64; Longden, *To the Victor*, 304; B. A. Jones, *A Journey from Blandford: A Chronicle of Personal Experiences from 1939–1946* (Fontwell, Sussex, UK: Woodfield, 1994), 109–11.

140. Backer, "World War II and the Triumph of Industrialized Food," 70.

141. Backer, 75–76, 53. See also Camille Begin, "Partaking of Choice Poultry Cooked à la Southern Style: Taste and Race in the New Deal Sensory Economy," *Radical History Review* 110 (May 2011): 127–53.

142. Longden, *To the Victor*, 309. On obtaining fresh food, see also Hills, *By Tank into Normandy*, 98.

143. Jones, *A Journey from Blandford*, 105. On the "Tommy Cooker," see Scully in *War on the Ground*, ed. Bruce, 165. On self-heating soup, see Evans, 59, IWM; and Longden, *To the Victor*, 304. General Brian Horrocks claimed British were much more successful than the Americans in getting hot meals brought up to the line. See Hills, *By Tank into Normandy*, 199.

144. Ryder, *Guns Have Eyes*, 91; Charles E. Carpenter, *As I Remember: The Memoirs of a WWII Soldier* (self-pub., 2011), 12.

145. Stewart, "Hurry Up and Wait," 80, MHI; Ray Rulis, "A Rifleman's Story," in *In Their Own Words*, ed. Agulnick et al., 131; Reburn, quoted in Humphrey, *Once upon a Time*, 108.

146. Leroy Coley, WWII Survey, 75th ID, MHI. See also Smith, "When the Rubber Meets the Road," 48, MHI; Clayton, letter dated January 4, 1945, MHI; Fisher and Fisher, *Food in the American Military*, 159–60; and Mauldin, *Up Front*, 168.

147. J. J. Kuhn, *I Was Baker 2: Memoirs of a World War II Platoon Sergeant* (West Bend, WI: DeRaimo, 1994), 146.

148. Private Papers of C. Newton, 18, IWM. See also Longden, *To the Victor*, 301.

149. Dyson, *Twins in Tanks*, 54; Mauldin, *Up Front*, 171.

150. Carter, *Those Devils*, 176. As Bill Mauldin once remarked, "Soldiers at the front read K-ration labels when the contents are listed on the package, just to be reading something." *Up Front*, 25, 47.

151. Paul Fussell has described infantry life during the war as "an experience of unprecedented ennui." See Fussell, *Wartime*, 77.

152. Bepulsi, *A GI's View*, 194.

153. Wharton, *Midnight Clear*, 17; Todd DePastino, *Bill Mauldin: A Life Up Front* (New York: W. W. Norton, 2008), 142.

154. Friedenberg, *Of Being Numerous*, 112–13; Millek, quoted in Stannard, *Infantry*, 19; Grady P. Arrington, *Infantryman at the Front* (New York: Vantage Press, 1959), 52.

155. Gerald Kersh, *Clean, Bright and Slightly Oiled* (London: William Heinemann, 1946), 62. See also Private Papers of A. A. Southam, 1, IWM, where he says, "After six weeks basic training I was judged capable of progressing to the infantry, a move that required an I.Q. minus rating."

156. Gantter, *Roll Me Over*, 12.

157. Gantter was in the Sixteenth Infantry Regiment, Company G, First Infantry Division. The division fought continuously in the Battle of the Bulge (or the Battle of Ardennes) from December 17, 1944, to January 28, 1945.

158. Robert Bowen, *Fighting with the Screaming Eagles: With the 101st Airborne from Normandy to Bastogne* (London: Greenhill Books, 2001), 17.

159. William Kunz, "Italy—50 Years Ago," 28, WWII Survey, 3rd ID, MHI.

160. Burgett, *Seven Roads to Hell*, 136; Smith, 18–19, MHI; Private Papers of J. M. Thorpe, pocket diary, 123, IWM (Thorpe survived his wounds); John Horne Burns, "The Trenchfoot of Michael Patrick," in *The Gallery* (1947; repr., New York: New York Review of Books, 2004), 12.

161. John T. Jones, "Personal Experience," 1, WWII Survey, 3rd AD, MHI. Schaps, *500 Days*, 81; Reeder, quoted in Stannard, *Infantry*, 199; Private Papers of E. A. Horrell, IWM. Horrell was retelling a story shared by Sid Carpenter about Bovey Tracey.

162. R. M. Wingfield, *The Only Way Out: An Infantryman's Autobiography of the North-West European Campaign, August 1944–February 1945* (London: Hutchinson, 1955), 186.

163. Roscoe C. Blunt Jr., *Foot Soldier: A Combat Infantryman's War in Europe* (Cambridge, MA: Da Capo Press, 2002), 118.

164. Frankel and Smith, *Patton's Best*, 89.

165. Quoted in Whiting, *Battle of Hurtgen Forest*, 25.

166. Pamer, quoted in Mark Harrison, *Medicine and Victory: British Military Medicine in the Second World War* (Oxford: Oxford University Press, 2004), 174.

167. Ryder, *Guns Have Eyes*, 151–52. See also Private Papers of Captain D. H. Deane, diary entry of November 18, 1944, IWM; and Harrison, *Medicine and Victory*, 175. For the American treatment of the problem, see Albert E. Cowdry, *Fighting for Life: American Military Medicine in World War II* (New York: Free Press, 1994), 137–38, 142. Sedation, rest, and food were the remedies used by American medics for combat exhaustion, a term they borrowed from the British Eighth Army. See also Cosmas and Cowdry, *The Medical Department*, 235, 336.

168. Petty, quoted in Delaforce, *Red Crown and Dragon*, 65; Courington, *Cruel Was the Way*, 48, 53; Mauldin, *Up Front*, 42; Edward Arn, *Arn's War: Memoirs of a World War II Infantryman, 1940–1946* (Akron, OH: University of Akron Press, 2006), 133;

Schaps, *500 Days*, 104. On exhausted soldiers, see Joanna Bourke, "Killing Frenzy: Wartime Narratives of Enemy Action," in *No Man's Land of Violence: Extreme Wars of the Twentieth Century*, ed. Alf Lüdtke and Bernd Weisbrod (Göttingen: Wallstein Verland, 2006), 105.

Chapter Two

1. Captain Harry C. Butcher, *My Three Years with Eisenhower* (New York: Simon and Schuster, 1946), 801. According to *Time*, February 26, 1945, Lieutenant General John C. H. Lee was also demanding that the cartoon be banned from *Stars and Stripes* because "Mauldin's weary, unshaven G.I.s were too slovenly and unsoldierly for General Lee's taste." Colleagues talked Lee out of pursuing his complaint. For Mauldin's praise of Eisenhower for keeping *Stars and Stripes* at least somewhat independent from the army, see undated speech, Speeches, box 8, Bill Mauldin Papers (hereafter BMP), Library of Congress. See also Andy Rooney on this topic in *My War* (New York: Public Affairs, 1995), 70.

2. *Time*, March 26, 1945. Will Lang wrote this article. He was waiting for Mauldin outside Patton's door to get the big scoop.

3. Solbert and Butcher, quoted in Bill Mauldin, *The Brass Ring* (New York: W. W. Norton, 1971), 248, 255. In *My Three Years*, Butcher described Patton's comment in a tamer way in his diary: "That fellow's a bad influence in the Army and if he comes into Third Army area, I'll throw him in jail for thirty days" (774). Mauldin was in Butcher's office when the call took place, so he overheard the conversation.

4. Butcher, *My Three Years*, 774.

5. Mauldin, *Brass Ring*, 247–56, 259–61.

6. Paul Fussell, *Wartime: Understanding and Behavior in the Second World War* (New York: Oxford University Press, 1989), 82.

7. Butcher, *My Three Years*, 801, 773–75; Mauldin, quoted in *Time*, March 26, 1945.

8. *45th Division News*, February 22, 1944.

9. Stephen E. Ambrose, foreword to Bill Mauldin, *Up Front* (New York: W. W. Norton, 2000) v, x. Mauldin's official biographer is Todd DePastino, who wrote *Bill Mauldin: A Life Up Front* (New York: W. W. Norton, 2008). There is some mention of the cartoonist in Brianna Buljung, "From the Foxhole: American Newsmen and the Reporting of World War II," *International Social Science Review* 86, nos. 1–2 (2011): 44–64. See also Karen Jensen, "The Best of Willie and Joe," *World War II* 22, no. 9 (January/February 2008): 38–43.

10. Ernie Pyle with David Nichols, *Ernie's War: The Best of Ernie Pyle's World War II Dispatches* (Norwalk, CT: Easton Press, 2000), 197.

11. Grady P. Arrington, *Infantryman at the Front* (New York: Vantage Press, 1959), 73–74.

12. For New York City, see Catherine McNeur, *Taming Manhattan: Environmental Battles in the Antebellum City* (Cambridge, MA: Harvard University Press, 2014). For London, see Eric Hopkins, *Industrialization and Society: A Social History, 1830–1951* (New York: Routledge, 2000). For Paris, see Michel Carmona, *Haussmann: His Life and Times, and the Making of Modern Paris* (Chicago: I. R. Dee, 2002).

13. The classic anthropological work on cleanliness and filth is Mary Douglas, *Purity and Danger: An Analysis of Concepts of Pollution and Taboo* (London: Routledge and Kegan Paul, 1966). For deodorization, see Alain Corbin, *The Foul and the Fragrant:*

Odor and the French Social Imagination (New York: Berg, 1986); Jonathan Reinartz, *Past Scents: Historical Perspectives on Smell* (Urbana: University of Illinois Press, 2014); and Robert Jütte, *A History of the Senses: From Antiquity to Cyberspace* (Cambridge, MA: Polity Press, 2005), 170–71. Mark S. R. Jenner has disagreed with the deodorization thesis. See his "Follow Your Nose? Smell, Smelling, and Their Histories," *American Historical Review* 116, no. 2 (April 2011): 335–51.

14. For a brief history of the US Army and hygiene, see Aaron Belkin, "Spoiling for a Fight: Filth, Cleanliness and Normative Masculinity," in *Bring Me Men: Military Masculinity and the Benign Façade of American Empire, 1898–2001* (New York: Columbia University Press, 2012), 125–50.

15. War Office, *Basic and Battle Physical Training, Part One, General Principles of Basic and Battle Physical Training, and Methods of Instruction* (London: War Office, 1944), 10; P. S. Bond, *Military Science and Tactics: Infantry Basic Course* (Washington, DC: P. S. Bond Publishing, 1944), 61, 82.

16. See Emma Newlands, "Preparing and Resisting the War Body: Training in the British Army," in *War and the Body: Militarisation, Practice and Experience*, ed. Kevin McSorley (London: Routledge, 2013), 36.

17. *Basic Field Manual: Soldier's Handbook* (Washington, DC: US War Office, 1944), 203; Bond, *Military Science*, 44–45.

18. John Leonard Foster and William Dilworth, Oral History Archive, Imperial War Museum (hereafter IWM), London. See also Private Papers of E. J. Rooke-Matthews, IWM. Rooke-Matthews talks about how when baths were taken, multiple recruits would have to share the same basin of water.

19. Private Papers of Lieutenant Colonel W. S. Brownlie, IWM.

20. Dilworth, Oral History Archive, IWM. Ironically, Mauldin himself didn't need to shave.

21. David Holbrook, *Flesh Wounds* (London: Methuen, 1966), 51; Private Papers of H. C. Abrams, 4, IWM; George W. Neill, *Infantry Soldier: Holding the Line at the Battle of the Bulge* (Norman: University of Oklahoma Press, 2000), 15.

22. Douglas Sutherland, *Sutherland's War* (London: Martin Secker and Warburg, 1984), 24; Anthony Cotterell, *What! No Morning Tea?* (London: Victor Gollancz, 1941), 31; Gerald Kersh, *Clean, Bright and Slightly Oiled* (London: William Heinemann, 1946), 62–63.

23. Norman Smith, *Tank Soldier* (Sussex, UK: Book Guild, 1989), 25.

24. Kersh, *Clean, Bright and Slightly Oiled*, 62–63.

25. Bond, *Military Science*, 84, 86. These beliefs were pervasive in American culture. Upon seeing *Up Front* syndicated in a local paper, one reader complained, "Our boys don't look like the way you draw them. They're not bearded and horrible-looking. They're clean fine Americans," *Saturday Evening Post*, March 17, 1945.

26. Mauldin, *Up Front*, 13.

27. Milo Green and Paul Gauthier, *Brickbats from F Company, and Other Choice Memorabilia Selections* (Corning, IA: Gauthier, 1982), 168. See also Morris Courington, *Cruel Was the Way* (Park Forest, IL: Velletri Books, 2000), 26–27.

28. Georges Gaudy, *Combats libérateurs* (Lyon: H. Lardenchet, 1948), 59. Gaudy was talking about the camp of the Thirty-Fourth "Red Bull" Infantry Division; Brian Harpur, *Impossible Victory: A Personal Account of the Battle for the River Po* (New York: Hippocrene Books, 1980), 81; W. A. Elliott, *Esprit de Corps: A Scots Guards*

Officer on Active Service, 1943–1945 (Norwich, UK: Michael Russell, 1996), 95; Fernand Pistor, *Correspondances de guerre: de Tunis à Marseille avec les troupes françaises d'Afrique du Nord, mai 1943–aôut 1944* (Pau: Les Amis de Fernand Pistor, 1978), 56.

29. Ross S. Carter, *Those Devils in Baggy Pants* (New York: Appleton-Century-Crofts, 1951), 128. For the same phenomenon in the Bulge, see Donald R. Burgett, *Seven Roads to Hell: A Screaming Eagle at Bastogne* (Novato, CA: Presidio Press, 1999), 156.

30. Ralph B. Schaps, *500 Days of Front Line Combat: The WWII Memoir of Ralph B. Schaps* (New York: iUniverse, 2003), 104; see also Maurice Merrit, *Eighth Army Driver* (New York: Hippocrene Books, 1984), 118. For the German soldiers complaining about their filth, see Hubert Gees, "Recollections of the Huertgen Forest: A German Soldier's Viewpoint," unpublished ms. excerpted in Huey E. Tyra, *Love Always, Ben: The Story of a Young World War II Soldier Who Gave His Life for God, Family and Country* (Gastonia, NC: P & H Publications, 2002), 172; and Hans Stock to his family, January 17, 1944, Museumsstiftung Post und Telekommunikation, Briefsammlung, Feldpost Zweiter Weltkrieg.

31. Reagler, quoted in Robert E. Humphrey, *Once upon a Time in War: The 99th Division in World War II* (Norman: University of Oklahoma Press, 2008), 107.

32. Carter, *Those Devils*, 128; Hans Stock to his family, January 17, 1944, Museumsstiftung Post und Telekommunikation, Briefsammlung, Feldpost Zweiter Weltkrieg.

33. Carter, *Those Devils*, 189. Showers were also welcomed a year later by the British and American troops crossing France and Germany. For more on the showers in Italy, see *Yank: The Army Weekly*, October 15, 1944; John Clayton, letter dated December 18, 1943, World War II Survey (hereafter WWII Survey), 3rd Infantry Division (hereafter ID), US Army Military History Institute (hereafter MHI), Carlisle Barracks, PA; and Schaps, *500 Days*, 82. Showers were also welcomed a year later by the British and American troops crossing France and Germany. See Raymond Gantter, *Roll Me Over: An Infantryman's World War II* (New York: Ivy Books, 1997), 43; Donald J. Willis, *The Incredible Year* (Ames: Iowa State University Press, 1988), 101; and Private Papers of B. F. Sully, 63, IWM.

34. Private Papers of Captain D. H. Deane, 4–5, IWM; Private Papers of J. M. Thorpe, pocket diary, 122, 135, IWM; Richard Sanner, *Combat Medic Memoirs* (Clemson, SC: Rennas Productions, 1995), 93. While everyone appreciated a shower, getting clean could be an adjustment. Raymond Gantter was only half-kidding when he wrote his wife after a shower that he was "cold without my dirt." See Gantter, *Roll Me Over*, 43.

35. Sean Longden, *To the Victor the Spoils: Soldiers' Lives from D-Day to VE-Day* (London: Robinson, 2007), 152. Longden wrote his narrative based on extensive interviews with veterans of the Twenty-First Army group.

36. Stuart Mawson, *Arnheim Doctor* (Gloucester, UK: Spellmount, 1981), 70.

37. Fussell, *Wartime*, 82 (Fussell fought in France, not Italy); Longden, *To the Victor*, 205; Pistor, *Correspondances de guerre*, 44–45; B. A. Jones, *A Journey from Blandford: A Chronicle of Personal Experiences from 1939–1946* (Fontwell, Sussex, UK: Woodfield, 1994), 121; Patrick Delaforce, *Marching to the Sound of Gunfire: North-West Europe, 1944–1945* (Phoenix Mill, UK: Sutton, 1996), 101; testimony of Wayne Kirby in Courington, *Cruel Was the Way*, 251.

38. Harpur, *Impossible Victory*, 93. On this issue, see also Patrick Delaforce, *The Fighting Wessex Wyverns: From Normandy to Bremerhaven with the 43rd Wessex Division* (Stroud, UK: Sutton, 1994), 191.

39. *45th Division News*, December 11, 1943.

40. Mauldin also wrote a column for the *45th Division News* titled "Quoth the Dogface."

41. Mauldin, undated speech, Speeches, box 8, BMP; Mauldin, *Brass Ring*, 195.

42. *Saturday Evening Post*, March 17, 1945. In S. B. Baskin, *Blood on the Olives: Sketches of Life with the 34th Bull Division* (n.p.: n.p., [1946?]), Baskin claimed that getting clean was a central part of a leave in Italy: "To the dirty, weary soldier, a shower and a change of clothes, topped with a pass to beautiful towns like Florence, reminded him of his previous life in the States" (n.p.).

43. Mauldin, *Up Front*, 78.

44. Mauldin, undated speech, Speeches, box 8, BMP.

45. Quoted in Mark M. Smith, *Sensing the Past: Seeing, Hearing, Smelling, Tasting, and Touching in History* (Berkeley: University of California Press, 2007), 66.

46. On the working-class composition of the American infantry, see DePastino, *Bill Mauldin*, 142–43. Former infantry soldier and literary critic Paul Fussell described his division as one of "hillbillies and Okies, dropouts and used-car salesmen and petty criminals." See Paul Fussell, "My War," in *The Boy Scout Handbook and Other Observations* (New York: Oxford University Press, 1982), 254. For the British infantry, see Alan Allport, *Browned Off and Bloody-Minded: The British Soldier Goes to War, 1939–1945* (New Haven, CT: Yale University Press, 2015), 208–13.

47. For these prejudices concerning filth, race, and class, see (among many other possibilities) Thomas Richards, *The Commodity Culture of Victorian England: Advertising and Spectacle, 1851–1914* (Stanford, CA: Stanford University Press, 1991), chap. 3; Anne McClintock, *Imperial Leather: Race, Gender and Sexuality in the Colonial Context* (New York: Routledge, 1995), chap. 5; and Timothy Burke, *Lifebuoy Men, Lux Women: Commodification, Consumption, and Cleanliness in Modern Zimbabwe* (Durham, NC: Duke University Press, 1996).

48. Mauldin, *Up Front*, 8, 35, 16.

49. *Stars and Stripes*, February 22, 1945; Don Robinson, *News of the 45th* (Norman: University of Oklahoma Press, 1944), 107.

50. *Stars and Stripes*, January 18, 1945; June 21, 1944.

51. Mack Bloom, "Air Raid," WWII Survey, 3rd ID, MHI; *Stars and Stripes*, October 25, 1944; Peter Schrijvers, *The Crash of Ruin: American Combat Soldiers in Europe during World War II* (New York: New York University Press, 1998), 4.

52. *Stars and Stripes*, April 29, 1944.

53. *Stars and Stripes*, February 10, 1944.

54. *45th Division News*, January 22, 1944.

55. *Time*, June 18, 1945; Mauldin, undated speech, Speeches, box 8, BMP; Mauldin, *Up Front*, 28.

56. Letter to Bill Mauldin from Edward C. Thurman: "I think you have brought before the public the misery and hardships of the infantry as much as anyone else." Mauldin, Correspondence, "T Miscellaneous," box 6, BMP.

57. Mauldin, *Up Front*, 5.

58. Bill Mauldin and Todd DePastino, *Willie and Joe: The World War II Years* (Seattle: Fantagraphics, 2011), 42; *Time*, November 6, 1944; Undated copies of "Star Spangled Banter" from the *45th Division News*, box 13, BMP.

59. Ernie Pyle wrote for *Stars and Stripes* as well as many other US newspapers. See Pyle's classic work *Brave Men* (New York: H. Holt, 1944); and Pyle with Nichols, *Ernie's War*.

60. Letter of Omar Bradley to Bill Mauldin, undated (early 1945), Correspondence, box 2, BMP. GIs often paired Mauldin and Pyle, as "their" cartoonist and columnist respectively. See, for example, letter from Private Charles M. Sallman to Mauldin, dated April 18, 1945, requesting that the cartoonist draw a memorial *Up Front* just after Pyle's death at Okinawa. Correspondence, "S Miscellaneous," box 6, BMP. See also letter from Private Edward C. Thurman to Mauldin, undated, Correspondence, "T Miscellaneous," box 6, BMP.

61. Pyle with Nichols, *Ernie's War*, 197–98; Will Lang, *Time*, November 6, 1944. Lang was the war correspondent for *Time* in the European theater of operations (ETO). For more on American journalists in the ETO, see Buljung, "From the Foxhole."

62. Frederick Painton, *Saturday Evening Post*, March 17, 1945.

63. Letter from Lt. Bach to Mauldin, dated December 29, 1944, Correspondence, "Stars and Stripes," box 6, BMP; undated letter from James P. Barney to Mauldin, Correspondence, "B Miscellaneous," box 2, BMP; letter from Alfred J. Kelly to Mauldin, March 30, 1945, Correspondence, "K Miscellaneous," box 4, BMP.

64. *Time*, June 18, 1945.

65. *Saturday Evening Post*, March 17, 1945.

66. Anonymous, *A Woman in Berlin: Eight Weeks in the Conquered City* (New York: Picador, 2000), 19.

67. John Horne Burns, "The Trenchfoot of Michael Patrick," in *The Gallery* (1947; repr., New York: New York Review of Books, 2004), 37.

68. See, for example, *Yank: The Army Weekly*, January 21, 1945.

69. J. G. Smith, *In at the Finish: North-West Europe 1944/45* (Montreux: Minerva Press, 1995), 234.

70. Mauldin, *Up Front*, 140.

71. *Stars and Stripes*, February 4, 1944.

72. *Time*, June 18, 1945.

73. *Stars and Stripes*, November 14, 1944.

74. For the concept of military masculinity, see (among many other choices), Belkin, *Bring Me Men*; and Thomas Kühne, *The Rise and Fall of Comradeship: Hitler's Soldiers, Male Bonding and Mass Violence in the Twentieth Century* (Cambridge: Cambridge University Press, 2017).

75. *Stars and Stripes*, February 24, 1944.

76. Mauldin, *Brass Ring*, 185.

77. *Stars and Stripes*, January 15, 1944. In a speech about *Up Front* after the war, Mauldin described his cartoons as "gibes at the hypocrisies of a silly caste system which simply had no place in a twentieth century army." Undated speech, Speeches, box 8, BMP.

78. Mauldin, *Up Front*, 35.

79. Mauldin, 35.

80. *Stars and Stripes*, September 23, 1944.
81. Robert Franklin, *Medic! How I Fought World War II with Morphine, Sulfa, and Iodine Swabs* (Lincoln: University of Nebraska Press, 2006), picture inset.
82. *Stars and Stripes*, February 21, 1945; Mauldin and DePastino, *Willie and Joe*, 365; Mauldin, undated speech, Speeches, box 8, BMP.

Chapter Three

1. John Horne Burns, "The Trenchfoot of Michael Patrick," in *The Gallery* (1947; repr., New York: New York Review of Books, 2004), 3–4, 12. Burns served in the infantry in Italy as a second lieutenant; his story was written just after the war, in 1947.
2. Private Papers of A. A. Southam, Imperial War Museum (hereafter IWM), London; Private Papers of A. G. Herbert, 98, IWM.
3. John Ellis, *On the Front Lines: The Experience of War through the Eyes of the Allied Soldiers in World War II* (New York: John Wiley and Sons, 1990), 180.
4. Graham A. Cosmas and Albert E. Cowdry, *The Medical Department: Medical Service in the European Theater of Operations* (Washington, DC: Center of Military History, 1992), 489.
5. Omar Bradley, *A Soldier's Story* (1951; repr., New York: Modern Library, 1999), 444–45; George Arnulf, *Un Chirurgien dans la tourmente* (Paris: Lavauzelle, 1981), 144.
6. Report of the General Board, United States Forces, European Theater, "Trench Foot (Cold Injury, Ground Type)," Study Number 94, Medical Section, 2–5.
7. Edward Arn, *Arn's War: Memoirs of a World War II Infantryman, 1940–1946* (Akron, OH: University of Akron Press, 2006), 143.
8. The military logic of "abstraction" is complex in terms of levels of command. Please see my discussion in the introduction.
9. Emma Newlands, "Preparing and Resisting the War Body: Training in the British Army," in *War and the Body: Militarisation, Practice and Experience*, ed. Kevin McSorley (London: Routledge, 2013), 35. See also Newlands, *Civilians into Soldiers: War, the Body and British Army Recruits, 1939–45* (Manchester: Manchester University Press, 2014); and Ute Frevert, *A Nation in Barracks: Modern Germany, Military Conscription and Civil Society*, trans. Andrew Boreham (New York: Berg, 2004).
10. Michel Foucault, *Discipline and Punish: The Birth of the Prison* (New York: Vintage Books, 1995), 135. See also Julian Reid, "Life Struggles: War, Discipline and Biopolitics in the Thought of Michel Foucault," *Social Text* 24, no. 1 (Spring 2008): 127–52; and Daniel Ussishkin, *Morale: A Modern British History* (Chicago: University of Chicago Press, 2018).
11. Bill Jardine, *Number, Rank and Name* (Suffolk, UK: Fine Publishing, 1990), 18.
12. Newlands, "Preparing and Resisting," 37.
13. P. S. Bond, *Military Science and Tactics: Infantry Basic Course* (Washington, DC: P. S. Bond Publishers, 1944), 86, 82.
14. War Office, *Basic and Battle Physical Training, Part One, General Principles of Basic and Battle Physical Training, and Methods of Instruction* (London: War Office, 1944), 22, 24.
15. Ian Hay, *The King's Service: An Informal History of the British Infantry Soldier* (London: Methuen, 1938), 239–56.

16. War Office, *Basic and Battle Physical Training*, 3.

17. John Guest, *Broken Images: A Journal* (London: Leo Cooper, 1949), 14; David Holbrook, *Flesh Wounds* (London: Methuen, 1966), 51.

18. One wartime British infantry manual was titled *Endurance Training* (London: War Office, 1945).

19. War Office, *Basic and Battle Physical Training*, 5.

20. Kenneth T. MacLeish calls this indifference to pain "anesthesia." See his "Armor and Anesthesia: Exposure, Feeling, and the Soldier's Body," *Medical Anthropology Quarterly* 26, no. 1 (2012): 49–68. In his analysis, MacLeish draws upon Susan Buck-Morss's notion of anesthesia in "Aesthetics and Anaesthetics: Walter Benjamin's Artwork Essay Reconsidered," *October* 62 (Autumn 1992): 3–41.

21. Paul Fussell, *Doing Battle: The Making of a Skeptic* (Boston: Little, Brown, 1996), 76.

22. As told by Paul Fussell in Richard M. Stannard, *Infantry: An Oral History of a World War II American Infantry Battalion* (New York: Twayne, 1993), xiv.

23. Bernard Friedenberg, *Of Being Numerous: World War II as I Saw It: Medical Detachment, 1st Battalion, 16th Regiment, 1st U.S. Infantry Division* (Pomona, NJ: Holocaust Resource Center, Richard Stockton College of New Jersey, 2008), 94.

24. Rocco Moretto, World War Two Survey Collection (hereafter WWII Survey), First Infantry Division (hereafter ID), US Army Military History Institute (hereafter MHI), Carlisle Barracks, PA; Eldred Banfield, Oral History Archive, IWM; Arn, *Arn's War*, 30.

25. Thomas Packwood, Oral History Archive, IWM.

26. Raymond Gantter, *Roll Me Over: An Infantryman's World War II* (New York: Ivy Books, 1997), 90; Michael Bilder, *Foot Soldier for Patton: The Story of a "Red Diamond" Infantryman with the U.S. Third Army* (Philadelphia: Casemate, 2008), 222.

27. In June 1944, the chief surgeon of the European theater informed army group commanders that care of the feet was "most important to the infantry." Chief Surgeon, "Care of the Feet," June 22, 1944, Record Group (hereafter RG) 112, Office of the Surgeon General, National Archives and Records Administration (hereafter NARA). See also Chief Surgeon, "Care of the Feet," August 28, 1945, RG 112, NARA.

28. Edward D. Churchill, *Surgeon to Soldiers: Diary and Records of the Surgical Consultant Allied Force Headquarters, World War II* (Philadelphia: J. B. Lippincott, 1972), 282; Bond, *Military Science*, 85.

29. Banfield, Oral History Archive, IWM.

30. Stephen W. Dyson, *Twins in Tanks: East End Brothers-in-Arms, 1943–1945* (London: Imperial War Museum, 1994), 144; John Majendie, quoted in Patrick Delaforce, *The Fighting Wessex Wyverns: From Normandy to Bremerhaven with the 43rd Wessex Division* (Stroud, UK: Sutton, 1994), 82.

31. Peter Ryder, *Guns Have Eyes: One Man's Story of the Normandy Landings* (London: Robert Hale, 1984), 139; Milo Green and Paul Gauthier, *Brickbats from F Company, and Other Choice Memorabilia Selections* (Corning, IA: Gauthier, 1982), 171; Nat Frankel and Larry Smith, *Patton's Best: An Informal History of the 4th Armored Division* (New York: Hawthorn Books, 1978), 83. On the issue of walking, see also Stanley Smith, "When the Rubber Meets the Road," 3rd ID, MHI; Wayne Harris, WWII Survey, 45th ID, MHI; George Biddle, *Artist at War* (New York: Viking, 1944), 211; William Warren Fee, *With the Eleventh Armored Division in the Battle of the Bulge: A Retrospective Diary* (Silver Spring, MD: self-pub., 1999), 53; and Robert Strong

Snyder, *And When My Task on Earth Is Done: The Day by Day Experiences of a Christian Written in His Diary Which Was Sent Home by the War Department* (Kansas City, MO: Graphic Laboratory, 1950), 99–100.

32. Biddle, *Artist at War*, 211; L. C. Pinner, *A Conscript at War* (Salisbury, UK: self-pub., 1998), 119; General Alexander, quoted in *London Times*, March 16, 1944; Arnold Whittaker, *Foxhole Promises: Stories from WWII Foxholes* (Marietta, GA: Deeds, 2011), 166.

33. Donald J. Willis, *The Incredible Year* (Ames: Iowa State University Press, 1988), 97.

34. Brian Harpur, *Impossible Victory: A Personal Account of the Battle for the River Po* (New York: Hippocrene Books, 1980), 88; Ryder, *Guns Have Eyes*, 153; Harpur, *Impossible Victory*, 37; R. W. Thompson, *Men under Fire* (London: Macdonald, n.d.), 75; see also 53, 86–87, 94, 96.

35. Dyson, *Twins in Tanks*, 144–45.

36. Walter Bernstein, *Keep Your Head Down* (New York: Viking, 1941–46), 148–49 (Bernstein was a journalist traveling with the troops); Donald R. Burgett, *Seven Roads to Hell: A Screaming Eagle at Bastogne* (Novato, CA: Presidio Press, 1999), 222; Private Papers of Leroy Stewart, "Hurry Up and Wait," 67, WWII Survey, 1st ID, MHI.

37. For French misery, see Jean Navard, *La Libération avec les chars: du débarquement en Provence jusqu'à Ulm, 15 août 1944–8 mai 1945 avec la 1re Armée française* (Paris: Nouvelles éditions latines, 1980), 198, 227.

38. Papers of G. F. R. House, letters dated November 13 and December 12, 1943, IWM; testimony of Bill Scully, in *War on the Ground, 1939–1945*, ed. Colin John Bruce (London: Constable, 1995), 164; Hans Bähr, *Die Stimmen des Menschen: Briefe und Augzeichnungen aus der ganzen Welt, 1939–1945* (München: R. Piper, 1966), entry dated March 15, 1944, 501; Ross S. Carter, *Those Devils in Baggy Pants* (New York: Appleton-Century-Crofts, 1951), 95, 98.

39. John Clayton, letter dated December 18, 1943, WWII Survey, 3rd ID, MHI. For other complaints about the rain and mud, see William Kunz, "Italy—50 Years Ago," WWII Survey, 3rd ID, MHI; and Biddle, *Artist at War*, 228.

40. Leonard J. Dziaba, WWII Survey, 8th ID, MHI; Maurice Piboule, *Du Maroc au Voralberg via Roma, 1942–1945: Journal de guerre d'un artilleur* ([Montluçon?]: self-pub., [1995?]), 33. Piboule found this diary in a German canteen and published it fifty years after the war. The author is unknown.

41. Jack Swaab, *Field of Fire: Diary of a Gunner Officer* (Phoenix Mill, UK: Sutton, 2005), 183; Hubert Gees, "Recollections of the Hurtgen Forest: A German Soldier's Viewpoint," unpublished ms. excerpted in Huey E. Tyra, *Love Always, Ben: The Story of a Young World War II Soldier Who Gave His Life for God, Family and Country* (Gastonia, NC: P & H Publications, 2002), 171.

42. Private Papers of A. Marshall, 113, IWM; Piboule, *Du Maroc*, 70; George Taylor, *Infantry Colonel* (Worcester, UK: self-pub., 1990), 155–56.

43. Hans Dollinger, *Kain, wo ist dein Bruder? Was der Mensch im Zweiten Weltkrieg erleiden Mußte—dokumentiert in Tagebüchern und Briefen* (München: List Verlag München, 1983), 294. See also the excerpt by the soldier Rudi Brill in the same collection, 304–5. For the German perspective on the cold, see Hans von Luck, *Panzer Commander: The Memoirs of Colonel Hans von Luck* (New York: Dell, 1980), 222, 228. For the French perspective on the cold, see Pierre Scherrer, *Royal Morvan: infanterie 1944* (Paris: Atelier alpha bleue, 1990), 118; and Henri Savournin, *Parachutiste avec la France combattante, 1939–1945* (Paris: Barre & Dayez, 1985), 206.

44. Willy Schröder, *Nur ein Kriegstagebuch: Rein menschliche Reflektionen* (Baden-Baden: Verlag Presse Informations Agentur, 1982), 133; see also 155.

45. John M. Coleton Jr., "A Battlefield Pledge Fulfilled . . . Forty Years Later," 20, WWII Survey, 87th ID, MHI. For the awful cold, see also testimony of Robert Conroy, in *In Their Own Words: The Battle of the Bulge as Recorded by Members of Company C*, ed. S. Agulnick, W. R. Condon, R. G. Conroy, and A. L. Bogardus (self-pub., 1996), 45; Stewart, "Hurry Up and Wait," 80, MHI; and Willis, *Incredible Year*, 91. Willis calls his chapter on the Ardennes "The Frozen Hell." See also Paul Cunningham, *Freezing in Hell: World War II, Ardennes: Battle of the Bulge, December 16, 1944–January 25, 1945* (Salisbury, MD: self-pub, 1998).

46. Robert T. Gravlin, "World War II as a Combat Engineer with the Third Armored Division," 24, WWII Survey, 3rd Armored Division (hereafter AD), MHI; John Davis, *Up Close: A Scout's Story: From the Battle of the Bulge to the Siegfried Line* (Bennington, VT: Merriam Press, 2008), 67; See also George W. Neill, *Infantry Soldier: Holding the Line at the Battle of the Bulge* (Norman: University of Oklahoma Press, 2000), 106–7.

47. Gantter, *Roll Me Over*, 108–9; Herbert, 79–80, IWM. For the British soldier's experience, see Robert Boscawen, *Armoured Guardsmen: A War Diary from Normandy to the Rhine* (South Yorkshire, UK: Pen and Sword, 2010), 132–33. See also Neill, *Infantry Soldier*, 95.

48. William F. McMurdie, *Hey, Mac! This Is Serious Business! A Guy Could Get Killed!* (Gig Harbor, WA: Red Apple, 2000), 111; Norman Smith, *Tank Soldier* (Sussex, UK: Book Guild, 1989), 161. On the cold, see also Patrick Delaforce, *Red Crown and Dragon: 53rd Welsh Division in North-West Europe, 1944–1945* (Brighton, UK: Tom Donovan, 1996), 141–43.

49. Homer Ankrum, *Dogfaces Who Smiled through Tears* (Lake Mills, IA: Graphic, 1987), 336, 365.

50. Among the many "official" descriptions of the condition, see US Army Ground Forces, *Prevention of Trench Foot and Frostbite* (Washington, DC: US Army War College, [1945?]), memo dated January 20, 1945, MHI.

51. GI J. J. Kuhn was disappointed when he couldn't get his new boots on, even if they were one and a half sizes bigger than his usual size, and even though he had elevated his feet all night. J. J. Kuhn, *I Was Baker 2: Memoirs of a World War II Platoon Sergeant* (West Bend, WI: DeRaimo, 1994), 147.

52. Leroy Coley, *A Little Bit of War: The Battle of the Bulge* (Centralia, WA: self-pub., 2003), 34; Dick Jepsen, *A Crusader in Europe* (Manhattan, KS: self-pub., 1996), 62; Henry Deloupy, *Les blindés de la Libération* (Paris: Service Historique de l'Armée de Terre, 1991), 112, diary entry of October 7, 1944.

53. Many were also too tired to remove shoes and boots at night. W. S. Brownlie explains yet another reason for the practice. If a soldier had to go to the bathroom in the middle of the night, putting on three pairs of socks and then boots "could result in an accident." See Brownlie, 76, IWM.

54. Roscoe C. Blunt Jr., *Inside the Battle of the Bulge: A Private Comes of Age* (Westport, CT: Praeger, 1994), 88; Private Papers of R. Walker, "The Devil of a War," 19, IWM. Herbert, 73, IWM.

55. Testimony of Rodger Lawrence in *In Their Own Words*, ed. Agulnick et al., 85; Noble Gardner, quoted in Charles Whiting, *The Battle of Hurtgen Forest: The Untold Story of a Disastrous Campaign* (New York: Orion Books, 1989), 52.

56. Frankel and Smith, *Patton's Best*, 103.

57. Office of the Chief of Military History, Department of the Army, *United States Army in World War II, The Technical Services, The Quartermaster Corps: Operations in the War against Germany* (Washington, DC: US Government Printing Office, 1965), 599–603.

58. In the MHI's WWII Survey, see, for example, Norman Maffei, 45th ID; David Shanshuck, 8th ID; Raymond Seidel, 1st ID; and Thomas P. Jacobs, 3rd AD. In *In Their Own Words*, ed. Agulnick et al., see testimonies of Robert Lawrence, 83, and Richard Root, 129. See also McMurdie, *Hey, Mac!*, 90.

59. Neill, *Infantry Soldier*, 109; General Board, "Trench Foot," 2.

60. Whittaker, *Foxhole Promises*, 38.

61. General Board, "Trench Foot," 3. The Americans borrowed "dubbing," or polish, from the British in order to waterproof boots.

62. Gantter, *Roll Me Over*, 195.

63. Clayton, letter dated December 18, 1943, MHI.

64. Testimonies of William Bomar and Robert Lawrence, in *In Their Own Words*, ed. Agulnick et al., 9, 85.

65. Testimony of Robert Lawrence, in *In Their Own Words*, ed. Agulnick et al., 83.

66. Erna Risch, *The Technical Services: The Quartermaster Corps: Organization, Supply and Services*, vol. 1 (Washington, DC: Center of Military History, United States Army, 1994), 106. See also General Board, "Trench Foot," 8, where the board argues that in the wet weather of the fall of 1944, none of the boots given to soldiers "were entirely satisfactory."

67. For the argument that the US Army was by no means uncaring about or indifferent to soldier's footwear, see Rachel Gross, "From Buckskin to Gore-Tex: Consumption as a Path to Mastery in Twentieth-Century American Wilderness Recreation" (PhD diss., University of Wisconsin–Madison, 2017), 118–20.

68. Risch, *Technical Services*, 104. French civilians preferred the GI rubber sole boot to that of the Germans because they made no noise when soldiers walked. See Mary Louise Roberts, *What Soldiers Do: Sex and the American GI in World War II France* (Chicago: University of Chicago Press, 2013), 39.

69. John Leonard Foster and Eldred Banfield, Oral History Archive, IWM. See the General Board, "Trench Foot," 9, in which the army admits that "the available information on the incidence of cold injury in the British forces indicates that it was much lower than that of the American forces." This is attributed to "better socks and shoes, a well-established combat rotation policy, strict command supervision and the carrying out of individual preventive measures." There were still complaints about British boots. Bill Dyson learned the hard way that his boot soles would get holes if he put them on his tank's hot engine hatch to warm his feet. See Dyson, *Twins in Tanks*, 124. David Evans complained that his soles had cracked, but he was quite happy with the new pair he was given. See Private Papers of D. Evans, 72, IWM.

70. William F. Ross and Charles F. Romanus, *The Technical Services: The Quartermaster Corps: Operations in the War against Germany* (Washington, DC: Center of Military History, United States Army, 1994), 608. See also "Again, Trench Foot," *Time*, January 1, 1945, 38.

71. Private Papers of Major Peter Pettit, "The Seine to VE Day," 40, IWM; Private Papers of Captain P. J. Cremin, letter to his wife, dated June 27, 1944, IWM; Sydney Jary, *18*

Platoon (Surrey, UK: Sydney Jary Ltd., 1987), 88. The Germans were also praised for their boots. See, for example, Thomas P. Jacobs, WWII Survey, 3rd AD, 20, MHI.

72. Ross and Romanus, *Technical Services*, 608. The incidence of trench foot was probably higher, Ross and Romanus note, because minor cases were not usually reported. Also, the authors claim, British rotations to the front line were never more than forty-eight hours, which would have prevented prolonged exposure to the elements.

73. Taylor, *Infantry Colonel*, 156. For the French case, see Fernand Pistor, *Correspondances de guerre: de Tunis à Marseille avec les troupes françaises d'Afrique du Nord, mai 1943–août 1944* (Pau: Les Amis de Fernand Pistor, 1978), 45.

74. "Knitting Second World War and Postwar," Fashion, Dress and Clothing Collection (hereafter FDCC), box 3, LBY Eph.C. 10, IWM.

75. FDCC, box 1, IWM. See also Coley, *A Little Bit of War*, 20.

76. The Quartermaster Corps recognized that sock supply was a major problem. See Ross and Romanus, *The Technical Services*, 189.

77. "With the Fifth Army," *London Times*, January 18, 1944. The paper further surmised that the socks were thin because, unlike the British, the Americans have "universal" central heating.

78. "Trenchfoot," November 29, 1944, AG 720, Health and the Prevention of Disease, Records of U.S. Army Operational, Tactical, and Support Organizations, Record Group (hereafter RG) 338, Records of US Army Commands, Fifth Army, Adjutant General Section, General Correspondence, NARA. For the sock exchange program, see "Exchange of Socks," Memorandum No. 94, November 10, 1944, RG 338, Unit Histories, 1940–1967, Infantry Divisions, 1940–1967, box 3925, NARA.

79. Ross and Romanus, *Technical Services*, 189.

80. Robert Houston, *D-Day to Bastogne: A Paratrooper Recalls World War II* (Smithtown, NY: Exposition Press, 1980), 116.

81. Bradley, *A Soldier's Story*, 445. Here Bradley takes responsibility for the "neglect" given to the soldiers' equipment, admitting that soldiers were "ill-prepared" for winter campaigning.

82. Common complaints were that the boots did not provide adequate arch support and that they made the feet sweat excessively while marching, then freeze when standing still. See Neill, *Infantry Soldier*, 147; Demetrius Lypka, *A Soldier Remembers: A Memoir of Service in the 1st Infantry Division, 1941–1945* (Chicago: Cantigny First Division Foundation, 2007), 195; Russell Cloer, WWII Survey, 3rd ID, MHI; Moretto, MHI; Mitchell Kaidy, WWII Survey, 87th ID, MHI; Anthony Harlinski, WWII Survey, 36th ID, MHI; testimony of William Bomar in *In Their Own Words*, ed. Agulnick et al.; John Ingles, *A Soldier's Passage: The Personal Memoir of an Artilleryman in Patton's Third Army* (self-pub., 1986), 73; and Robert E. Humphrey, *Once upon a Time in War: The 99th Division in World War II* (Norman: University of Oklahoma Press, 2008), 140–41. The Quartermaster Corps and the Medical Board recognized these problems with the Arctic boots and tried to make improvements. Unfortunately the war ended before changes could be made. See Risch, *Technical Services*, 106, 108; and General Board, "Trench Foot," 6.

83. Ross and Romanus, *Technical Services*, 189.

84. See testimony of Richard Wies in Whittaker, *Foxhole Promises*, 93.

85. Bilder, *Foot Soldier for Patton*, 163–64.

86. Gantter, *Roll Me Over*, 195.

87. Neill, *Infantry Soldier*, 146; Jack Capell, *Surviving the Odds: From D-Day to VE-Day with the 4th Division in Europe* (Claremont, CA: Regina Books, 2007), 158.

88. Charles Whiting, *Poor Bloody Infantry* (Staplehurst, UK: Spellmount, 2007), 233; Jepsen, *Crusader in Europe*, 62.

89. Stewart, "Hurry Up and Wait," 91–92, MHI. See also "Winterwarfare," *Yank*, February 11, 1944; and Roscoe C. Blunt Jr., *Foot Soldier: A Combat Infantryman's War in Europe* (Cambridge, MA: Da Capo Press, 2002), 128.

90. McMurdie, *Hey, Mac!*, 90.

91. Ernie Pyle with David Nichols, *Ernie's War: The Best of Ernie Pyle's World War II Dispatches* (Norwalk, CT: Easton Press, 2000), 178.

92. Richard Flemming, WWII Survey, 88th ID, MHI; Donald W. Lyddon, "My Memories of World War II," 28, WWII Survey, 28th ID, MHI.

93. On this point, see Bill Mauldin, *Up Front* (New York: W. W. Norton, 2000), 135–37.

94. Ross and Romanus, *Technical Services*, 189.

95. Lee Otts and Bruce Egger, WWII Survey, 26th ID, MHI.

96. "Winterwarfare," *Yank*, February 11, 1944; Ross and Romanus, *Technical Services*, 602.

97. Neill, *Infantry Soldier*, 250, 257–58; Mel Richmond and Jake Langston, quoted in Humphrey, *Once upon a Time*, 214; Capell, *Surviving the Odds*, 158.

98. Yet at the same time they did not want to cause collective death through their weakness. See Thomas Kühne, "Protean Masculinity, Hegemonic Masculinity: Soldiers in the Third Reich," *Central European History* 51 (2018): 403.

99. John Khoury, *Love Company, L Company, 399th Infantry Regiment, of the 100th Infantry Division during World War II and Beyond* (Maywood, NJ: Chi Chi Press, 2003), 77. On this issue, see also Humphrey, *Once upon a Time*, 111.

100. Ryder, *Guns Have Eyes*, 151; Charles B. MacDonald, *Company Commander* (Washington, DC: Infantry Journal Press, 1947), 27, 33, 37.

101. Snyder, *And When My Task*, 147; Leff Murray, *Lens of an Infantryman: A World War II Memoir with Photographs from a Hidden Camera* (Jefferson, NC: McFarland, 2007), 61.

102. Dale Lundhigh, *Show Me the Hero: An Iowa Draftee Joins the 90th Infantry Division during WW II in Europe* (Bloomington, IN: AuthorHouse, 2009), 25–26; Bilder, *Foot Soldier for Patton*, 187.

103. Fee, *With the Eleventh Armored Division*, 44; testimony of William Condon in *In Their Own Words*, ed. Agulnick et al., 28.

104. Blunt, *Inside the Battle of the Bulge*, 121–22.

105. Memo from Chief Surgeon, European Theater of Operations, November 22, 1944, Records of Headquarters, European Theater of Operations, US Army, Historical Division Administrative History, 1942–1946, Surgeon's Section, Bulletins, Memos and Information Letters, 1944–1945 (hereafter Surgeon's Section), box 5759, RG 498, NARA.

106. *Stars and Stripes*, November 29, 1944; General Board, "Trench Foot," 2.

107. Letter from Omar Bradley to Courtney Hodges, First Army, Adjutant General Section, General Correspondence, 1940–1957 (hereafter AGS, Correspondence), box 302, RG 338, NARA.

108. Memo dated November 24, 1944, and letter from Courtney Hodges to V Corps Commander, November 23, 1944, AGS, Correspondence, box 302, RG 338, NARA.

109. Circular Letter No. 71, May 1944, Surgeon's Section, box 5267, RG 498, NARA; letter to Hawley from Twelfth Army Group Medical Section, dated November 19,

1944, and "Prevention of Trench Foot," dated November 23, 1944, Surgeon's Section, box 5759, RG 498, NARA.

110. Captain William L. Hawley, Memo on Trench Foot in Third and Seventh Armies, Surgeon's Section, box 5759, RG 498, NARA.

111. Undated memo from Headquarters Com Z to the War Department, Surgeon's Section, box 5759, RG 498, NARA; letter from AGWAR (Adjutant General War Department) to ETOUSA (European Theater of Operations United States Army), "Trench Foot in Our Armies," December 11, 1944, Surgeon's Section, box 5759, RG 498, NARA.

112. Letter from Omar Bradley to Courtney Hodges, First Army, AGS, Correspondence, box 302, RG 338, NARA.

113. Letter to V Corps Commander from Courtney Hodges, First Army, AGS, Correspondence, box 302, RG 338, NARA.

114. Colonel Bruce, Conservation of Manpower, October 12, 1944, Fifth Army, AGS Correspondence, box 419, RG 338, NARA.

115. *Oxford English Dictionary*. Manpower was reckoned as being equal to between an eighth and a tenth of one horsepower.

116. Letter from Omar Bradley to Courtney Hodges, First Army, AGS, Correspondence, box 302, RG 338, NARA.

117. Preventive Medical Bulletin #12, "Trench Foot," Fifth Army, AGS, Correspondence, box 419, RG 338, NARA.

118. Letter from G. S. Patton to Paul Hawley, dated December 1, 1944, Surgeon's Section, box 5759, RG 498, NARA.

119. The notion that Army Medical Services aimed primarily to conserve manpower for war was by no means limited to the Second World War. For the First World War, for example, see Ana Carden-Coyne, *The Politics of Wounds: Military Patients and Medical Power in the First World War* (Oxford: Oxford University Press, 2014), 20.

120. Outgoing Classified Message, Surgeon's Section, box 5759, RG 498, NARA.

121. Dwight D. Eisenhower, *Crusade in Europe* (1948; repr., Baltimore: Johns Hopkins University Press, 1997), 316.

122. For an example of an urgent supply demand, see memo dated November 11, 1944, First Army, AGS, Correspondence, box 302, RG 338, NARA. For complaints about "foot discipline," see undated memo from Headquarters Com Z to the War Department, Surgeon's Section, box 5759, RG 498, NARA.

123. Arnulf, *Un Chirurgien*, 144–46.

124. Letter from W. G. Livesay to Commanding General, Fifth Army, dated November 29, 1944, and memo from Headquarters 91st ID, dated November 30, 1944, Fifth Army, box 419, RG 338, NARA.

125. Hawley, quoted in "Prevention of Trench Foot," dated November 23, 1944, Surgeon's Section, box 5759, RG 498, NARA; Preventive Medicine Bulletin #12, dated October 31, 1944, Records of U.S. Army Commands, Fifth Army, AGS, Correspondence, RG 338, NARA; and see also here Preventive Medical Bulletin #10, September 23, 1944: "The man who fails to follow the rules is knowingly tripping a natural booby-trap that may destroy one or both of his feet."

126. Letter to Hawley from Twelfth Army Medical Section, November 19, 1944, Surgeon's Section, box 5759, RG 498, NARA.

127. "No Purple Heart for Purple Foot," *Stars and Stripes*, December 6, 1944.

128. General Board, "Trench Foot," 10, 7.

129. Quoted in Ross and Romanus, *Technical Services*, 191.

130. Testimony of William Condon in *In Their Own Words*, ed. Agulnick et al., 31.

131. Ankrum, *Dogfaces Who Smiled*, 337.

132. Quoted in Whiting, *Battle of Hurtgen Forest*, 52.

133. Preventive Medicine Bulletin #12, October 31, 1944, Fifth Army, AGS, Correspondence, box 419, RG 338, NARA.

134. "Again, Trench Foot," *Time*, January 1, 1945, 38.

135. Blunt, *Foot Soldier*, 141.

136. Humphrey, *Once upon a Time*, 142.

137. William Wharton, *A Midnight Clear* (New York: HarperCollins, 1982), 128–29; Frankel and Smith, *Patton's Best*, 81.

138. Lester Atwell, *Private* (New York: Simon and Schuster, 1958), 167–68. The incident also appears in Whiting, *Battle of Hurtgen Forest*, 222–23.

139. Swann, quoted in Humphrey, *Once upon a Time*, 212.

140. Harpur, *Impossible Victory*, 16; Private Papers of H. C. Abrams, 30, IWM.

141. Stanley Whitehouse and George B. Bennett, *Fear Is the Foe: A Footslogger from Normandy to the Rhine* (London: Robert Hale, 1995), 126.

142. Robert Bradley, WWII Survey, 30th ID, MHI; Gantter, *Roll Me Over*, 106. See also William McConahey, *Battalion Surgeon* (Rochester, MN: self-pub., 1966), 61. For self-inflicted injuries by German soldiers, see Magnus Koch, *Fahnenfluchten: Deserteure der Wehrmacht im Zweiten Weltkrieg—Lebenswege und Entscheidungen* (Paderborn: Verlag Ferdinand Schöningh, 2008), esp. 40–43.

143. Jesse Caldwell, "Combat Diary," WWII Survey, 87th ID, MHI. See also Anthony Beevor, *Ardennes 1944: The Battle of the Bulge* (New York: Viking, 2015), 118.

144. Whiting, *Battle of Hurtgen Forest*, 168–69.

145. James Fry, *Combat Soldier* (Washington, DC: National Press, 1968), 11–12; Whitehouse and Bennett, *Fear Is the Foe*, 126.

146. Whiting, *Battle of Hurtgen Forest*, 168–69; Davis, *Up Close*, 88.

147. Burns, "The Trenchfoot of Michael Patrick," 4.

148. General Board, "Trench Foot," 15. On this issue, see also MacDonald, *Company Commander*, 132–35.

149. Khoury, *Love Company*, 76. On this point, see also Wharton, *Midnight Clear*, 129.

150. Burns, "Trenchfoot of Michael Patrick," 4.

151. Arn, *Arn's War*, 157–58.

152. On the bulk of the American infantry as coming from the lower or working classes, see Peter R. Mansoor, *The GI Offensive in Europe: The Triumph of American Infantry Divisions, 1941–1945* (Lawrence: University Press of Kansas, 1999), 40–41.

153. Bond, *Military Science*, 61.

154. Burgett, *Seven Roads to Hell*, 53, 118, 120–21.

Chapter Four

1. Private Papers of J. M. Thorpe, pocket diary, 128, Imperial War Museum (hereafter IWM), London. Stewart Montgomery also landed at the hospital in the middle of the night. See Stewart Montgomery, Sound Archive, reel 10, IWM.

2. According to Robert Macay, British military censorship had relaxed somewhat by 1944, but the British people were still kept from knowing much of the bad news brought by the war. See his *Half the Battle: Civilian Morale in Britain during the Second World War* (Manchester, UK: Manchester University Press, 2002), 149. See also George P. Thomson, *Blue Pencil Admiral: The Inside Story of the Press Censorship* (London: Sampson Low, Marston, ca. 1960), 8–37; and Ian McLaine, *Ministry of Morale: Home Front Morale and the Ministry of Information in World War II* (London: George Allen and Unwin, 1979), 240–81. Most recently, Henry Irving has downplayed the power of censorship in the war, describing Britain as a "relatively open society" at that time. See "The Ministry of Information on the British Home Front," in *Allied Communication to the Public during the Second World War: National and Transnational Networks*, ed. Simon Elliot and Marc Wiggam (London: Bloomsbury Academic, 2020), 30. See also David Welch, *Persuading the People: British Propaganda in World War II* (London: British Library, 2016). In the American case, see George H. Roeder Jr., *The Censored War: American Visual Experience during World War Two* (New Haven, CT: Yale University Press, 1993).

3. Keith Wheeler, *We Are the Wounded* (New York: E. P. Dutton, 1945), 4. Wheeler was a US Marine wounded in the Pacific theater, so he is not speaking of the ETO here.

4. Elaine Scarry, *The Body in Pain: The Making and Unmaking of the World* (New York: Oxford University Press, 1985), 70–71. See also Kevin McSorley and Sarah Maltby, "War and the Body: Cultural and Military Practices," *Journal of War and Culture Studies* 5, no. 1 (2012): 3.

5. See, for example, Omar Bradley, *A Soldier's Story* (1951; repr., New York: Modern Library, 1999), 482, when he talks about the Battle of the Bulge: "At a cost of 482 killed, 2,449 wounded, Tony McAuliffe had withstood the attacks of three German divisions." See also Field-Marshal the Viscount Montgomery of Alamein, *El Alamein to the River Sangro: Normandy to the Baltic* (New York: St. Martin's Press, 1948), 358. Military historians have reproduced this language. According to Rick Atkinson, for example, the capture of Cherbourg came at the "price of 22,000 VII Corps casualties." St.-Lô, he claims, was a "disappointment: at a cost of forty thousand casualties." Rick Atkinson, *The Guns at Last Light: The War in Western Europe, 1944–1945* (New York: Holt, 2013), 121, 129; see also 137.

6. Scarry, *The Body in Pain*, 71. Stephen Ambrose describes the Sixteenth Regiment on Omaha Beach in this way: "What was left of A, F, G, and E companies of the 116th huddled behind obstacles." Stephen Ambrose, *D-Day: June 6, 1944, the Battle for the Normandy Beaches* (London: Simon and Schuster, 2016), 337.

7. See Atkinson, *Guns at Last Light*, 123. Atkinson is again reproducing the language of military command. For example, General Bernard Montgomery described German armor as having "already received a heavy battering and was tired and dispirited." See Montgomery, *El Alamein*, 263, 324, 366; and Bradley, *A Soldier's Story*, 444, 477.

8. Anthony Beevor, *D-Day: The Battle for Normandy* (New York: Viking, 2009), 62, 69, 71, 95, 108, 110–11, 197. See also Ambrose, *D-Day*, 331, 334, 337; and Atkinson, *Guns at Last Light*, 144.

9. "Thoughts on Four Years of War Surgery—1939–1943," *British Medical Journal*, July 8, 1944. On the banality of most wounds, see John M. Kinder, "The Embodiment of War: Bodies for, in, and after War," in *At War: The Military and American Culture in*

the Twentieth Century and Beyond, ed. David Kieran and Edwin A. Martini (New Brunswick, NJ: Rutgers University Press, 2018), 227.

10. My interest in the wounded rests not in how they "experienced" injury or "what happened" to them when they were wounded. For this approach, see Emma Newlands, "'Man, Lunatic or Corpse': Fear, Wounding and Death in the British Army, 1939–45," in *Men, Masculinities and Male Culture in the Second World War,* ed. Linsey Robb and Juliette Pattinson (London: Palgrave Macmillan, 2018), 48. Nor am I interested in the wounded from the perspective of advances in military medicine, that is, how sulfide drugs, penicillin, and plasma transfusions reduced rates of death. The classic work on the British medical treatment of wounded soldiers is Mark Harrison, *Medicine and Victory: British Military Medicine in the Second World War* (Oxford: Oxford University Press, 2004); see also Julie Anderson, *War, Disability and Rehabilitation in Britain: 'Soul of a Nation'* (Manchester, UK: Manchester University Press, 2016).

11. Sean Longden, *To the Victor the Spoils: Soldiers' Lives from D-Day to VE-Day* (London: Robinson, 2007), 43.

12. David Holbrook, *Flesh Wounds* (London: Methuen, 1966), 244. See also how David Evans describes the effect of an artillery attack inside a tank. Private Papers of D. Evans, 108–9, 127, IWM.

13. As Nat Frankel and Larry Smith asked: "What is it that makes a grizzly death grizzly? It is not the blood and guts, the untimeliness, the pain. It is, rather, the complete loss of human dignity, of even looking human." See Frankel and Smith, *Patton's Best: An Informal History of the 4th Armored Division* (New York: Hawthorn Books, 1978), 66. On this issue, see also Ralph Ingersoll, *The Battle Is the Pay-Off* (New York: Harcourt Brace, 1943), 184.

14. Douglas Allanbrook, *See Naples* (Boston: Houghton-Mifflin, 1995), 116. On gore, see also Carolyn Nordstrom, *A Different Kind of War Story* (Philadelphia: University of Pennsylvania Press, 1997).

15. Testimony of Rex Wingfield, in Patrick Delaforce, *Marching to the Sound of Gunfire: North-West Europe, 1944–1945* (Phoenix Mill, UK: Sutton, 1996), 91.

16. Private Papers of S. R. Verrier, diary entry of July 11, 1944, IWM; testimony of Roly Curtiss, in Patrick Delaforce, *Monty's Iron Sides: From the Normandy Beaches to Bremen with the 3rd Division* (Phoenix Mill, UK: Sutton, 1995), 145.

17. On the "million-dollar wound," see Peter Ryder, *Guns Have Eyes: One Man's Story of the Normandy Landings* (London: Robert Hale, 1984), 108. According to Fiona Reid, in the First World War, the French called the same type of wound "une bonne blessure" and the Germans "heimat schusse." See Fiona Reid, "'My Friends Looked at Me in Horror': Idealizations of Wounded Men in the First World War," *Peace and Change* 41, no. 1 (2016): 70.

18. Longden, *To the Victor,* 42.

19. Private Papers of J. Allen, 22, IWM; Private Papers of E. J. Rooke-Matthews, IWM; Private Papers of W. S. Scull, 11, IWM.

20. R. M. Wingfield, *The Only Way Out: An Infantryman's Autobiography of the North-West Europe Campaign, August 1944–February 1945* (London: Hutchinson, 1955).

21. See Thorpe, pocket diary, 135, IWM: "I was wounded but not too badly. I would sooner have been able to have stayed with my crew till the end, but it was not to be." See also Longden, *To the Victor,* 44.

22. Longden, *To the Victor*, 42. See also testimony of Jim Wisewell, in Delaforce, *Marching*, 69.

23. Ryder, *Guns Have Eyes*, 125; Private Papers of E. J. Rooke-Matthews, IWM; Mary Morris, *A Very Private Diary: A Nurse in Wartime* (London: Wedenfeld and Nicholson, 2014), 94; see also 126.

24. See, for example, Arthur Reddish, *Normandy 1944: From the Hull of a Sherman* (Wanganui, NZ: Battlefield Associates, 1995), 31, 63, 82.

25. Jean Navard, *La Libération avec les chars: du débarquement en Provence jusqu'à Ulm, 15 août 1944–8 mai 1945 avec la 1re Armée française* (Paris: Nouvelles éditions latines, 1980), 99; anonymous, quoted in Longden, *To the Victor*, 43.

26. Newlands, "'Man, Lunatic or Corpse,'" 50–51.

27. Longden, *To the Victor*, 231–32. German soldier Martin Pöppel was hit in the pelvis during an accident, but "a grab down there reassures me that everything is still there." See his *Heaven and Hell: The War Diary of a German Paratrooper* (Staplehurst, UK: Spellmount, 1988), 170. For soldiers who did return home with sexual dysfunction, see Elissa Mailänder, "Whining and Winning: Male Narratives of Love, Marriage, and Divorce in the Shadow of the Third Reich," *Central European History* 51 (2018): 496–99.

28. Thorpe, pocket diary, 25–26, IWM; Scull, 14, IWM; Evans, 165, 181, IWM.

29. Arthur W. Frank, *The Wounded Storyteller: Body, Illness, and Ethics* (Chicago: University of Chicago Press, 1995), 55–56, 60–61. See also Ana Carden-Coyne, "Men in Pain: Silence, Stories and Soldiers' Bodies," in *Bodies in Conflict: Corporeality, Materiality and Transformation*, ed. Paul Cornish and Nicholas J. Saunders (New York: Routledge, 2014), 53–65.

30. Robert Boscawen, *Armoured Guardsmen: A War Diary from Normandy to the Rhine* (South Yorkshire, UK: Pen and Sword, 2010), 204–6. Because the 105 mm was a "rear" artillery gun, and the 88 mm was a heavy anti-tank gun, Boscawen was more likely to be looking down the barrel of four 88s.

31. Ryder, *Guns Have Eyes*, 148; Private Papers of Major H. W. Freeman-Attwood, 25, IWM. See also Private Papers of R. Walker, "The Devil of a War," 31, IWM: "Owing to the savage fighting taking place in the village it would be several hours before we could be evacuated from our hillside location."

32. See Ryder, *Guns Have Eyes*, 124–25; W. A. Elliott, *Esprit de Corps: A Scots Guards Officer on Active Service, 1943–1945* (Norwich, UK: Michael Russell, 1996), 117; testimony of Bill Scully, in *War on the Ground, 1939–1945*, ed. Colin John Bruce (London: Constable, 1995), 155–56.

33. John Hall, *Soldier of the Second World War: The Memoirs of a Junior Officer Who Fought in the Front Line from 'D' Day in Normandy to V.E. Day with Many Individual Infantry and Armoured Regiments of the British, Canadian and Polish Armies* (Bournemouth, UK: self-pub., 1986), 64; Private Papers of L. F. Roker, diary entry of April 14, 1945, IWM; Scull, 11, IWM.

34. Evans, 178, IWM.

35. Testimony of Paul Hall, 31, in Patrick Delaforce, *The Fighting Wessex Wyverns: From Normandy to Bremerhaven with the 43rd Wessex Division* (Stroud, UK: Sutton, 1994), 31.

36. Testimonies of Harry Jones and Geoffrey Steere, in Delaforce, *Marching*, 68, 142. Private Papers of E. A. Horrell, IWM.

37. Allen, 19, IWM. See also Lieutenant Colonel George Y. Feggetter, "Diary of an RAMC Surgeon at War, 1942–1946," 102, RAMC 1776, Wellcome Library (hereafter Wellcome), London. See also Walker, "The Devil of a War," 31, IWM: "At the moment of the explosion, I thought I had been kicked by a mule as a piece of shrapnel tore a hole through my left upper arm"; and also Patrick Delaforce, *Red Crown and Dragon: 53rd Welsh Division in North-West Europe, 1944–1945* (Brighton, UK: Tom Donovan, 1996), 84.

38. Thorpe, pocket diary, 123, IWM; and see Delaforce, *Fighting Wessex Wyverns*, 53.

39. Montgomery, Sound Archive, reel 10, IWM.

40. Allen, 19, IWM; Walker, "The Devil of a War," 32, IWM; Scull, 11, IWM; Wingfield, *Only Way Out*, 183.

41. Montgomery, Sound Archive, reel 10, IWM; Elliott, *Esprit de Corps*, 117; Horrell, IWM.

42. On this point, see Wingfield, *Only Way Out*, 183.

43. Private Papers of P. G. Thres, "Memoirs, 1940–1946," 42–43, IWM. See also testimony of Scully, in *War on the Ground*, ed. Bruce, 156. For the profuse bleeding of facial wounds, see "Early Treatment of War Wounds of the Upper Part of the Face," *British Medical Journal*, August 7, 1943.

44. Montgomery, Sound Archive, reel 10, IWM; Hall, *Soldier of the Second World War*, 64.

45. Quoted in Ronald Lewin, *The War on Land: The British Army in World War II, an Anthology of Personal Experience* (New York: William Morrow, 1970), 274.

46. Evans, 107–9, IWM; Private Papers of A. G. Herbert, 23, IWM; Private Papers of A. Marr, 12, IWM; Private Papers of C. Newton, 19, IWM.

47. So did the French. See Navard, *La Libération*, 232.

48. Frankel and Smith, *Patton's Best*, 94–96.

49. Peter Holyhead, Sound Archive, reels 3 and 4, IWM; Newton, 35, IWM; Roker, diary entry of April 14, 1945, IWM.

50. Allen, 19–20, IWM; Walker, "The Devil of a War," 32, IWM.

51. Allen, 20, IWM.

52. Evans, 24–25, IWM; testimony of Leslie Skinner, in Delaforce, *Marching*, 42–43; Ryder, *Guns Have Eyes*, 124.

53. Brian Harpur, *Impossible Victory: A Personal Account of the Battle for the River Po* (New York: Hippocrene Books, 1980), 58; Wingfield, *Only Way Out*, 186.

54. Scull, 15, IWM; Ryder, *Guns Have Eyes*, 125; Montgomery, Sound Archive, reel 10, IWM; Private Papers of Captain D. H. Clark, 51, IWM.

55. Boscawen, *Armoured Guardsmen*, 206–11; Roker, diary entry of April 14, 1945, IWM. The Panzerfaust was a German anti-tank weapon used in the war during the years 1943 to 1945.

56. Roker, diary entry of April 14, 1945, IWM.

57. Newton, 33–34, IWM.

58. Scull, 14, IWM.

59. Roker, diary entry of December 13, 1944, IWM.

60. Rooke-Matthews, IWM; Thorpe, pocket diary, 123, IWM; Evans, 167, IWM. See also Ryder, *Guns Have Eyes*, 127.

61. On this point, see Paul Fussell, *Doing Battle: The Making of a Skeptic* (Boston: Little, Brown, 1996), 149.

62. Ryder, *Guns Have Eyes*, 149; Newton, 35, IWM; Thorpe, pocket diary, 123–24, IWM.

63. For an excellent wartime description of the British medical system, see "Medical Services for the Western Front," *British Medical Journal*, June 17, 1944. The official history of the Royal Army Medical Corps in Italy and northern Europe, 1943–45, is F. A. E. Crew, *The Army Medical Services*, vols. 3 and 4 (London: Her Majesty's Stationery Office, 1962).

64. Montgomery, Sound Archive, reel 10, IWM.

65. As Nurse Mary Morris put it in her diary: "We all work hard at the job of repairing bodies so that they will be fit enough to go back to the front and fight all over again." Morris, *Diary*, 145.

66. Stanley Whitehouse and George B. Bennett, *Fear Is the Foe: A Footslogger from Normandy to the Rhine* (London: Robert Hale, 1995), 168.

67. F. A. E. Crew, *The Army Medical Services*, vol. 1, *Administration* (London: Her Majesty's Stationery Office, 1953–55), 148, 215–16.

68. Rooke-Matthews, IWM; Thres, "Memoirs, 1940–1946," 42, IWM; Michael Hunt, quoted in Longden, *To the Victor*, 42. On this point, see also testimony of Roy Nash, in Delaforce, *Marching*, 196.

69. "The Wounded from Alamein: Observations on Wound Shock and Its Treatment," *Bulletin of War Medicine* 4, no. 5 (1944).

70. "The Immediate Surgical Treatment," *Bulletin of War Medicine* 4, no. 5 (1944).

71. Clark, 45, IWM; see also 52.

72. Stuart Mawson, *Arnheim Doctor* (Gloucester, UK: Spellmount, 1981), 71; see also 81.

73. J.A.R. [James Alexander Ross], *Memoirs of an Army Surgeon* (Edinburgh: W. Blackwood, 1948), 202, 210.

74. On the stress of triage, please see also Private Papers of P. J. Cremin, letter dated June 27, 1944, IWM; and Private Papers of Captain D. G. Aitken, 19, IWM.

75. See Rachel Millet, *Spearette: A Personal Account of the Hadfield-Spears Ambulance Unit, 1940–1945* (Cambridgeshire, UK: Fern House, 1998), 82. At the time, Millet worked in an ambulance unit. Sorting continued at the base hospitals to the further rear, where nurses and orderlies also picked which soldiers should be sent again to the surgeon, and which could be simply undressed and put to bed. On this point, see also Morris, *Diary*, 93.

76. Mawson, *Arnheim Doctor*, 64.

77. Feggetter, "Diary of an RAMC Surgeon," 116, RAMC 1776, Wellcome.

78. Stanley Aylett, *Surgeon at War, 1939–1945* (London: Metro, 2015), 210–12.

79. J. C. Watts, *Surgeon at War* (London: George Allen and Unwin, 1955), 93.

80. In fact, all Western armies follow the practice of triage.

81. Copies of Reports by Medical Officers of 1st Airborne Division on Operation Market and Their Subsequent Experiences, September 17, 1944–May 8, 1945, RAMC 696, Wellcome.

82. Morris, *Diary*, 102; Millet, *Spearette*, 99; Brenda McBryde, *A Nurse's War* (London: Sphere Books, 1979), 102. Patrick Delaforce tells of another incident when a German patient spat up into the face of a Jewish medical officer. The medical officer, according to another medical official, "exhibited surprise but not anger." See Delaforce, *Red Crown and Dragon*, 44.

83. See Private Papers of Major A. R. Kennedy, 89, IWM: "Among the wounded we began to get one or two German prisoners and this of course was encouraging. We were quite obviously advancing and the Germans were quite obviously suffering a good deal of pounding."

84. J.A.R., *Memoirs*, 210.

85. Charles Donald, "The Diagnosis of Doubtfully Penetrating Abdominal Wounds," *British Medical Journal*, June 9, 1945. On this issue, see also McBryde, *A Nurse's War*, 78.

86. J.A.R., *Memoirs*, 211; Millet, *Spearette*, 83; Aylett, *Surgeon at War*, 258.

87. J.A.R., *Memoirs*, 211; Watts, *Surgeon at War*, 97.

88. Aitken, 16, 19, IWM.

89. Mostyn Thomas, quoted in Delaforce, *Red Crown and Dragon*, 71; McBryde, *A Nurse's War*, 107.

90. J.A.R., *Memoirs*, 209.

91. Private Papers of G. Cowell, diary entry of June 6 and 7, 1944, IWM.

92. Aitken, 19–20, IWM. See also Aitken's recording on Thursday, June 8: "Then called out again at 8:15; another ship arriving. Only 39 cases this time, 30 stretcher cases (no deaths) and 9 walking wounded."

93. Mawson, *Arnheim Doctor*, 45, 81.

94. Aylett, *Surgeon at War*, 257 (see also 263); McBryde, *A Nurse's War*, 101 (see also 106–7), 81.

95. See John C. Buchanan, Sound Archive, reel 6, IWM: "When you go back to these places you're impersonal. You're just a number."

96. Private Papers of J. A. Garrett, diary entry of October 29, 1944, IWM; Cowell, diary entry of June 7 and 11, 1944, IWM; Cremin, letter dated August 3, 1944, IWM; Private Papers of E. H. P. Lassen, diary entry of June 9 and 21, 1944, IWM. A.D.S. stands for "Advanced Dressing Station."

97. Feggetter, "Diary of an RAMC Surgeon," 96, RAMC 1776, Wellcome; Watts, *Surgeon at War*, 103–4. Nurses also knew the numbers. Rachel Millet told her diary that in the early months of 1945, she recorded 1,880 admissions; at one point she was treating 400 soldiers with only 200 beds. See *Spearette*, 167.

98. Newlands, "'Man, Lunatic or Corpse,'" 57.

99. Watts, *Surgeon at War*, 93.

100. Private Papers of H. C. Abrams, 53–54, IWM.

101. Copies of Reports by Medical Officers of First Airborne Division on Operation Market and their subsequent experiences, September 17, 1944–May 8, 1945, 33, Wellcome.

102. Copies of Reports by Medical Officers, Appendix G, Wellcome.

103. Copies of Reports by Medical Officers, Appendix J, Wellcome.

104. Lassen, diary entry of June 9, 1944, IWM; Clark, 45–46, IWM; Cremin, letters dated June 14 and 28, 1944, IWM.

105. On this point, see Aitken, 37, 21, IWM.

106. Aylett, *Surgeon at War*, 257; Clark, 52, IWM; J.A.R., *Memoirs*, 216; Aitken, 21, IWM; Millet, *Spearette*, 123; McBryde, *A Nurse's War*, 77 (see also 89); Morris, *Diary*, 96.

107. J.A.R., *Memoirs*, 199; Aylett, *Surgeon at War*, 297; Feggetter, "Diary of an RAMC Surgeon," 25, 114, RAMC 1776, Wellcome; G. M. Warrick, from Copies of Reports by Medical Officers, 17, Wellcome; Mawson, *Arnheim Doctor*, 155; J.A.R., *Memoirs*, 198. See also Aitken, 17, 26, IWM.

108. Diary of service in the Royal Army Medical Corps during World War II, carbon copy of typescript identified as E. Grey Turner on the pouch, diary entry of February 15, 1944, 105, GC/96/1, Wellcome.

109. RAMC typescript account of the work of the Royal Pioneer Corps at the Battle of Monte Cassino, extract from "A War History of the Royal Pioneer Corps, 1939–1945," Wellcome.

110. "The Two-Stage Operation in the Treatment of Wounds in the Italian Campaign," *Bulletin of War Medicine* 6, no. 1 (September 1945).

111. "The Changing Character of War Wounds," *British Medical Journal*, January 1, 1944; "Thoughts on Four Years of War Surgery"; "Abdominal Wounds in War," *British Medical Journal*, January 16, 1943.

112. Captain Archibald Stewart, box 4, "Cases of Interest," Italy 1944, MS 8030, Wellcome.

113. "The Two-Stage Operation."

114. "Penetrating Shell Wound of Neck Involving Larynx, " *Bulletin of War Medicine* 5, no. 1 (April 1944). See also Watts, *Surgeon at War*, 88, on wound pathways. Surgeons also described wounding as a matter of physics. R. Walton measured tissue damage by calculating the speed of the foreign agent against the counterforce of bodily tissue. Speaking of abdominal wounds, he noted that a shell fragment had "a very high initial velocity, which, however, is soon lost against the resistance of the tissues, so that the fragment may not traverse the body but remains embedded within it." Larger masses, continued Walton, "having a much higher momentum[,] will probably pass through the body and not only cause wide destruction of the viscera but form large jagged wounds of exit." See "Abdominal Wounds in War."

115. Feggetter, "Diary of an RAMC Surgeon," 218, RAMC 1776, Wellcome.

116. Although penicillin was discovered in 1928, it could not be produced synthetically until 1957. Until that time, scientists relied on a fermentation method in a large deep tank to produce the drug.

117. McBryde, *A Nurse's War*, 141.

118. "Abdominal Wounds in War."

119. J.A.R., *Memoirs*, 195. See also Watts, *Surgeon at War*, 99.

120. Mawson, *Arnheim Doctor*, 115.

121. Feggetter, "Diary of an RAMC Surgeon," 125, RAMC 1776, Wellcome.

122. "The Two-Stage Operation."

123. Often the wounds weren't sutured because conditions in field hospitals were too dirty to clean the wound properly.

124. "The Two-Stage Operation"; "Treatment of Wounds by Delayed Suture," *British Medical Journal*, December 16, 1944. For "frosting" the wound, see also Feggetter, "Diary of an RAMC Surgeon," 120–21, RAMC 1776, Wellcome.

125. Arthur S. MacNalty, foreword to Crew, *The Army Medical Services*, vol. 4, *Campaigns Northwest Europe*, xi.

126. Richard Charles, "Gunshot Wound of the Innominate Artery," *British Medical Journal*, December 4, 1943. For another example of showcasing surgical skill, see "Two Cases of Gunshot Wound Resulting from Unusually Large Missiles," *British Medical Journal*, July 15, 1944.

127. See Donald, "The Diagnosis of Doubtfully Penetrating Abdominal Wounds." Watts considered doing this procedure on a man with abdominal wounds but ultimately rejected it as indecisive. See Watts, *Surgeon at War*, 98.

128. Private Papers of Captain R. Barer, letter dated November 26, 1944, IWM. "Hb" here stands for hemoglobin, the metabolic substance that carries oxygen in the blood.

129. J.A.R., *Memoirs*, 196; Aylett, *Surgeon at War*, 303–4; E. Grey Turner, Diary of service in the Royal Army Medical Corps, GC/96/1, Wellcome; J.A.R., *Memoirs*, 200.

130. J.A.R. *Memoirs*, 213.

131. Testimony of Jim Wisewell, in Delaforce, *Marching*, 69.

132. Barer, letter dated August 13, 1944, IWM; Aylett, *Surgeon at War*, 295; McBryde, *A Nurse's War*, 87.

133. David Holbrook, *Flesh Wounds* (London: Methuen, 1966), 244–45.

Chapter Five

1. As British historian Lucy Noakes has said, "The dead are often absent from histories of wartime Britain." See her "Valuing the Dead: Death, Burial, and the Body in Second World War Britain," *Critical Military Studies* (forthcoming). This article gives a full account of British army interment practices during the war. Luc Capdevila and Danièle Voldman also bemoan the lack of historiography of death and war in their *War Dead: Western Societies and the Casualties of War* (Edinburgh: Edinburgh University Press, 2006), xiii. In the American case, see Christina S. Jarvis, *The Male Body at War: American Masculinity during World War II* (DeKalb: Northern Illinois University Press, 2004), chap. 5.

2. GIs who remember seeing multiples of dead bodies often describe them as "stacked like cordwood." Their memories were no doubt shaped by the same phrase referred to in narratives of Nazi mass murder. See, for example, Roscoe C. Blunt Jr., *Inside the Battle of the Bulge: A Private Comes of Age* (Westport, CT: Praeger, 1994), 156; Michael Bilder, *Foot Soldier for Patton: The Story of a "Red Diamond" Infantryman with the U.S. Third Army* (Philadelphia: Casemate Books, 2012), 108–9; Walter L. Brown, *Up Front with U.S.: Day by Day in the Life of a Combat Infantryman in General Patton's Third Army* (self-pub., 1979), 318; James Graff, *Reflections of a Combat Infantryman: A Soldier's Story of C. Co. 134th Inf. 35th Div.* (self-pub., 1977), 7. On photographs of the liberation of death camps, see also Barbara Zelitzer, *Remembering to Forget: Holocaust Memory through the Camera's Eye* (Chicago: University of Chicago Press, 1998). A rich scholarly resource on corpses resulting from violence and genocide is www.corpsesofmassviolence.eu.

3. Lieutenant, quoted in Rick Atkinson, *The Guns at Last Light: The War in Western Europe, 1944–1945* (New York: Henry Holt, 2013), 86; Charles B. MacDonald, *Company Commander* (Washington, DC: Infantry Journal Press, 1947), 29; Raymond Gantter, *Roll Me Over: An Infantryman's World War II* (New York: Ivy Books, 1997), 28.

4. Maurice Blanchot, *The Space of Literature* (Lincoln: University of Nebraska Press, 1982), 256.

5. Thomas W. Laqueur, *The Work of the Dead: A Cultural History of Mortal Remains* (Princeton, NJ: Princeton University Press, 2015), 80.

6. Julia Kristeva, *Powers of Horror: An Essay on Abjection* (New York: Columbia University Press, 1982), 3–4.

7. See Max Hastings, *Overlord: D-Day and the Battle for Normandy* (London: M. Joseph, 1984), 216: "On the battlefield, men were reluctantly fascinated by the look

of the dead." He gives the example of a lieutenant who, despite himself, could not help admiring the "physical splendor" of the SS infantry, even as they lay dead.

8. Quoted in Paul Fussell, *The Boys' Crusade: The American Infantry in Northwestern Europe, 1944–1945* (New York: Modern Library, 2003), 64.

9. Quoted in Fussell, 62–63.

10. The best general explanation of the history of the Graves Registration Service is Edward Steere, *The Graves Registration Service in World War II* (Washington, DC: Office of the Quartermaster General, Historical Section, 1951). For the Civil War, see Drew Gilpin Faust, *This Republic of Suffering: Death and the American Civil War* (New York: Random House, 2008). For a history of burial practices in Europe, see Capdevila and Voldman, *War Dead*, 6–10.

11. David Colley, *Safely Rest* (New York: Caliber, 2004), 179–80.

12. Colley, 4–5.

13. On this point, see Fussell, *Boys' Crusade*, 122; and Don Robinson, *News of the 45th* (Norman: University of Oklahoma Press, 1944), 113. When possible German soldiers were also given individual graves, sometimes quite elaborate ones.

14. Robert McGowan Littlejohn, *Graves Registration in the European Theater of Operations* (Harwood, MD: n.p., 1955), 3. Littlejohn was assigned by General Eisenhower to be commanding general of Graves Registration Command, centered in Paris, in 1945. Means to identify a soldier included examining clothing for laundry marks and trademarks, the use of dental records, the fluoroscoping of remains to detect hidden objects in the skin, hair analysis, fingerprinting on a body in decomposed state, and interviews with soldiers who had fought near the site of death. See Littlejohn, 16–17. For efforts to identify American soldiers, see also "Graves Registration," *Quartermaster Review*, May/June 1946, 26.

15. Steere, *Graves Registration Service*, 22.

16. See "Company History, 603 Qm. Reg. Co., 1943–1945," in Charles Butte, *Collection of Publications, Letters, and Writings of the 603rd Quartermaster Graves Registration Company* (Cincinnati, OH: C. D. Butte, 1997), 31–33.

17. Steere, *Graves Registration Service*, 24.

18. Atkinson, *Guns at Last Light*, 85.

19. Steere, *Graves Registration Service*, 102–3. See Eudora Richardson and Sherman Allan, *Quartermaster Supply in the European Theater of Operations in World War II*, vol. 8, *Graves Registration* (Camp Lee, VA: Quartermaster School, 1948), 30. See also "Company History," in Butte, *Collection of Publications*, 33.

20. See First U.S. Army, *Report of Operations, 20 October 1943–1 August 1944* (n.p.: n.p., [194?]), 102, and Annex 7. See also "Administrative Circular," no. 86, November 24, 1943, in Littlejohn, *Graves Registration*, 4–5.

21. Steere, *Graves Registration Service*, 103, 105.

22. Joseph James Shomon, *Crosses in the Wind: The Unheralded Saga of the Men in the American Graves Registration Service in World War II* (New York: Stratford House, 1947), 14. Shomon was captain of the 611th Graves Registration unit deployed in France. See also Steere, *Graves Registration Service*, 26. The idea was that caskets would take up cargo space needed for war matériel. See the testimony of James Stryder, an African American engineer, about collecting the dead in Normandy, in Colley, *Safely Rest*, 182–83.

23. Gerald Plautz, Adjutant Generals Office, Departmental Records Branch (hereafter AGO), US Army.

24. Atkinson, *Guns at Last Light*, 69. Fear that the sight of decomposing bodies was a threat to morale was also a major concern of the British army. See Emma Newlands, "'Man, Lunatic or Corpse': Fear, Wounding and Death in the British Army, 1939–1945," in *Men, Masculinities and Male Culture in the Second World War*, ed. Linsey Robb and Juliette Pattinson (London: Palgrave Macmillan, 2018), 60–63; Dominick Dendooven, "'Bringing the Dead Home': Repatriation, Illegal Repatriation and Expatriation of British Bodies during and after the First World War," in *Bodies in Conflict: Corporeality, Materiality and Transformation*, ed. Paul Cornish and Nicholas J. Saunders (New York: Routledge, 2014), 66–79; Noakes, "Valuing the Dead," 13–14.

25. Tom Dowling, "The Graves We Dug," *Army*, January 1989, 36–39. According to Colley, Tom Dowling called Graves Registration "the most gruesome duty of the war." See Colley, *Safely Rest*, 174; and Bilder, *Foot Soldier for Patton*, 200–201. See also Shomon, *Crosses in the Wind*, 34. Sometimes commanders were assigned to clean up bodies when GR units could not arrive right away. See, for example, William McConahey, *Battalion Surgeon* (Rochester, MN: self-pub., 1966), 69.

26. "Company History," in Butte, *Collection of Publications*, 40.

27. Shomon, *Crosses in the Wind*, 41.

28. Gantter, *Roll Me Over*, 5.

29. Richardson and Allan, *Quartermaster Supply*, 31; Shomon, *Crosses in the Wind*, foreword. On American World War II cemeteries in France, see Kate Clarke Lemay, *Triumph of the Dead: American World War II Cemeteries, Monuments, and Diplomacy in France* (Tuscaloosa: University of Alabama, 2018).

30. GR workers found it extremely difficult to line up the crosses in a perfectly symmetrical manner. According to one GR soldier, each planting required four people: one to hammer the cross into the clod-filled ground; one to hold the cross; and two to stand at various angles and make checks on the position. See US Army, 612th Graves Registration Company, *C'est la Guerre!: 612th Graves Registration Company, World War II, 1943–1945* (Bonn, Germany: Cathaus, n.d.), 44.

31. Blake Ehrlich, "Shall We Bring Home the Dead of World War II?" *Saturday Evening Post*, May 31, 1947. On the return of the dead soldiers, see also Robert McBane, "These Honored Dead," *Army Information Digest*, August 1946, 23–30; Herbert L. Schon, "The Return of Our War Dead," *Quartermaster Review* 26 (July/August 1946): 16–18, 85–86.

32. Laqueur, *Work of the Dead*, chap. 9. See also Noakes, "Valuing the Dead," 5.

33. George H. Roeder Jr., *The Censored War: American Visual Experience during World War Two* (New Haven, CT: Yale University Press, 1993), chap 1.

34. Colley, *Safely Rest*, 192. For the preparation of the corpse prior to turning it over to the family, see United States, American Graves Registration Service, Distribution Center No. 1, *Standing Operating Procedure, American Graves Registration Division, Distribution Center No. 1* (Brooklyn: New York Port of Embarkation, [1945?]), 51–52.

35. Richard Borek, Eugene Fidler, Maynard Flanigan, Dominic Giovinazzo, Lloyd Johnson, Donald Harvey, AGO, US Army.

36. Dominic Giovinazzo, AGO, US Army.

37. George W. Neill, *Infantry Soldier: Holding the Line at the Battle of the Bulge* (Norman: University of Oklahoma Press, 2000), 123.

38. Robert D. Kellett, AGO, US Army.

39. US Army, Quartermaster Corps, Army Effects Bureau, *Effects Warehousing: A Study* (Kansas City, MO, 1945), 2, 5. See also Colley, *Safely Rest*, 175; Richardson and Allan, *Quartermaster Supply*, 65.

40. Plautz, AGO, US Army.

41. George Zatko, Dickie Kramer, Gilbert Smith, Arnold Schmall, Ernest Schultz, AGO, US Army.

42. Richardson and Allan, *Quartermaster Supply*, 85.

43. Shomon, *Crosses in the Wind*, 137–38.

44. Elmer Fidler, James Kurz, Gilbert Hinrichs, AGO, US Army.

45. Ernie Pyle, *Brave Men* (Lincoln: University of Nebraska Press, 2001), 390–94. The piece was originally written in 1944.

46. Littlejohn, *Graves Registration*, 6.

47. Steere, *Graves Registration Service*, 111.

48. "Graves Registration during World War II in Europe," in Butte, *Collection of Publications*, 2, 5.

49. "Company History," in Butte, *Collection of Publications*, 33.

50. Steere, *Graves Registration Service*, 112.

51. "Company History," in Butte, *Collection of Publications*, 34.

52. Ralph B. Schaps, *500 Days of Front Line Combat: The WWII Memoir of Ralph B. Schaps* (New York: iUniverse, 2003), 98.

53. General Board, "Report on Graves Registration Service," unpublished ms., 10, US Army Military History Institute, Carlisle Barracks, PA; Shomon, *Crosses in the Wind*, 35. On this issue, see also "Company History," in Butte, *Collection of Publications*, 33, 39; US Army, *C'est la Guerre!*, 43.

54. Colley, *Safely Rest*, 177.

55. Blunt, *Inside the Battle of the Bulge*, 156–57.

56. "Company History," in Butte, *Collection of Publications*, 45.

57. For the non-combat roles played by African Americans in the war, see Maggie M. Morehouse, *Fighting in the Jim Crow Army: Black Men and Women Remember World War II* (Lanham, MD: Rowman and Littlefield, 2000); Phillip McGuire, ed., *Taps for a Jim Crow Army: Letters from Black Soldiers in World War II* (Santa Barbara, CA: ABC-Clio,1983); Ulysses Lee, *The Employment of Negro Troops* (Washington, DC: Office of the Chief of Military History, US Army, 1966).

58. On the prevalence of African Americans in Grave Registration units, see Shomon, *Crosses in the Wind*, 63–64.

59. Dowling, "The Graves We Dug," 38–39. For another eyewitness account of the bodies floating off the shore of Normandy, see "Company History," in Butte, *Collection of Publications*, 31.

60. Dowling, "The Graves We Dug," 38–39. See also Colley, *Safely Rest*, 178.

61. Testimony of Louis Blaise, 83, 1366 W, Comité vérité historique, Liberté 44, *La Manche témoigne* (hereafter *MT*), Archives de la Manche (hereafter ADM), St.-Lô, France.

62. Testimony of Christian Letourneur, 732, *MT*, ADM.

63. Marcelle Hamel-Hateau, "Des mémoires d'une petit maîtresse d'école de Normandie: souvenirs du débarquement de juin 1944," 16, Le Mémorial de Caen, France.

64. Testimony of Christian Letourneur, 732, *MT*, ADM.

65. "Graves Registration," in Butte, *Collection of Publications*, 5.

66. "Américains—Normands—Omaha—1944," René Mouillard, Mémorial de Caen, Séries FN—France Normandie, Trevières; Elbert E. Legg, "Graves Registration in Normandy France, June 1944," in Butte, *Collection of Publications*, 10; "Company History," in Butte, 39.

67. Testimony of Madame LeBourg, 391, *MT*, ADM.

68. Claude Paris, *Paroles de braves: d'Omaha la sanglante à Saint-Lô, capitale des ruines, 7 juin–18 juillet 1944* (Condé-sur-Noireau: Éditions Charles Corlet, 2007), 155.

69. Mark Goodman, "Unit History of Company A," 50, World War II Survey, 5th Infantry Division, US Army Military History Institute, Carlisle Barracks, PA.

70. Michel Béchet, *L'attente: "Overlord" vécu à cent kilomètres du front* (Montsûrs: Résiac, 1994), 84.

71. Testimony of Marcelle Hamel-Hateau, 8, Mémorial de Caen.

72. Anonymous testimony, 1017–18, 1366 W, *MT*, ADM.

73. Béatrice Poule, ed., *Cahiers de mémoire: vivre et survivre pendant la Bataille de Normandie* (Caen: Conseil Général du Calvados, 1994), 73.

74. Institut d'histoire du temps présent, Paris, France, ARC 1074–62 Alliés (2), *Voici nos alliés, Les États-Unis*, no. 2; and ARC 074 Alliés (7), Saint-John de Crèvecoeur, *Qu'est-ce qu'un américain?* [reprint of 1774 text] (Washington, DC: OWI, 1943).

75. Ken Parker, *Civilian at War* (Traverse City, MI: self-pub., 1984), 50.

76. Paul Fussell, *Wartime: Understanding and Behavior in the Second World War* (New York: Oxford University Press, 1989), 270–71.

77. Blunt, *Inside the Battle of the Bulge*, 33; Donald R. Burgett, *Seven Roads to Hell: A Screaming Eagle at Bastogne* (Novato, CA: Presidio Press, 1999), 138; George Biddle, *Artist at War* (New York: Viking, 1944), 206; Spencer Wurst, *Descending from the Clouds: A Memoir of Combat in the 505 Parachute Infantry Regiment, 82nd Airborne Division* (Haverton, PA: Casemate, 2004), 239. See also Paul E. Cunningham, *Freezing in Hell: World War II, Ardennes: Battle of the Bulge, December 16, 1944–January 25, 1945* (Salisbury, MD: self-pub., 1998), 215.

78. Bilder, *Foot Soldier for Patton*, 93; Blunt, *Inside the Battle of the Bulge*, 12–13.

79. Paul Fussell "My War," in *The Boy Scout Handbook and Other Observations* (New York: Oxford University Press, 1982), 43; Andrew Wilson, quoted in Hastings, *Overlord*, 220. As Hastings points out, "It had become brutally apparent to every man in the First Army that service in an infantry unit was an almost certain sentence to death or wounds" (246).

80. Jim Gavin, quoted in Charles Whiting, *The Battle of Hurtgen Forest: The Untold Story of a Disastrous Campaign* (New York: Orion Books, 1989), 220–21; William F. McMurdie, *Hey, Mac! This Is Serious Business! A Guy Could Get Killed!* (Gig Harbor, WA: Red Apple, 2000), 68.

81. Audie Murphy, *To Hell and Back* (1949; repr., New York: Henry Holt, 1977), 50; Brown, *Up Front with U.S.*, 318; Robert Bowen, *Fighting with the Screaming Eagles: With the 101st Airborne from Normandy to Bastogne* (London: Greenhill Books, 2001), 171; Paul Boesch, *Road to Huertgen, Forest in Hell* (Houston: Gulf, 1962), 200; Morris Courington, *Cruel Was the Way* (Park Forest, IL: Velletri Books, 2000), 32.

82. Blunt, *Inside the Battle of the Bulge*, 137–38.

83. As Thomas Laqueur has put it, the corpse "is to us unbearably abject." See Laqueur, "The Deep Time of the Dead," *Social Research* 78, no. 3 (Fall 2011): 799–820.

84. Henry Deloupy, *Les blindés de la Libération* (Paris: Service Historique de l'Armée de Terre, 1991), 122; Jean Navard, *La Libération avec les chars: du débarquement en Provence jusqu'à Ulm, 15 août 1944–8 mai 1945 avec la 1re Armée française* (Paris: Nouvelles éditions latines, 1980), 132; Fussell, "My War," 259; Bowen, *Fighting with the Screaming Eagles*, 171; Rex Flower, quoted in Patrick Delaforce, *Marching to the Sound of Gunfire: North-West Europe, 1944–1945* (Phoenix Mill, UK: Sutton, 1996), 85; Robert E. Humphrey, *Once upon a Time in War: The 99th Division in World War II* (Norman: University of Oklahoma Press, 2008), 135; André Chamson, *La Reconquête, 1944–1945* (Paris: Éditions Plon, 1975), 122.

85. Orval Eugene Faubus, *In This Faraway Land* (Conway, AR: River Road, 1971), 162–63. See also Ross S. Carter, *Those Devils in Baggy Pants* (New York: Appleton-Century-Crofts, 1951), 245.

86. Quoted in Fussell, *Boys' Crusade*, 119–20.

87. In *Road to Huertgen*, 191–92, Boesch was shocked at the way a GR unit handled a dead body: "They obviously had no concern with harming the remains, for they were dragging him to their trailer on his back with stout ropes tied to his wrists and ankles." See also Dale Helm, *From Foxhole to Freedom: The World War II European Journal of Captain H. Dale Helm of Indiana* (Indianapolis: Guild Press of Indiana, 1996), 38.

88. Paul Fussell, *Doing Battle: The Making of a Skeptic* (Boston: Little, Brown, 1996), 108.

89. Bilder, *Foot Soldier for Patton*, 161; foot soldier, quoted in Murphy, *To Hell and Back*, 223; Lester Atwell, *Private* (New York: Simon and Schuster, 1958), 153–54; Biddle, *Artist at War*, 128.

90. Bob Sheldrake, quoted in Delaforce, *Marching*, 65. See also Patrick Delaforce, *Monty's Iron Sides: From the Normandy Beaches to Bremen with the 3rd Division* (Phoenix Mill, UK: Sutton, 1995), 174.

91. Hubert Gees, "Recollections of the Huertgen Forest: A German Soldier's Viewpoint," unpublished ms. excerpted in Huey E. Tyra, *Love Always, Ben: The Story of a Young World War II Soldier Who Gave His Life for God, Family and Country* (Gastonia, NC: P & H Publications, 2002), 174.

92. Brendan Phibbs, *The Other Side of Time* (Boston: Little and Hart, 1987), 7–8.

93. Phibbs, 10.

94. Phibbs, 11–12.

95. Phibbs, 16.

96. Phibbs, 21, 22.

97. As Thomas W. Laqueur has argued, care of the dead creates a unified purpose in the community, a space in which to affirm their mutual humanity. See his *Work of the Dead*, 22: "Bodies create a community of memory . . . together they make a claim on space and on the attention of the living."

INDEX